6.00

ESSAY

ON

THE RATE OF WAGES:

WITH

AN EXAMINATION

OF THE

CAUSES OF THE DIFFERENCES

IN THE

CONDITION OF THE LABOURING POPULATION

THROUGHOUT THE WORLD.

"We cannot refrain from expressing an opinion that another and a greater matter than that between the advocates and opponents of poor-laws remains behind—namely, an examination of the *necessity* which is supposed to entail *pauperism* on society."—*Athenæum, July 18, 1835.*

BY H. C. CAREY.

AMS PRESS
NEW YORK

Reprinted from the edition of 1835, Philadelphia
First AMS EDITION published 1970
Manufactured in the United States of America

International Standard Book Number: 0-404-01392-9

Library of Congress Card Catalog Number: 77-119647

AMS PRESS, INC.
NEW YORK, N.Y. 10003

ESSAY

ON

THE RATE OF WAGES.

In the discussion now and for a long time past
carried on between the political economists and the
practical men, or advocates of the mercantile theory,
the former have generally confined themselves to indicating what *would be* the result of the adoption of
their views, while the latter have pointed triumphantly to experience, calling upon us to admire the
prosperity that *has been* produced by their system,
and to hesitate before abandoning one that has been
the cause of such admirable results, and which has
the additional recommendation of having been sanc-
tioned by our forefathers. They call for facts, re-
garding them as universally confirmatory of the truth
of their doctrines, and look upon their opponents as
theorists, reasoning in opposition to all experience,
and willing to hazard the happiness and prosperity
of nations in the endeavour to prove the correctness
of visionary notions, that will not bear examination.
Thus, in the inquiry now prosecuting by the French
Minister of the Interior, M. Barbet, one of the wit-

nesses summoned, says, " We are exceedingly sorry that the persons who, in their writings, have attacked the existing system, have not come before the council to defend their opinions here. *If instead of a system founded on probabilities and surmises, they had opposed to us facts,* we could have answered them."

The object of the following essay is to furnish the facts, as called for by M. Barbet: not a few isolated facts, as has generally been done by the advocates of " things as they are," but " the truth and the whole truth," as far as it can be ascertained, in regard to the policy of some of the principal nations of the earth, and to its results, as seen in *the rate of wages,* or *reward of labour.* As introductory thereto, it is proposed to examine what are the circumstances which tend to determine the rate of wages. Both of these subjects have been treated by Professor Senior in his lectures delivered before the University of Oxford,* and as he is among the latest and highest authorities, I propose, in order that the reader may compare our views, and judge between us, to give mine in the form of a review of the doctrines enunciated in those lectures.

* Three Lectures on the Rate of Wages; delivered before the University of Oxford—Easter Term, 1830. By Nassau William Senior. Second edition: London: 1831.

Lecture on the Cost of obtaining Money; delivered before the University of Oxford, in Easter Term, 1829, by Nassau W. Senior. Lond. 1830.

CHAPTER I.

" Most men, in all ages, have sat down to the Gospel with a set of prejudices, which, like so many inquisitors, have laid the Christian religion on a bed like that of Procrustes: and as it suited them, either mutilated it by violence, or extended it by force." So said the learned and excellent Alexander Knox, in a letter to Bishop Jebb, and so may be said of most writers on Political Economy. Almost all approach the subject with " a set of prejudices," and instead of patiently collecting facts, and constructing theories therefrom, the theory is first constructed— the bed of Procrustes is made—and then as many facts are taken as tend to support it, omitting all notice of those which have a contrary tendency. Had this not been the case, it would not, in our day, be in the power of a distinguished professor to characterize the doctrine of wages as " *the most difficult*, as well as the most important branch of political economy."*

Adam Smith asserted that the rate of wages was regulated by the proportion which the supply of labour bore to the demand; a theory which has been controverted by writers of our time, on the ground that in no case where an article can be freely produced can any *permanent* influence upon price be

* Lectures on Wages, p. 3.

produced by excess of demand, and that any rise must cause increased production that will sink the price again to the cost. That this argument is generally correct, there can be no doubt, but in order to make it fit man, it has been necessary to distort some facts, and overlook others, which are in direct opposition to it. Had subsequent writers followed the author of the Wealth of Nations, confining themselves to an examination of the various disturbing causes, the work of man, that operate among the several nations of the earth to produce the inequalities that exist in the proportion between the supply and demand, the " difficulty" would have been obviated.

There can be no difference of opinion as to the " importance" of this subject, and its peculiar importance at this time, when there is so strong a tendency to the transfer of the reins of government from the hands of the few to those of the many. With the single exception of the United States, the privilege of making laws has heretofore been confined to certain classes, who, blinded by false views of their own interest, have generally acted as if government had been established for their peculiar benefit, and hence have arisen corn laws and monopolies of all kinds; restrictions on importations and exportations; wars, and their attendant, heavy taxation. It is not to be doubted, that many of those who promoted this system, have honestly believed that it was for the benefit of the nation over which they were placed; and that, with better information, they would have adopted a widely different course. They might, and probably would, have discovered, that "*laissez nous faire*," the reply of the French merchants to Colbert, was sound and judicious; and that all that could be desired by any people of their government, was to let them alone, and confine its attention to the security of person and property; not allowing any man to "kick the shins or pick the pocket" of his neighbour with impunity. Had they done so, the governments of Europe would be deemed blessings, instead of curses, as is now too frequently the case. It remains to be seen, whether in those in which the people have attained a higher degree of influence than they have heretofore possessed, they will do better than has been done for them in times past by their hereditary lawgivers; and whether or not it will be so, depends upon a correct understanding of their own interest. If they can be made to see, that the course heretofore pursued has had a tendency to *depress* the rate of *wages*, and to keep the mass of the people in a state of poverty, it may be hoped that there will be a disposition to make trial of a different one, and ascertain its effects. If it can be shown that restrictions and monopolies—wars, and heavy taxation—low wages, poverty, and wretchedness—go hand in hand;—while free trade—freedom of action—peace—moderate taxation—high wages, and abundance, are all associated, there can be little doubt which will be their choice.

Heretofore, a large portion of the people of Great Britain have believed that a state of war was that in which the nation was most prosperous; and they have been content to barter the advantages of peace for the glories of Blenheim or Ramilies, Vittoria or

Waterloo. Intoxicated with glory, and deafened by shouts of victory, and the roar of cannon celebrating their triumphs, they have squandered hundreds of millions seeking that prosperity which stood at their doors waiting the return of reason. Like the drunkard, feeling after every such debauch the injurious effects of excitement, they have been disposed to attribute those effects to the absence of stimulus, and not to the stimulus itself. Thus at each return of peace, the nation has found itself burthened with increased debt, requiring increased taxes, tending to lessen the enjoyments of the people; but those inconveniences have been attributed not to the war, but to the peace. The necessary consequence of this has been a proneness to embrace the first opportunity of recommencing hostilities, and causes the most insignificant—the taking of Oczakow—the seizure of the Falkland Islands—or the denial of the right to cut logwood in the Bay of Honduras—have been sufficient to set the nation in a flame. When, at length, the French Revolution occurred, it was gladly seized upon as affording an opportunity to interfere in the affairs of the continent, in accordance with the system that has prevailed since the accession of the House of Orange, and the war then commenced was persevered in, until its close found the nation in a state of prostration, and the people by whom it was most desired, reduced to the alms-house.

" Ships, colonies, and commerce," was the cry of Napoleon, echoed by the British ministry, and gladly re-echoed by the people, always accustomed to associate the idea of prosperity with that of extended dominion. During the whole of the last century, this erroneous association led the nation to do that which each member of it would have deemed madness in an individual, because it was supposed that the rules which should govern the actions of individuals, could not be applied to those of nations. Had they seen a man wasting his means and incurring heavy debts in the prosecution of hazardous enterprises, the benefit of which was doubtful, even should they succeed to the full extent of his anticipations, while his farm was untilled, or his business neglected; they would have said that he must become bankrupt, and his credit would have been destroyed. Yet the people who would argue thus in regard to an individual, neglected the means of prosperity within their grasp, seeking to increase their store at the expense of their neighbours; and the addition of a new colony, although, like Gibraltar, Malta, or St. Helena, productive only of cost, was deemed sufficient to entitle the minister to the gratitude of the nation. Every acquisition was accompanied by an increase of debt and consequent increase of taxation, tending to prevent the proper cultivation of the farm at home, until at length it was found necessary to apply the same system to this country, the attempt at which lost her these immense possessions, and added greatly to her embarrassments. Had she been content prior to the war of 1756 to cultivate her own resources, she would never have experienced the want which led to that attempt. It is true she might not have added Canada to her already extended dominion, but she might have retained these provinces, perhaps even

to the present time; or, when they had become too
strong to be longer held as colonies, the separation
might, and probably would, have been a peaceable
one, each party governing itself, but remaining one
for all purposes of commerce.   The battle of Plassy
substituted dominion in the east for that which she
lost in the west, but what has it added to her prosperity? Nothing! It has enabled many men to bring
home large fortunes, acquired at the cost of the
cries, and groans, and curses, of the unfortunate
Hindoos, plundered by order of a Clive or a Hastings; but to the substantial comforts of the mass of
the people, it has added nothing in any shape, while
it has withdrawn from them immense sums for the
support of an odious and oppressive monopoly. Sub-
sequently, the wars of the French revolution made
large additions to the possessions of the nation, on
the one hand, and corresponding additions to its
embarrassments, on the other: increasing the care
and anxiety of the governors, and preventing that
improvement in the condition of the governed that
would otherwise have taken place.

   Had the laws which govern the rate of wages, and
the effect of the various disturbing causes which prevent the action of those laws, been properly understood, wars could never have been popular.   Mr.
M'Culloch says, with great truth, that "the labourers are masters of their own fortunes, and that there
is little reason to hope for any great improvement
until they shall be made to understand correctly the
laws which govern the rate of wages, and the fact
that it rests with them to determine what that rate

shall be." Had they understood them, they would
have seen that a state of peace was that in which
they must prosper most, and would have been indis-
posed to join in a pursuit that might bring them
"glory," but that would inevitably deprive them of
a part of their bread and meat. Had they been understood by those who are in "high places," and
upon whom rested the cares of government, they
would have seen that the prosperity and happiness
of the people, in which would consist their own true
glory, were not to be promoted by empty triumphs,
nor by the addition of barren islands to their already
extensive possessions. They would have seen that
peace alone could do it, and had they done so, they
might perhaps have retained the same intimate connexion with this country that once existed, with an
intercourse unfettered by corn laws on the one side,
or the system of minimums on the other; and the
people of Great Britain, instead of groaning under
the pressure of taxation, for the support of the government, the land owners, paupers, and monopolists,
might now be the happiest and freest from taxation
of any nation in the world. It is, indeed, impossible
to imagine the height of prosperity which she might
have attained, had she kept aloof from the intrigues
and contentions of the Continent during the last century, as she might well have done; and had the
thousands of millions expended in paying men for
carrying muskets, been left in the hands of their owners to be applied as they might judge most likely to
conduce to their comfort and advantage. Unfortunately, however, the triumphs of peace are little

valued, and Sir Robert Walpole, who could maintain
a peace for twenty years, is little thought of when
compared with the elder Pitt, whose first wish was
for extended territory, and who is best known for
carrying the nation triumphantly through a war; and
the names of Alexander and of Cæsar are familiar
to thousands who never heard of Antoninus, or of
Marcus Aurelius.*

Had this subject been properly understood, we
should long since have seen the end of protective
tariffs; but as nothing can be more evident to the un-
enlightened than the advantage to be derived from
making their neighbours pay them high prices, so
nothing is more easy than to excite popular feeling
in favour of a system of protection; and the same
man who would deem absurd such a system in his
own family, would advocate its adoption by the large
family, termed a nation; as if those principles of trade
which were true with regard to ten or twenty persons, could be untrue when applied to twenty thousand or two hundred thousand. It is a disgrace to
our age to see two such nations as those of Great
Britain and France each hedging round its commerce
by restrictions that limit their exchanges to a million
or two of pounds per annum; thus doing all in their
power to frustrate the beneficent designs of the Deity,
who, in giving to different parts of the earth different
powers of production, paved the way for that inter-

---

* During the long peace maintained by Cardinal Fleury, France
recovered a little; the insignificant administration of this weak
minister proving that the ruler of a nation may achieve much good
by abstaining from the commission of evil.—*Say*, p. xxxv.

course which is most beneficial to mankind. "Commerce," says Mr. M'Culloch, "is the grand engine by which the blessings of civilization are diffused, and the treasures of knowledge and of science conveyed to the remotest corner of the habitable globe; while by making the inhabitants of each country dependent on the assistance of those of others, for a large share of their comforts and enjoyments, it forms a principle of union, and binds together the universal society of nations by the common and peaceful ties of mutual interest and reciprocal obligation."

In another point of view, it is highly desirable that it should be understood. *Wages and profits* have been represented by many political economists as natural antagonists, the Ormuzd and Ahriman of political economy, one of which could rise only at the expense of the other. Such has been the belief of the great mass of the people who receive wages, which belief has given rise to trades' unions, so numerous in England, and obtaining in the United States; as well as to the cry of *the poor against the rich*. A large portion of those who pay, as well as those who receive wages, believe that the rate is altogether arbitrary, and that changes may be made at will. To this belief we are indebted for the numerous " strikes," or " turns out" we have seen, the only effect of which has been loss to both employers and workmen.* Had the journeymen tailors of Lon-

* From a pamphlet recently published by Mr. Pratt, in relation to Savings Banks, it is found, " that the few counties which exhibit a falling off in the amount of their deposits are precisely those in which trades'-unions and turns-out have prevailed to the greatest ex-

don understood the laws by which the distribution of
the proceeds between the workman and the capitalist
is regulated, they would have saved themselves and
their employers the enormous loss that has arisen out
of their recent combination, and would have retained
their situations instead of seeing themselves pushed
from their stools by the influx of Germans, who seized
gladly upon the places vacated by their English fellow workmen. Believing, as they do, that their wages
are depressed for the benefit of their employers, they
believe also that those employers are bound to give
them a portion of their profits in the advance of
wages, when, in fact, the employers are also sufferers by the same causes which produce the depression,
and are unable to advance them, however willing
they may be. If the real causes of the depression
were understood, instead of combining against their
employers, they would unite with them to free their
country from those restrictions and interferences
which produce the effect of which they complain, and
would thus secure permanent advantage, instead of
a temporary advance of wages, which is all that can
be hoped for from combination, even if successful,
which is rarely the case. Fortunately, in the United
States there have been fewer interferences, and there

tent. Among parts of the country where unions appear to have
flourished at the expense of the savings banks, we may enumerate
Derbyshire and Durham, in the latter of which there has been a decrease of 917 out of 3651 accounts. As might naturally be supposed,
the waste of capital has occurred principally among the smaller and
poor depositors; the diminution in the number of accounts under
£ 50, being 719, and the decrease in sums below £ 100, amounting
to 830 of the entire 917."

is therefore less to alter, than in any other country; and if the workmen and labourers could be made to understand the subject, they would see that the division between themselves and the capitalist, or the rate of wages, is regulated by a law immutable as are those which govern the motion of the Heavenly bodies; that attempts at legislative interference can produce only disadvantageous effects; and, that the only mode of increasing wages is by rendering labour more productive, which can only be accomplished by allowing every man to employ his capital and talent in the way which he deems most advantageous to himself. They would see that all attempts on the part of the capitalist, to reduce wages below the natural rate, as well as all on their part to raise it above that rate, must fail, as any such reduction must be attended with an unusual rate of profit to the employer, which must, in its turn, beget competition among the possessors of capital, and raise the rate of wages; while such elevation in any employment must reduce the rate of profit so far as to drive capital therefrom, and reduce wages again to the proper standard.

They should see in the fact that the great majority of the master workmen have risen by their own exertions to the situations they at present occupy, abundant evidence that nothing is wanting to them but industry and economy. They should desire nothing but freedom of action for themselves, and that security both of person and property which prompts the capitalist to investment; and so far should they be from entertaining feelings of jealousy towards those who, by industry and economy, succeed in making

B

themselves independent, that they should see with pleasure the increase of capital, certain that such increase must produce new demands for their labour, accompanied by increased comfort and enjoyment for them. With such a system the population of this country might increase still more rapidly than it has done; the influx of people from abroad might be triple or quadruple what it has been, and each successive year find the comforts of the labouring population in a regular course of increase, as the same causes which drive the labourers of Europe here, to seek that employment and support denied them at home, impel the capitalist to seek here a market for his capital, at the higher rate of interest which our system enables us to pay him with profit to ourselves. The great influx of foreign labour at the present time has caused some uneasiness, but without good reason. The capitalist should bear in mind that if the supply of labour did not keep pace with the growth of capital, the profits of the latter would be diminished; and the labouring classes should recollect that if the labourers remained at home the capital would probably remain with them, and that, at all events, *every man who, by his arrival in this country, increases the number of producers, and of competitors for employment, also increases the number of consumers or employers.* Such people consume nearly, if not quite, the whole amount of their wages, and are therefore employers to nearly the same extent that they are competitors. This remark applies with equal force to the opposite side of the Atlantic, from which vast numbers of consumers are sent off in the hope of lessening the number of producers.

Had these laws been understood by the opposers of the tariff at the south, Mr. M'Duffie and his friends would not have asserted that " the tariff system had raised the price of labour, in the free states, to fifty cents per day, while it had forced it down in the planting states to twelve and a half cents per day." Had they endeavoured to prove to the people of the north, that *all were equal sufferers* by the system, they might have been listened to much more readily, although, by such an argument, they would not have produced so much effect upon the people of the southern states. It was, probably, this erroneous idea that produced the lamentably inconsistent course of the most active friends of free trade in promoting the passage of the gold bill, for the purpose of granting a bounty upon a southern product. It may be hoped that the result of this departure from principle will prevent any such conduct in future. The friends of free trade should never forget the admirable advice of Burke: " We ought to be bottomed enough in prinple, not to be carried away upon the first prospect of any sinister advantage. For depend upon it, that if we once give way to a sinister dealing, we shall teach others the same, and we shall be overcome and overborne."

In opposition to the doctrine of Adam Smith, that " demand and supply govern the rate of labour, and that where capital increased most rapidly the increased demand for labour would lower the rate of profits, by which the labourer would be benefited,"

Mr. M'Culloch says, that no competition among capitalists can lessen the rate of profit, except temporarily, because, the rate of wages can never exceed the *necessary* rate, [or, according to M. Say, "the limit of *strict necessity*"] which is that which will enable the labourer to purchase food and clothing; and that if they should chance at any time to exceed it, there would be an increase of population sufficient to reduce them again. He says, "the cost of production will always regulate price, and if price go beyond cost, the production will be increased." At the same time he tells us that the food and clothing of a labourer are now vastly greater than they were three centuries since; that is, that the cost of a labourer is now greater than it was. We know that there has been a steady increase in the comforts of the labouring classes for centuries; that it is still going on, and that *their increased price has not increased production sufficiently to check the advance,* nor does it appear likely so to do. In every tolerably well governed state there has been a steady increase of price and augmentation of comfort, causing increased production, and yet that increase of production is attended with an equally steady improvement of condition.

Following out the doctrine that the labourer receives only necessary wages, and that, in the event of any circumstance causing a fall below that rate, there will be a reduction in the supply of labour, which will cause wages to advance, Mr. M'Culloch asserts, that all taxes on wages, or upon articles used by the labourer, must be paid out of profits, and that as wages must rise with any increase of taxation, profits must fall. If this be correct, it is of little importance to the labourer what is the extent of taxation. Receiving only necessary wages, i. e. sufficient to support life, they cannot be reduced; and all taxes being paid by his employer, what interest can he have in the good government of the nation? The experience of England has shown, however, that such taxation is not accompanied by a fall of profits, as within the last century, in which taxation has been so much increased, the rate of interest has advanced, and is now considerably higher than it was in the early part of the 18th century. During the reign of George I., interest frequently did not exceed 3 per cent. In 1731–2, the bank furnished money to the government at 3 per cent. In June 1739, the 3 per cents. were as high as 107. In 1743, a period of war, they were at 97. In 1744, a loan was contracted at $4\frac{3}{8}$. After the close of the war in 1749, the interest on the public debt was reduced to 3 per cent. after 1757, with a condition, that the creditors should receive 4 per cent. for one year, and $3\frac{1}{2}$ per cent. thereafter until 1757. In 1757, after the nation had been two years engaged in an expensive war, the rate was very little more than 3 per cent. Since 1815, the 3 per cents. have fluctuated from $56\frac{1}{8}$ to $93\frac{3}{4}$ per cent. From a statement furnished to Parliament by the Bank of England, of the half yearly prices of stocks, it appears that from August 1815 to February 1832, a period of 17 years, the prices were—

Once between 50 and 60 per cent.
5 times " 60 and 70 per cent.
12 times " 70 and 80 per cent.

11 times between   80 and 90 per cent.
5 times   "   90 and $93\frac{7}{8}$ per cent.

From August 1825 to February 1832, the highest price was $91\frac{5}{8}$, and the lowest $76\frac{7}{8}$, and the average of the fourteen half yearly returns 86.   In France, prior to the war of 1756, East India stock commanded so high a price as to yield little over 4 per cent. interest.   In Hindostan, where taxation is high, it produces no increase of wages, while the moderation of it, in the United States, does not depress them.

Mr. M'Culloch says, that the great object of government should be to secure to its people *high profits,* which would enable them to increase their capital most rapidly; but according to his doctrine, and that of M. Say, who styles them "conflicting interests," high profits must be accompanied by low wages.   It is difficult to determine precisely what is meant, when he speaks of wages, and what by profits, and, after a careful perusal of what he has written upon this subject, I am uncertain whether he considers the man who cultivates a dozen acres of flax as receiving profits, or if he would confine that term to the capitalist who makes it into linen.

The great mass of the agriculturists of this country are small capitalists, as are those of France, Italy, and Germany, paying rent, and finding their own implements.   The shoemaker, the tailor, the engraver, and the engineer, have a capital in that quantity of previous labour, which enables them to obtain higher wages than a common labourer.   There are daily examples of the fact, that skill in any department of business is deemed equivalent to capital, in the partnerships that are formed, where one party furnishes the moneyed capital, and the other the skill to manage it. A large portion of the classes mentioned obtain, in their double capacity of labourer and capitalist, moderate wages, as I would term their compensation; but I do not know whether Mr. M'Culloch would consider them as living on wages or profits.

The moneyed capitalist of India receives enormous profits, while the smaller capitalist, who cultivates a few acres, has barely sufficient to support a miserable existence. There, capital does not increase. In England, Holland, and the United States, capital is furnished at a much lower rate of interest, by the large capitalists, but the smaller one, such as we have mentioned above, who, perhaps earns only tolerable wages, is much better paid, and there capital does increase, as is evidenced by a rapid increase of population, accompanied by improved means of living. It would be necessary, in order to make the theory of Mr. M'Culloch correct, to consider all those great classes of which we have spoken, capitalists, living by profits; but, if so, the class living by wages is a comparatively small one. I should be disposed to consider them as living by wages, and to say that, *where wages are highest, there capital increases most rapidly.* The most rapid increase of capital is in the United States and Great Britain, where wages are highest. This is entirely in opposition to the doctrines of Messrs. Say, Malthus, Ricardo, and M'Culloch, as, if wages did not exceed " the limit of strict necessity," there could be no accumulation from *that* source, and as, according to them, where wages are high profits must be low, there could be little expectation from *them*.

Mr. M'Culloch asserts, that *real* wages, (*by which he means proportional wages*,) have fallen in Great Britain within the last fifty years, while the tables in his own Commercial Dictionary show that *real* wages, or *the quantity and quality of commodities attainable by the labourer*, have steadily increased. That increase has been small in food, because of the corn laws, but it has been very great in almost all other articles of consumption.* No better evidence need be desired of the improvement that has taken place in the situation of the labouring classes generally, than the fact that the Savings Banks of England have a capital exceeding fifteen millions,† and those of France,‡ instituted more recently, a capital

---

* The Edinburgh Review, Vol. 56, in a Review of Dr. Chalmers's Political Economy, furnishes extracts from various works on the situation of Scotland, about *the middle of the last century*, showing that the people were in the lowest state of wretchedness, and "often felt what it was to want food." Now they are universally well fed and well clothed, their cottages are comfortable; and they are all in the enjoyment of luxuries that formerly were never tasted, even by rich proprietors.

† Upwards of 20,000 of the depositors were agricultural labourers, who, there is reason to believe, were generally heads of families.— *Report Poor Law Commissioners*, p. 229.

‡ " M. Peuchet, the ablest of French statistical writers, says, ' Ils se mangent aujourd'hui plus de pain, plus de viande en France qu'autrefois. L'homme des campagnes qui ne connoissoit qu'une nourriture grossiere, une boisson peu saine, à aujourd'hui de la viande, du pain, du blé, du vin, du bon cidre, ou de la bière. Les denrées coloniales se sont repandues aussi dans les campagnes depuis l'augmentation de la richesse des cultivateurs.' If we turn to

of four millions, of pounds sterling, the accumulation of those classes. It is a very general impression, that the condition of the labouring classes of England had deteriorated since the close of the war, but the Agricultural Committee of the House of Commons, of which Mr. Jacob was chairman, state in their report of August 2d, 1833, that, "It appears, that in all parts of the country—in the most distressed as well as the most prosperous—the condition of the labourer is in no instance worse than it was five or ten years ago, and that in most cases their condition is greatly improved. The wages of labourers, the witnesses state, have not been reduced in proportion to the reduction in the price of the necessaries of life, and in many parts of the country *no reduction whatever has taken place in their money wages since the war.* This state of things is the more extraordinary, as the superabundance of labour is represented to be greater than ever, and the number who are out of employ, and who are provided for by the poor's rate, is very considerably increased." The improvement in the situation of the people of England would be immense, had she not wasted her energies in the prosecution of wars of the most expensive and ruinous character, the natural consequence of which has been enormous taxation, which absorbs a large portion of her increased production. Her corn laws,

Russia, Prussia, and Germany, the change for the better is even more striking than in France; and while the numbers of the people are increasing, their comforts and enjoyments are increasing still more rapidly."—*Ed. Rev. Vol.* 56, *p.* 65.

too, the object of which is to raise the price of that most important article of consumption, prevent the improvement that might, even under the pressure of her great taxation, take place. In the United States, where taxation is small, and trade comparatively free, a much more fair comparison may be made, and it is the only country in which it can be done with any thing like an approach to correctness. The reward of the labourer is vastly greater at this time, when there are fifteen millions of people, than it was forty years since, when there were only four millions; and although the increased price has produced increased production, as well as large importations of labour, there has been a constant augmentation of the means of living. Agricultural labour has not varied materially in these forty years in its *money price*, but the variation that has taken place has been in its favour, the wages of men having been very steadily about nine dollars per month and their board, but higher wages are now not very unusual. The wages of house servants and of females have greatly advanced, being nearly double what they were forty years since. The expenditure of all these classes being confined almost altogether to the purchase of clothing, in which there has been a prodigious reduction of price, it follows that the increase of comforts within their reach must have been very great. From the year 1783 to 1790, the wages of carpenters and brick-layers were from 62½ to 75 cents per day: at present the wages of carpenters are from $1 12½ to $1 25, and of bricklayers from $1 37 to $1 50 per day. During that time the price of wheat has experienced great variations, but the average of ten years from 1784 to 1793 inclusive, and 1824 to 1833 also inclusive, both periods of peace, is rather lower in the latter period than in the former. The following list of prices is made on an average of January, July, and December of each year.

1784,	$ 6 26	
1785,	5 82	
1786,	5 56	
1787,	5 56	
1788,	4 89	general
1789,	5 07	average,
1790,	5 91	$5 57
1791,	5 42	
1792,	4 97	
1793,	6 26	
1824,	5 00	
1825,	4 84	
1826,	4 92	
1827,	5 17	
1828,	5 67	general
1829,	6 25	average,
1830,	4 91	$5 32
1831,	5 41	
1832,	5 67	
1833.	5 34	

From this it will be seen that the quantity of wheat that can be obtained by the mason and carpenter is now double what could be obtained fifty years since. In manufactured articles, the increase is vastly greater. A change to the same extent would have taken place in England, but for restrictions and heavy taxation; yet Mr. M'Culloch insists, not only that wages have fallen, but that they must fall. Mr. Senior says, very justly, in regard to this theory, " Since the publication of Mr. Ricardo's work, it has been received as an axiom among the dabblers in Political Economy, that according to the established doctrines of the science, high wages and high profits are incompatible, and therefore that either the leading doctrines of political economy are false, or the interest of the labourer and capitalist are directly opposed to each other. The former opinion has been embraced by the large class, who do not attend to what they read, and the latter by the still larger class, who do not attend to what they see."*

* Lectures on Wages, p. 4.

CHAPTER II.

THE proposition with which Mr. Senior commences his Lectures on Wages, and which it is the object of them to establish, is one that is entitled to unqualified assent. It is that " the rate of wages (i. e. the quantity and quality of commodities obtainable by the labourer and his family) depends on the extent of the fund for the maintenance of labourers, compared with the number of labourers to be maintained." Of this proposition, he says, " it is so nearly self-evident, that it may appear scarcely to deserve a formal statement, still less to be dwelt on as if it were a discovery. It is true that it is obvious and trite, but perhaps on that very account its obvious consequences have been neglected."

Self-evident as it appears, it may not be amiss to pause for a moment to illustrate it. It will be evident, that if any given community now producing 100,000 bushels of wheat, shall increase the quantity to 120,000, without an increase of number, the quantity for each, an equal division being made, will be increased one-fifth. It will be equally evident, that if at the end of a certain period, they shall, by any improvement in cultivation, have doubled their product, while their numbers have only increased fifty per cent., the share of each will be increased one-third.

As, however, the arrangements which take place

c

in society are often of a much more complicated character, and render it necessary to make a division between the farmer who owns, and the labourer who tills the soil, it will be proper to examine how that is regulated, and what determines the extent of the fund for the support of the labourer. In a prosperous community like that above mentioned, there is a constant increase of capital, and as every owner desires to receive compensation for the use of his portion, each will seek some mode of employing it. One will purchase new lands, while another will turn his attention to the further improvement of those he already possesses, and both will require additional labour, the former desiring to rent his lands to some one who will pay him rent, and the latter wishing to pay wages to some one to work for him. Both parties will be in the labour market as competitors for the new population, who will have thus the opportunity of becoming either farmers or labourers, and *unless those who want them in the latter capacity will give a fair share of the proceeds of their labour, they will prefer the former.* Such is exactly the case in the United States, and it is as much so in the mechanic arts as in agriculture.

If capital increased much more rapidly than population, labour would rise, and the share of the capitalist would fall. If it fell below the rate obtainable elsewhere, so much would be sent abroad as would bring it again to a level. If no such means could be found of investing it, the share of the capitalist would continue to fall until some means should be found to supply the place of the labourer, or of rendering his

labour more productive. Such we have seen to be the case in England, where interest had fallen in the early part of the last century, considerably below its present rate, and might still have remained so, had not the spinning-jenny and the steam engine substituted capital for labour, and by increasing the produce of labour, had the same effect as multiplying the labourers. Since those changes capital has increased most rapidly, but with it there have been new improvements of a similar kind, as the power loom, the steam-vessel, the rail-road, and the locomotive engine, by which it has been made productive, increasing the demand for, and consequent price of, capital, and at the same time reducing the cost of all articles of consumption to the labourer, by which the same effect has been produced as if his money wages had been increased, and the prices of commodities had remained stationary. Had these improvements not taken place, the rate of interest would now be low, but although the *proportion* of product assigned to the labourer would be greater, the *amount* would be by no means so great, on account of the unproductiveness of capital. It has been already shown that although the money price of agricultural labour has not changed materially in this country within forty years, the share of the labourer of all the articles of consumption has greatly increased, and the general fund of commodities assigned for the support of the whole body of labourers must have increased in the same ratio, all of which has arisen out of the fact that with the aid of capital human labour has been rendered so very productive.

The more advantageously the capital and labour
of a country are applied, the greater must be the
amount of production, and the more rapid must be
the increase of capital. If it advance more rapidly
than population, the demand for labour will always
be such as to secure to the labourer nearly as large a
share of the proceeds of it as if he worked on his own
account; because, if he could obtain more by doing so,
he would not fail to embrace the first opportunity. The
division of produce is therefore regulated by the supply
of labour in the market; and the quantity and quality
of commodities assigned to the use of the whole body
of labourers, will depend upon the relation which
exists between the demand and the supply.

———

Mr. Senior cautions his readers that there are various "popular errors" with which he deems this doctrine to be inconsistent, and which are—

" *First.* It is inconsistent with the doctrine, that the rate of wages
depends on·the proportion which the number of labourers bears to
the amount of *capital* in a country. The word capital has been
used in so many senses, that it is difficult to state this doctrine precisely; but I know of no definition of that term which will not include many things that are not used by the labouring classes; and
if my proposition be correct, no increase or diminution of *these* things
can directly affect wages. If a foreign merchant were to come to
settle in this country, and bring with him a cargo of raw and manufactured silk, lace, and diamonds, that cargo would increase the
capital of the country; silks, lace, and diamonds, would become more
abundant, and the enjoyments of those who use them would be increased; but the enjoyments of the labourers would not be directly
increased: indirectly, and consequentially, they might be increased.
The silk might be re-exported in a manufactured state, and commo-

dities for the use of labourers imported in return; and then, and not till then, wages would rise; but that rise would be occasioned, not by the first addition to the capital of the country, which was made in the form of silk, but by the substituted addition made in the form of commodities used by the labourer."

In another place the investment in diamonds is given as a reason why wages are not in the proportion of *revenue* to population. Such doctrines, as well as that advanced in regard to absenteeism, which will be considered hereafter, and that of M. Say in regard to capital employed in foreign trade, have a tendency to give a character of empiricism to the science, and it is to be regretted that teachers whose doctrines are so generally correct, should sanction with their names others so erroneous.

If a land-holder employ a hundred labourers in producing corn, and ten in working a diamond mine, of what importance is it to the labourer whether his employer retain his profit in diamonds or corn? Or if the whole be employed in producing corn, and he export part of the produce, and receive diamonds in exchange, how can it affect the wages of the labourer? Suppose, instead of giving his corn for diamonds, he were to give it in exchange for a library, would the situation of the labourer be benefited? Or, suppose he employed only one hundred of them in agriculture, and ten in building himself a new house, would they benefit by this mode of investment? The extent of the fund assigned to the whole body of labourers, must depend upon the amount of production, and the proportion which exists between the supply of labour, and the demand for it, and it is totally unimportant to them whether that production be in the form of corn and potatoes, or diamonds and gold, and whether the landlord retain his share in the first or the last. It is entirely unimportant whether he retain his diamonds, or invest the proceeds of them in enlarging his house. In the former case he would gratify his love of display, while in the latter his sole object might be to increase the comfort of his family. In all nations, and in al' stages of society, a portion of revenue will be applied to the increase of convenience or ornament. The Indian and the slave have as much love of display as is found in Grosvenor Square, or the *Chaussée d'Antin.* The cottager will give a portion of his time or his money towards ornamenting or extending his cottage, or, grown richer, will replace it by a new house, of brick or stone; the mechanic will purchase carpets and mirrors; the merchant his carriage, and his lady her diamonds; every man will have his watch, and those who have been accustomed to have them of silver, will replace them by others of gold, and in all these cases the object may be the same; yet Mr. Senior would hardly be disposed to say that the price of labour was not in proportion to capital, because a part of the increase was appropriated to replacing wooden houses by others of brick or stone!

There is no objection arising out of the investment of a portion of the capital or revenue of a nation in diamonds, that does not lie equally against its employment in the construction of houses of four stories, where those of two would as well answer the purpose of their occupants, or against the formation of libraries or museums, or the use of mahogany for furniture

In place of cedar or pine; or, in fact, against every species of expenditure above that of the log-house, and the blanket necessary for preservation against the inclemency of winter.

The chief, if not the only, cause of error that would exist in estimating wages to be in the ratio of capital to population, is that which arises out of governmental interferences; and if two countries *equally free from them*, but differing in capital, could be found, wages would be found to differ in the same ratio. In England, the nominal rate of wages, when the labourer subsists himself, does not differ very materially from that of the United States; but after the division between him and the capitalist has taken place, a large amount is withdrawn for the service of the state, another for the support of the land owner, a third for that of the East India Company, and a fourth for that of the West India planters in their competition with the growers of sugar in the East Indies, all of which tend greatly to reduce the quantity of commodities that falls to his share, and it follows that the general fund for the support of the labourers is very much reduced. In the United States, where the ratio of capital, land included, to population, is, perhaps, smaller than in England, the " fund" is much larger; because, after the division has taken place, a comparatively small portion is claimed for state and other purposes, and the labourer has of course, a larger sum to invest in the purchase of commodities.

CHAPTER III.

THE second error to which Mr. Senior deems his doctrine to be opposed, is, "that wages depend on the proportion borne by the number of labourers to the *revenue* of the society of which they are members:" his reasoning in regard to which is as follows:—

"*Secondly.* It is inconsistent with the doctrine, that wages depend on the proportion borne by the number of labourers to the *revenue* of the society of which they are members. In the example last suggested of the introduction of a new supply of laces or diamonds, the *revenues* of those who use lace or diamonds would be increased; but as wages are not spent on those articles, *they* would remain unaltered. It is possible, indeed, to state cases in which the revenue of a large portion of a community might be increased, and yet the wages of the labourers might fall, without an increase of their numbers. I will suppose the principal trade of Ireland to be the raising produce for the English market; and that for every two hundred acres ten families were employed in raising, on half the land, their own subsistence, and on the remainder corn and other exportable crops requiring equal labour. Under such circumstances, if a demand should arise in the English market for cattle, butchers'-meat, and wool, instead of corn, it would be the interest of the Irish landlords and farmers to convert their estates from arable into pasture. Instead of ten families for every two hundred acres, two might be sufficient: one to raise the subsistence of the two, and the other to tend the cattle and sheep. The revenue of the landlords and the farmers would be increased, but a large portion of the labourers would be thrown out of employment; a large portion of the land formerly employed in producing commodities for their use would be devoted to the production of commodities for the use of England; and the fund for the maintenance of Irish labour would fall, notwithstanding the increase of the revenue of the landlords and farmers."

Having already, (p. 33,) considered the objection arising out of the investment of a portion of the *revenue* of a nation in diamonds, I shall here notice only the case of the Irish labourers, which is entirely in opposition to his own views, expressed in relation to machinery. He says no improvement in that can depress the *general* rate of wages, and as the land is only a machine, it follows, that if the owner can find a mode of using it, that will render it doubly productive, he is in the same situation with a man who doubles or trebles the product of labour by an improvement in the power-loom, or any other machine. By the saving which he makes in this case, he is enabled to increase his capital, and afford an equal, if not an increased, amount of employment, although not perhaps to the very same persons whom this improvement deprives of wages. What the labourer has to complain of, is the want of capital. If capital in land were abundant, he would transfer his labour to some other part of Ireland, or if he had a little moneyed capital, the result of his savings, he might transfer himself to Canada; but as land cannot be had in one place, and he has not what would enable him to seek it in another, he is deprived of employment. In the United States no injurious effect would be produced by a determination of the whole people of Pennsylvania to abstain from tillage, and devote themselves to grazing, as the labourer would speedily remove to Ohio, Indiana, or Missouri.

Great Britain possesses abundant capital in land, but her people are too much impoverished by taxation to be able to seek it, and when they are not so,

they know that they cannot be permitted to exchange
their corn for hardware or cotton goods, except on
payment of a heavy duty in addition to freight and
other expenses, because the land owners do not deem
it for their interest to permit such exchange. The
following remarks by Mr. Senior, in relation to machinery, will be found to apply with equal force to the
case he has above supposed:—

" Nature has decreed that the road to good shall be through evil
—that no improvement shall take place in which the general advantage shall not be accompanied by partial suffering. The obvious
remedy is to remove those whose labour has ceased to be profitable,
to a country that will afford room for their exertions. Few inventions, during the present century, have conferred greater benefits on
the labouring classes than that of the power-loom. By diminishing
the expense of clothing, it has been a source, not merely of comfort,
but of health and longevity. But its proximate effect was to spread
ruin among the hand-weavers; to reduce almost all of them to a
mere subsistence, and many to the most abject want. Ever since
its introduction, thousands have been pining away under misery,
not alleviated even by hope; 'with no rational expectation, but that
the ensuing year would be more calamitous than the passing one:
and this without fault, and even without improvidence."

The true causes why wages are not in the proportion of revenue to population, are, first, differences
in the ratio of capital to population; second, in the
extent of taxation for the support of government and
for other purposes; and, third, in the mode of assessing the contributions for those purposes.

In a country in which the ratio of capital to population is large, the demand for labour ensures to
the workman a full share of the produce of his labour, as is the case in the United States, but in one in
which it is small, there is little demand for labour, and

the competition for the use of landed or other capital
being great, its price is enhanced, and the capitalist
is enabled to obtain an undue proportion of the produce, as in Ireland.

In two countries alike in the proportions which
capital and revenue bore to population, which could
not be the case, unless there was also equality in the
security of person and property, as well as of freedom
of trade and of action, there would be an equality of
wages, unless prevented by difference in the government expenditure. The revenue at any given time
being equal, if one should from that time forward
expend ten millions, and the other one hundred millions, the portion which the labourers would be obliged to contribute would form a deduction from the
quantity of commodities obtainable by them, and
render wages unequal. If one nation remained at
peace with an army of six thousand men, and the
other went to war, and employed half a million of
men in carrying muskets, the production or revenue
would be lessened, and the share of each man reduced.

During the whole time that this state of things
continued, there would be a constantly increasing
difference in the ratio of capital to population in the
two nations, with a constantly increasing difference
of wages, and at the expiration of half a century it
would be difficult to imagine that there had been at
any time an equality of condition between them.

Unproductive expenditure of any kind, has the
same effect; but that of government usually so far
exceeds that of all others as to attract exclusive con-

sideration. If economy in government be advantageous, that of individuals is also in a very high
degree promotive of the increase of capital, and of
the improvement of the condition of the labouring
classes. If in one country the labourers expend their
surplus in gin, and the land-holders in the support of
a numerous train of servants, while in another, the
one class is prudent and sober, and the other moderate
in expenditure, the difference will soon be perceived
in the greater rapidity with which capital will grow,
and with it the competition in the market of labour.

The third cause of difference mentioned above, is
the mode of assessing contributions for the support
of government and for other purposes. While taxes
are chiefly on consumption, governments will select such objects as are extensively consumed, and
will afford large revenue. An examination of the
revenue systems of the different countries of Europe
and America, will show that the chief part of the
revenue is collected upon articles chiefly used by the
labouring classes, while those which are used exclusively by the wealthy are almost untaxed, on
account of the small amount they would yield, and
the greater liability to fraud in the importation of the
finer articles. All taxes and impositions of whatsoever
kind being paid by the consumer, it follows that
the labouring classes bear an undue proportion of the
public burthen. Such is the case under all governments, but less so in the United States than in England, and less in the Netherlands than in France.

CHAPTER IV.

THE third error to which Mr. S. adverts, is, " that the non-residence of landlords, funded proprietors, mortgagees, and other unproductive consumers, can be detrimental to a country that *does not export raw produce.*" He admits its disadvantage in relation to a country like Ireland, which exports corn, but denies the injurious effect upon England, because she exports only manufactures. This distinction being original, his views are given in his own words:—

" *Thirdly.* It is inconsistent with the prevalent opinion, that the non-residence of landlords, funded proprietors, mortgagees, and other unproductive consumers, can be detrimental to the labouring inhabitants of a country *that does not export raw produce.*

" In a country which exports raw produce, wages may be lowered by such non-residence. If an Irish landlord resides on his estate, he requires the services of certain persons, who must also be resident there, to minister to his daily wants. He must have servants, gardeners, and perhaps gamekeepers. If he build a house, he must employ resident masons and carpenters; part of his furniture he may import, but the greater part of it must be made in his neighbourhood: a portion of his land, or what comes to the same thing, a portion of his rent, must be employed in producing food, clothing, and shelter for all these persons, and for those who produce that food, clothing, and shelter. If he were to remove to England, all these wants would be supplied by Englishmen. The land and capital which was formerly employed in providing the maintenance of Irish labourers, would be employed in producing corn and cattle to be exported to England to provide the subsistence of English labourers. The whole quantity of commodities appropriated to the use of Irish labourers would be diminished, and that

D

appropriated to the use of English labourers increased, and wages would, consequently, rise in England, and fall in Ireland.

" It is true that these effects would not be co-extensive with the landlord's income. While, in Ireland, he must have consumed many foreign commodities. He must have purchased tea, wine, and sugar, and other things which the climate and the manufacturers of Ireland do not afford, and he must have paid for them by sending corn and cattle to England. It is true, also, that while in Ireland he probably employed a portion of his land and of his rents for other purposes, from which the labouring population received no benefit, as a deer park, or a pleasure garden, or in the maintenance of horses or hounds. On his removal, that portion of his land which was a park would be employed partly in producing exportable commodities, and partly in producing subsistence for its cultivators; and that portion which fed horses for his use might be employed in feeding horses for exportation. The first of these alternatives would do good; the second could do no harm. Nor must we forget that, through the cheapness of conveyance between England and Ireland, a portion, or perhaps all, of those whom he employed in Ireland, might follow him to England, and, in that case, wages in neither country would be affected. The fund for the maintenance of labourers in Ireland, and the number of labourers to be maintained, would both be equally diminished, and the fund for the maintenance of labourers in England, and the number of labourers to be maintained, would both be equally increased.

" But after making all these deductions, and they are very great, from the supposed effect of the absenteeism of the Irish proprietors on the labouring classes in Ireland, I cannot agree with Mr. M'Culloch that it is immaterial. I cannot but join in the general opinion that their return, though it would not affect the prosperity of the British empire, considered as a whole, would be immediately beneficial to Ireland, though perhaps too much importance is attached to it.

" In Mr. M'Culloch's celebrated examination before the committee on the State of Ireland, (Fourth Report, 814, Sess. 1825,) he was asked, ' Supposing the largest export of Ireland were in live cattle, and that a considerable portion of rent had been remitted in that manner, does not such a mode of producing the means of paying rent contribute less to the improvement of the poor than any exten-

sive employment of them in labour would produce?' He replies,—
'Unless the means of paying rent are changed when the landlord
goes home, his residence can have no effect whatever.'

" 'Would not,' he is asked, 'the population of the country be
benefited by the expenditure among them of a certain portion of
the rent which (if he had been absent) has (would have) been remitted (to England)?' 'No,' he replies, 'I do not see how it could
be benefited in the least. If you have a certain value laid out
against Irish commodities in the one case, you will have a certain
value laid out against them in the other. The cattle are either exported to England, or they stay at home. If they are exported, the
landlord will obtain an equivalent for them in English commodities;
if they are not, he will obtain an equivalent for them in Irish commodities; so that in both cases the landlord lives on the cattle, or on
the value of the cattle: and whether he lives in Ireland or in England, there is obviously just the very same amount of commodities
for the people of Ireland to subsist upon.'

" This reasoning assumes that the landlord, while resident in
Ireland, himself personally devours all the cattle produced on his
estates; for on no other supposition can there be the very same
amount of commodities for the people of Ireland to subsist upon,
whether their cattle are retained in Ireland or exported.

" But when a country does *not* export raw produce, the consequences of absenteeism are very different. Those who derive their
incomes from such a country cannot possibly spend them abroad
until they have previously spent them at home.

" When a Leicestershire landlord is resident on his estate, he
employs a certain portion of his land, or, what is the same, of his
rent, in maintaining the persons who provide for him those commodities and services, which must be produced on the spot where they
are consumed. If he should remove to London, he would want the
services of Londoners, and the produce of land and capital which
previously maintained labourers resident in Leicester, would be sent
away to maintain labourers resident in London. The labourers
would probably follow, and wages in Leicestershire and London
would *then* be unaltered; but until they did so, wages would rise in
the one district, and fall in the other. At the same time, as the
rise and fall would compensate one another, as the fund for the
maintenance of labour, and the number of labourers to be main-

tained, would each remain the same, the same amount of wages would be distributed among the same number of persons, though not precisely in the same proportion as before.

" If he were now to remove to Paris, a new distribution must take place. As the price of raw produce is lower in France than in England, and the difference in habits and language between the two countries prevents the transfer of labourers from the one to the other, neither the labourers nor the produce of his estates could follow him. He must employ French labourers, and he must convert his share of the produce of his estates, or, what is the same thing, his rent, into some exportable form in order to receive it abroad. It may be supposed that he would receive his rent in money. Even if he were to do so, the English labourers would not be injured, for as they do not eat or drink money, provided the same amount of commodities remained for their use, they would be unaffected by the export of money. But it is impossible that he could receive his rent in money, unless he choose to suffer a gratuitous loss. The rate of exchange between London and Paris is generally rather in favour of London, and scarcely ever so deviates from par between any two countries as to cover the expense of transferring the precious metals from the one to the other, excepting between the countries which do, and those which do not possess mines. The remittances from England to France must be sent, therefore, in the form of manufactures, either directly to France, or to some country with which France has commercial relations. And how would these manufactures be obtained? Of course in exchange for the landlord's rent. His share of the produce of his estates would now go to Birmingham or Sheffield, or Manchester, or London, to maintain the labourers employed in producing manufactures, to be sent and sold abroad'for his profit. An English absentee employs his income precisely as if he were to remain at home and consume nothing but hardware and cottons. Instead of the services of gardeners and servants, upholsterers and tailors, he purchases those of spinners, weavers, and cutlers. In either case his income is employed in maintaining labourers, though the class of labourers is different; and in either case, the whole fund for the maintenance of labourers, and the number of labourers to be maintained, remaining unaltered, the wages of labour would not be affected.

" But, in fact, that fund would be rather increased in quantity, and rather improved in quality.' It would be increased, because land previously employed as a park, or in feeding dogs and horses, or hares and pheasants, would now be employed in producing food or clothing for men. It would be improved, because the increased production of manufactured commodities would occasion an increased division of labour, the use of more and better machinery, and the other improvements, which we long ago ascertained to be its necessary accompaniments."

This distinction will not hold good. The laws of political economy are of universal application, and cannot be changed to suit the particular circumstances of a state. *Whatever has a tendency to prevent the growth of capital, is injurious, while every thing that promotes its growth is advantageous.* This is the test; and if it can be shown that absenteeism has a tendency to prevent its growth, in however small a degree, there will be no difficulty in stating what is the law which governs in this case, which has been styled "the opprobrium of political economy." If the landlord receive 1000 quarters of corn, and, as a resident, consume the whole, while, as an absentee, he lives upon 500, applying the remainder to the improvement of his land, there can be no doubt his absenteeism is advantageous. The question is not, however, between a wasteful resident and an economical absentee, but between two men of the same habits of expenditure; one living abroad, and the other at home. In the one case the 1000 quarters of corn, or its equivalent, are sent to Paris, and the amount is invested in the purchase of commodities. The corn having been sold at its wholesale, and its proceeds applied to the purchase of other articles at retail, prices, it is probable that he receives a

wholesale value, equivalent to 800 quarters of corn,
while his tradesmen of Rue Vivienne, or Rue Riche-
lieu, add to their capital the remaining 200 quarters.
The resident landlord does the same thing at Cork,
Dublin, or Limerick, dividing his 200 quarters among
his countrymen, by which their capital is increased.
It might be fairly estimated, that one-fifth of the
amount transmitted to absentee landlords, is thus
distributed, *in the form of profits*, among foreign
tradesmen.   The abstraction, in this manner, of a
fifth of the whole rents of absentee proprietors,
which would undoubtedly be left with the tradesmen,
is felt severely in Ireland, where the growth of population is rapid, and of capital small; but in Great
Britain and the United States, the growth of capital
and increase of demand for labour are so great, that
although the same result is produced, the effect is too
insignificant to be remarked. It can hardly be doubted
for a moment, that if all the landlords of Ireland were
to conclude to live at home for one year, and expend
the same amount among their tenants and tradesmen,
that they had been accustomed to expend among
the people of London, Paris, or Rome, there would be
a greater increase of capital among the mechanics
and tradesmen of Ireland, than if they had remained
abroad.   Less money would be spent in those cities,
and there would be a smaller increase of capital than
usual.   In like manner the absentees of New York
and Philadelphia contribute to the support of the hotel
keepers and tradesmen of Quebec and Montreal. If
they remained at home, and spent the same sum, the

profits would remain with the tradesmen of their own cities.

Absenteeism is thus injurious wherever it occurs, tending to impede the growth of capital, but *its effect is felt in the ratio of population to capital,* and is almost unfelt when that ratio is small, as in England and the United States.

A very material deduction is also made by absenteeism from the means of obtaining employment and consequent reward. To illustrate this, the following case may be stated:—An island containing ten millions of acres is the property of one thousand landholders, and has a labouring population of one million of persons. The average share of each would be ten acres, producing 300 bushels of grain, of which fifty go to the landlord. The fund for the support of the labouring population would be 250 millions, leaving fifty millions for the capitalists or land-holders. These persons, however, being resident, have occasion for gardeners, coachmen, footmen, &c., and employ each fifty in various capacities, leaving only 950,000 persons for cultivation, who divide among themselves the whole of the land and its product, after paying rent, giving 263 bushels to each. As the wages of the cultivator amount to 263 bushels, it is probable that the persons employed by the landlord, would have as much; and as their number would be 50,000, they would receive among them 13 millions of bushels *out of the fund originally assigned to the landlord,* increasing that for the support of the labouring population to 263 millions, leaving only 37 millions to the landlords for their support, and for the increase of their capital.

If their savings, and those of their tenants, should enable capital to keep pace with population, the lands would be improved, roads and canals would be constructed, manufactories would be built, the amount of production would be increased, and with it the fund for the labourer, and wages would continue unaltered; if they went beyond it, they would rise, but if they fell short of it, they would fall.

If, however, these one thousand persons should go abroad, leaving their servants, &c., behind them, the thirteen millions of bushels which they had been accustomed to pay for services, would be paid to foreigners, and there would remain only 250 millions to be divided among a million of labourers. The capital in land would remain the same, while the competition for it would be increased; the labourer would be willing to pay a higher price for its use, perhaps 60 bushels, instead of 50, thus reducing his share from 263 to 240. A further increase of population would increase the competition, and as there would be a steady excess of demand over supply, the landlord's share would probably rise to 80, 100, or 120 bushels, reducing the fund out of which the labourers were supported, from 263 millions, to 180 or 200 millions.

All accumulation on the part of the labourer would be thereby effectually prevented, and if the landlord should expend or invest abroad, the whole of his revenue, there could be no increase of capital from that source. If, under such circumstances, population continued to advance, they might be reduced to patches of an acre or two, the gross produce of which would do no more than afford subsistence, although the unfortunate cultivator would be willing to give one half of it, in preference to being ejected from the land. Such is precisely the condition to which Ireland has been reduced by the extravagance and absenteeism of its landed proprietors.

If the absenteeism existed without the extravagance; if the profligate and wasteful landlord were replaced by the honest, active, and intelligent agent; if the residence abroad produced habits of economy that would admit of the investment in improvements of various kinds, by the agent, of a part of the revenue, absenteeism would be a blessing instead of a curse. The following passage from Mr. Inglis's new work, "Ireland in 1834," confirms these views. Mr. I. visited Ireland strongly impressed with the necessity of poor-laws to counteract the ill effects of absenteeism, and is in this case a most unexceptionable witness.

" It must not be imagined that the people on all absentee estates are in a worse condition than they are upon those estates where there is a resident landlord. The condition of the peasantry depends *on the circumstances under which the lands are occupied*, much more than upon the residence of proprietors, and I cannot say that it is generally an easy matter to guess whether the landlord be absentee or resident. Some of the most comfortable tenantry in Ireland are found on absentee properties, and some of the most miserable on estates upon which the proprietor resides; there is no doubt, however, that where a well-disposed and *unembarrassed* landlord resides, fewer unemployed labourers are found, the condition of the labourer is better, and *the retail trade of the most adjacent towns is materially benefited.*—Vol. II. p. 256.

In the United States capital in land is abundant,

circulating capital increases with great rapidity, and the demand for labour is consequently great. Should the capitalist conclude to live abroad, his coachman, footman, gardener, and all others who have been accustomed to live out of his income, can readily find employment, and notwithstanding the fact that nearly the whole of the exports consist of *raw produce*, it is scarcely of the slightest importance whether he lives abroad or at home. The foreign capitalist who places his funds in the United States is an absentee, but if he were to reinvest the proceeds here, so far as not required for his subsistence, he would be nearly as useful as if he were to remove here with his capital; notwithstanding which, there is a constant jealousy of the investment, by foreigners, of their capital in either bank stocks or real estate. In some of the states there is an absolute prohibition to hold them. It is difficult to conceive of a greater absurdity. The men who oppose a tariff upon cotton goods, would prohibit the importation of capital! The British government has wisely offered inducements to foreigners to invest their surplus funds in its stocks, and large amounts are so invested, yet it would be difficult to point out any difference between the absentee landlord, who left his estate in Surrey or Kent, and the absentee fund-holder who left his money in London. Yet the same persons who inveigh against the former, would deem it injudicious to prevent investments of the latter description.

Having shown, by the case of this country, that the position of Mr. S. in regard to countries exporting raw produce, is not correct, the question arises, would

it be more so, if the population above supposed to
exist were *exclusively engaged in manufactures, and
exported nothing else.* If the one thousand landed
proprietors were converted into an equal number of
capitalists, owning extensive manufacturing establishments, and their portion of the profits were remitted
to them in cottons, instead of, as in the other case,
grain, what would be the difference? It is obvious
that their interest, or rent, or profits, could perform
but one operation instead of two, as suggested by Mr.
Senior. It would be difficult to imagine any disadvantage arising out of the transmission of rent from
Ireland, that would not arise in such a case as the
one now stated. No law of political economy can be
correct unless universally so, and that propounded
by Mr. S. is certainly not so as regards the United
States, which exports only raw produce; nor, even
according to his own theory, would it be so in relation to one which was exclusively engaged in manufactures, and exported nothing else; nor as regards
the capitalist of England, who lives abroad, having
lent his capital to an English *manufacturer*, who *exports the interest in the produce of his manufacture;*
nor to the agriculturist of Ireland, who exported the
interest in corn.

The people of Ireland suffer under the absenteeism
of the landlord, who leaves his capital behind him,
and those of Great Britain under the *forced* absenteeism of capital, the owner of which stays at home.
The absurd system of corn laws, by preventing exchanges, prevents the employment of capital in manufactures, and it is therefore sent abroad to seek that

reward which is denied to it at home. It is sent to the United States to aid in the construction of canals and rail roads, and the erection of manufactories, and the labour that might be employed at home, is sent to assist in using that capital, and in consuming that corn, a market for which is refused in Great Britain.*

* Since writing the above, I have looked into Pebrer's work on the British Empire, and find the following remark in corroboration of the views above given. "There is found an immense excess of capital, the very source of production, causing distress instead of prosperity among its owners. An extraordinary excess of labour, the very cause of wealth, producing poverty, ruin, and misery among the labourers, themselves a great and powerful empire, when knowledge, invention, and art, have multiplied in a boundless manner the means for the enjoyment of life, and for the satisfaction of all its wants, comforts, and luxuries; but when the very perfections of these springs of human and social happiness occasion misfortune, distress, and perpetual agitation, among the members of that great empire itself." page v. The object of Mr. Pebrer's work is to ascertain the cause of the difficulties under which Great Britain labours, and to point out a remedy. Laying aside all consideration of the impediments in the way of freedom of action and of exchange, he attributes the whole difficulty to excess of taxation, which he supposes to have the effect of *raising the price of labour*, and preventing the sale of their manufactures. He holds up the case of Spain as a warning, and says : " It is to her bad fiscal laws, to her bad system of imposts, to the taxes on consumption, which *enhanced wages*, and prevented the sale of her manufactures, that the misfortunes of Spain must be attributed; these, and no other, were the true causes of that wide spread devastating laziness, which still desolates and impoverishes a land worthy of a better fate." p. 542. Considering wages as always at a minimum, and the heavy taxes on consumption as the cause of their high rate in England, the remedy is to be found in the abolition of those taxes, which can only take place when the debt shall have been paid off. To accomplish this object *in part*, it is proposed to raise 500 millions of pounds by a tax on all property in Great Britain *and the Colonies*, which latter are to be induced to

It is this abstraction of capital which causes the redundance of labour, and yet it has been *seriously* proposed in the Quarterly Review to tax all capital invested in machinery, as a means of raising the price of labour! This would drive it abroad still more rapidly, and wages would rise here while those of Great Britain would fall below their present standard. No great improvement is likely to take place until the corn laws are repealed and the workman is allowed to procure food from those who will give it him at the lowest price.   Mr. Senior advocates this and the repeal of the poor laws, but deems it necessary to prepare therefor by a free exportation of the surplus population.   He says, " The only *immediate* remedy for an actual excess of population is an ancient and approved one ; *coloniam deducere.*" In the existing state of things, colonization may be beneficial

agree to it by the prospect of advantage to their commerce.   Such an arrangement would have one good effect, that of throwing the burthens of the government upon the holders of property, who have been accustomed to shuffle them off upon the unfortunate labourers, but it would not reduce wages in the manner supposed by Mr. P. Although the ultimate effect would be to raise wages by reducing the cost of articles of consumption, it is not improbable that the first effect produced by such an arrangement might be to depress them. The two years in which it is proposed that this assessment should be paid, would probably be "years of confusion," arising out of the transfer of property under circumstances little calculated to satisfy the owners of it, or to give confidence to the trading community, and it is not improbable that the loss to the nation, arising out of such a measure, would be greater than the whole amount raised by it. *Let Great Britain throw off the shackles which interfere with the free action of her people, and the free exchange of her productions, and her debt will cease to be of moment to her.*

E

to both the mother country and the colonies, and as
the people have been deprived of the means of transferring themselves, it may perhaps be well to let it be
done at public expense, but it is highly improbable
that the nation will be more prepared for the abolition
of the corn laws after sending away half a million of
people, than at the present time. Unless the removal
of restrictions proceed *pari passu* with the removal
of the population which is rendered surplus by restriction, it certainly will not.

The capital which is thus driven abroad by the
corn laws of England, is employed in the United
States to remove restraints imposed by nature upon
the trade in corn and other articles of produce. They
laboured under a deficiency of circulating capital, and
the consequence was that communications in many
parts of the country were very bad, and the difference
in the prices of corn very considerable. When it was
proposed to make some of the great public improvements that have since been completed, it was supposed that the effect would be to raise the price of lands
in the west, and in a corresponding degree reduce
those nearer the cities which had before been very
valuable, or precisely the same effect that is now anticipated in England from a repeal of the corn laws. New
York and Pennsylvania have completed their great
works, *by which they have repealed their corn laws*, and
so far from the repeal having had the effect of reducing
the price of lands within forty, fifty or one hundred miles
of their capitals, those lands have materially advanced
in price in consequence of the general prosperity, to
which those improvements have largely contributed

by increasing the facilities of communication and interchange. A similar repeal of the English corn laws would, without doubt, be attended with similar effects, and land owners would find that the prosperity which would be the result of such a change of system, would cause their lands to be more valuable than they had been under the restrictive system, and in addition, they would have the satisfaction of knowing that their rents were not forced contributions from the unfortunate manufacturers for their benefit. The experience of the United States should satisfy the people of England, first, that no loss is likely to arise to the land owners from the freedom of trade in corn, and second, that absenteeism is not necessarily productive of evil, as nearly all the great public works of this country have been made with the capital of absentees.

It is singular that English writers who are so nervous in regard to English and Irish absenteeism, should have so little thought of the effect of it in India. *The landlord of all India is an absentee,* and his agents are little better, as all their surplus profits are transferred to England, with a view of returning home as soon as their capital shall be sufficient, to make way for a new swarm who will do the same. If so much effect be produced in Ireland, what must be the consequence in India?

CHAPTER V.

THE fourth error adverted to by Mr. S. is, "That
the general rate of wages can be reduced by machinery." Few persons now doubt the advantages
of machinery to the labourer, and if those who still
continue to do so, would reflect that the greater the
amount of production, the greater must be the fund
of commodities to be divided between the capitalist
and the labourer, and, that the rate of interest, which
indicates the usual rate of profit, has not varied materially for many years, showing that the capitalist
cannot take an extraordinary share of the increased
product, they would see that the fund for the support
of the labourers must be increased in the full proportion of the increased production, and consequently,
that the share of each must be larger. The greatly
increased consumption of all articles used by that
class ought to be sufficient evidence on this head.
The average consumption of cotton goods in Great
Britain, from 1816 to 1820, was 227 millions of yards,
and that of 1824 to 1828, four hundred millions! It
is not improbable that it is now 500 millions, or
about twenty yards per annum to each individual.
The value of this immense quantity, at five pence a
yard, would little exceed ten millions of pounds sterling, while at 2s. 6d., *the price about thirty years since*,
it would be about sixty millions; or at 6s. the yard,

the price about forty-five years since, it would amount
to one hundred and fifty millions of pounds. To the
improvements in machinery of the last half century
alone it is owing that the people of Great Britain have
been able to bear such an excessive amount of taxation, under which any other nation must have sunk.
" Every new invention and discovery, by which the
production of commodities can be facilitated, and
their value reduced, enables individuals to spare a
larger quantity of them for the use of the state."—*Parnell,* p. 11.

It is but a short time since that one of the most respectable and intelligent editors in the Union, in noticing some improvement in machinery, expressed
his regret that human labour should in this manner
be superseded; that locomotive engines should take
the place of thousands of men and of horses who had
been accustomed to be employed in the transportation
of merchandise. Yet this same editor is among the
ablest advocates of one of the principal canals now in
the course of construction. A little reflection would
satisfy him and all other opponents of machinery that
the same objection which lies against the use of locomotive power, would lie against the rail road itself,
and equally against the canal—the turnpike—the
common road, and even the horse path. If the object be to employ the greatest number of persons in
doing a given amount of transportation, dispense entirely with carriages and roads for them, and let the
whole be done on the backs of mules, as is in a great
measure the case in Spain; or still further, dispense

with horses and mules, and employ manual labour
exclusively as in China.

The fifth error is, " That it can be reduced by the
import of foreign commodities."

" *Fifthly.* Closely connected with this mistake, and occasioned
by the same habit of attending only to what is temporary and partial, and neglecting what is permanent and general; of dwelling on
the evil that is concentrated, and being insensible of the benefit that
is diffused, is the common error of supposing that the general rate
of wages can be reduced by the importation of foreign commodities.
In fact the opening of a new market is precisely analogous to the
introduction of a new machine, except that it is a machine which
it costs nothing to construct or to keep up. If the foreign commodity be not consumed by the labouring population, its introduction
leaves the general rate of wages unaffected; if it be used by them,
their wages are raised as estimated in that commodity. If the absurd laws which favour the wines of Portugal to the exclusion of
those of France were repealed, more labourers would be employed
in producing commodities for the French market, and fewer for the
Portuguese. Wages would temporarily fall in the one trade, and
rise in the other. The clear benefit would be derived by the drinkers
of wine, who, at the same expense, would obtain more and better
wine. So if what are called the protecting duties on French silks
were removed, fewer labourers would be employed in the direct production of silk, and more in its indirect production, by the production of the cottons, or hardware, with which it would be purchased.
The wearers of silk would be the only class ultimately benefited;
and as the labouring population neither wear silk nor drink wine,
the general rate of wages would, in both cases, remain unaltered.
But if the laws which prohibit our obtaining on the most advantageous terms tea and sugar, and corn, were altered, that portion of
the fund for the maintenance of labour, which consists of corn, sugar, and tea, would be increased. And the general rate of wages,
as estimated in the three most important articles of food, would be
raised."

It is an error to suppose that the wearers of silk

would be the only persons ultimately benefited in this case. If the labour of twenty thousand persons be now required to produce silks, which, under a different system, could be obtained in exchange for the labour of ten thousand employed in the production of cottons, the whole amount of production of the remaining ten thousand would be added to the fund of commodities. If the importation of silks were doubled in consequence thereof, it would be equivalent to a large increase in the amount of production, and although the labourer might not obtain a silk gown for his wife, there would be a larger portion of cotton goods for his share; but the experience of this country proves that even the wife of the labourer may, with a system of free trade, obtain one of silk. If it remained the same, the wearers of silks would add to their capital one half of the sum they had been accustomed to expend for them, and this increase of capital, by increasing the demand for labour, would tend to produce an augmentation of wages. The laws of political economy are universal in their application, and none more so, than that restraints upon the freedom of trade are injurious to all classes of society, and all measures tending to the removal of those restraints, advantageous, even to those who consume none of the particular articles the importation of which is thereby promoted.

———

The sixth error indicated by Mr. Senior is, " That the unproductive consumption of landlords and capitalists is beneficial to the labouring classes, because it finds them *employment*." No benefit can arise from

employment, unless it tend to increase the amount of
production. Where it does this, it has a tendency to
raise wages, while any species of employment that
tends to decrease production, must reduce them.
Many persons are honestly opposed to machinery,
but if they would reflect, that the quantity produced
is greatly increased by the use of it, while it does
not increase the number of consumers, they would
see that the effect must be to increase the quantity of
commodities that falls to the share of each labourer.
If those persons who are opposed to machinery
would take the trouble to examine what would be
the effect upon the growers of cotton and consumers
of cotton goods, (among whom are, of course, the
cotton manufacturers,) the owners of ships, and proprietors of canal and rail road stocks, and the immense number of persons that are employed in navi-
gating those ships, and directing the canal boats, rail-
road cars and engines, of abolishing the spinning
jenny and power loom, under the mistaken notion of
increasing the demand for manual labour, they
would never again say a word on the subject.

The seventh and last error is that of Mr. Ricardo,
that it is better to be employed in the production of
services, than in that of commodities, or, as Mr. Senior says, " better to be employed in standing behind
chairs, than in making them; or as soldiers and
sailors, than as manufacturers." Mr. M'Culloch,
allowing his views of the conflicting interests of
wages and profits to mislead him also, says, that
" the demand for a large number of men, for the

supply of armies and fleets, must raise wages, in consequence of the increased demand which it produces, and that the increase of wages must come from profits." As the amount of real wages depends upon the quantity and quality of the commodities obtainable by the labourer, and as that depends upon the total amount of production, this theory must remain unsusceptible of proof, until it can be shown that in any given community a greater amount of commodities will be produced where one-half of the population is employed in standing behind chairs, or shouldering muskets, than when the whole are employed in the business of production; or when the half shall be shown to be greater than the whole. If Mr. M'Culloch's views on this subject were generally received, it would not be extraordinary that wars should be popular among the labouring classes, but if they could be made to understand their own interests, they would be sensible that " War is mischievous to every class in the community; but to none is it such a curse as to the labourers."—*Senior.*

> " War is a game, which, were their subjects wise,
> Kings would not play at."—*Cowper.*

CHAPTER VI.

THE reader has seen, that in the Lectures on Wages which have been considered, Mr. Senior has taken the quantity and quality of commodities as the measure of wages, but in that "On the Cost of Obtaining Money," which it is proposed now to consider, he assumes *the money price of labour* as the standard of comparison. It must be obvious, however, that the cost of obtaining silver is only the cost of obtaining commodities that will exchange for it, and that whether a day's labour be estimated as equal to a bushel of wheat, or to so much silver as can be obtained for it at the nearest store, the result is the same. Where they have reference to the same places, and at the same times, Mr. S. considers them as convertible terms, and his object in using the money price in the present instance, is to assume *that* as a measure of the *powers of production* of the several countries. There is, however, a very serious objection to its use for that purpose, arising out of the different *modes* of taxation, in different countries, even when the *amount* is the same.

In India almost the whole taxation is direct, and is taken in the form of rent, *before* the labourer receives his share. In England, on the contrary, direct taxation is small, while that upon consumption is large, and is taken from the labourer *after* he has received his share. To show the effect of this, I will suppose the following case. A man in England raises three hundred bushels of wheat, fifty of which go to his landlord as rent, and twenty to the state as land tax, leaving him two hundred and thirty bushels as the rewards of his labour, or wages and interest of capital. In exchanging this for tea, sugar, coffee, &c. he pays, I will suppose, as a tax on consumption, eighty bushels, leaving him one hundred and fifty bushels. In India, another man, raising the same quantity, would have paid one hundred and fifty bushels as rent and tax, leaving his wages exactly the same, although apparently above one third less. Again, where the *mode of taxation* is the same, money wages, although they may be taken as a measure of the powers of production, cannot be taken as an evidence of the extent of *real wages,* unless allowance be made for the difference of *amount of taxation.* In England, money wages are nearly as high as in the United States, yet the greater amount of the claims of the state makes a vast difference in the quantity and quality of commodities at the labourer's command, which is the only measure of real wages.

In the following extract will be found Mr. Senior's views as to the actual amount of wages, and the causes of the difference that exists :—

" The average annual wages of labour in Hindostan are from one pound to two pounds troy of silver a year (from fourteen to twenty-eight dollars). In England they are from nine pounds to fifteen pounds troy ($126 to $210—average $168, or £35). In Upper Canada and the United States of America, they are from twelve pounds troy to twenty pounds ($168 to $280—average $224, or £46 13*s*.).

Within the same time the American labourer obtains twelve times, and the English labourer nine times as much silver as the Hindoo.

" The difference in the cost of obtaining silver, or, in other words, in the wages of labour in silver, in different countries, at the same period, has attracted attention, though not perhaps so much as it deserves, and various theories have been proposed to account for it.

" It has been attributed to the different degrees of labour requisite to obtain the necessaries of the labourer. In Hindostan it has been said, he requires little clothing or fuel, and subsists on rice, of which he obtains a sufficient quantity with little exertion. But how then do we account for his wages in North America being twenty-five per cent. higher than they are in England, while the labour requisite to obtain necessaries is not much more than half as great in the former country as in the latter? How do we account for the low amount of wages in silver in China, where the labour necessary to obtain necessaries is proverbially great?

" It has been attributed to the different densities of population. In Hindostan and in Ireland, it has been said, labourers multiply so rapidly, that the market is overstocked with labour, and the price falls from the increased supply. But if this were an universal rule, as the population of England has doubled in the last seventy or eighty years, wages ought to have fallen, whereas they have doubled or trebled in that interval. They have kept on increasing in North America during a still greater increase of population. They are, perhaps, twice as high in Holland as in Sweden, though the population of Holland is ten times as dense as that of Sweden.

" It has been attributed to the different pressure of taxation : but taxation is no where so light as in America, where wages are the highest. It is, probably, heavier in Hindostan than in England, yet wages are nine or ten times as high in England as in Hindostan. So that it might seem that wages are highest where taxation is lowest; but, on the other hand, taxation is lighter in France than in England, yet wages are lower, and lighter in Ireland than in France, yet wages are lower still. It appears, therefore, that there is no necessary connexion between taxation and wages.

" It has been attributed to the different rates of profit. The average rate of profit in England is supposed to be about one-tenth, or about eleven per cent. per annum. In Hindostan and America it is higher. We will suppose it to be one-sixth, or twenty per cent. per annum, which is probably far too high an estimate. This difference would account for the labourer, whose wages have been advanced for a year, receiving nine-tenths of the value of what he produces in England, and only five-sixths in America and Hindostan, or rather is only a different expression of the same fact, but it does not afford even a plausible solution of the present question.

" If the difference in wages were solely occasioned by a difference in the rate of profit, whatever is lost by the labourer would be gained by the capitalist, and the aggregate value in silver of a commodity produced by an equal expenditure of wages and profits, or, in my nomenclature, by an equal sum of labour and abstinence, would be every where the same; and in that case, how could both wages and profits be higher in North America than in England?

" Taking North America as the standard, and that the value in silver of the produce of a year's labour of one man, his wages having been advanced for a year, is two hundred and eighty ounces of silver, the value in silver in Hindostan and in England, of the produce of a year's labour of one man, his wages having been advanced for a year, would also be two hundred and eighty ounces, and as the labourer receives only twenty-four ounces of silver in Hindostan, and only one hundred and eighty ounces in England, the Hindoo capitalist must receive, on the sum advanced by him in payment of wages, a profit of more than two hundred and fifty-six ounces, or above one thousand per cent. per annum; and the English capitalist more than one hundred ounces, being more than sixty per cent. per annum, which we know to have no resemblance to the fact. If my statements and suppositions as to the average wages of labour, and the average profits of capital in England, Hindostan, and America be correct, a commodity unaffected by any monopoly produced by the labour of one man for a year, his wages having been advanced for a year, must sell in Hindostan for from one pound two ounces, to two pounds four ounces of silver; that is, for from twelve to twenty-four ounces as the wages of the labour, and from two to four ounces as the profit of the capital employed. In England such a commodity must sell for from about nine pounds nine ounces, to about sixteen pounds three ounces. In America for from fourteen pounds to twenty-three pounds four ounces. In other words, the same sum of labour and abstinence, or, in other words, the same

F

sacrifice of ease and of immediate enjoyment, obtains in America twenty-three pounds four ounces; in England sixteen pounds three ounces; and in Hindostan two pounds four ounces. And this difference is the phenomenon to which I am calling your attention.

"It has been attributed to the different prices, in silver, of necessaries. Provisions, it is said, are dearer, that is, exchange for more silver in England than in France; therefore, the labourer must receive more silver to enable him to purchase them. But provisions are cheaper in America than in England, and yet the labourer receives much less silver in England than in America. The productiveness of the worst soil cultivated, the period for which capital is advanced, and the rate of profit being given, it is clear that the average price in silver of corn, must depend on the average wages in silver of labour, not the wages of labour on the price of corn. On my hypothesis, that the services of an English labourer for a year, his wages having been advanced for a year, are worth about nine pounds nine ounces of silver, the corn produced by him in a year on the worst land, his wages having been advanced for a year, must be worth nine pounds nine ounces of silver, and cannot be permanently worth either more or less. If his wages fall one-half, the rate of profit remaining the same, the corn must be worth four pounds ten ounces and a half. If they double, it must be worth nineteen pounds six ounces. But in all cases, the productiveness of the worst land cultivated, the period for which wages are advanced, and the rate of profit remaining the same, the average amount in silver of wages must regulate the average value in silver of corn, and not the value in silver of corn the amount of wages. To suppose the contrary, is in fact the vulgar error of putting the cart before the horse, or mistaking the effect for the cause. To use Adam Smith's illustration, 'It is not because one man keeps a coach while his neighbour walks a-foot, that the one is rich and the other is poor; but because the one is rich he keeps a coach, and because the other is poor he walks a-foot.'

"If the population of England should maintain its present rate of advance; if our numbers should continue to increase at the rate of more than five hundred persons every twenty-four hours, and the absolute prohibition of foreign corn, for which a violent faction is now clamouring, should be conceded, there can be no question that even though wages should not rise, the price of corn would advance.

The constantly increasing additional quantity which must be raised to supply an annual addition of fifty thousand families, would be raised at a constantly increasing proportionate expense. According to the theory which I am considering, the wages of the labourer would rise in proportion. For what purpose would they rise? To enable him to consume the same quantity as before, though the whole quantity raised would bear a less proportion than before to the whole number of producers? On such a supposition wages might be ten guineas a day, and corn ten guineas a peck. According to the present administration of our poor-laws, which allots to each individual a definite quantity of corn, to be given by the landlord as relief when not paid by the employer as wages, the whole amount received by the labourer in the two forms of relief and wages might rise, not indeed ad infinitum, but until it had absorbed the whole amount of rent and tithes,—had converted the landlords and clergy into trustees for the poor. And this is the state of things which, under the united influence of corn laws, even such as they are now, poor laws, and an increasing population, seems gradually approaching. But in the absence of poor laws, what reason would there be for expecting a rise in wages? Because the labourer would want more? But would the labourer's wants give to the capitalist the power or the will to pay him more? Does the Manchester manufacturer pay his fine spinners 30s. a week, and his coarse spinners 15s. because the fine spinner eats twice as much as the coarse spinner? He pays the fine spinner 30s. because the produce f his labour is worth 30s., and a further sum equal to the average profit obtained by a manufacturing capitalist, and because, if he were to offer less, other capitalists would engage his labourers, and his machinery would stand idle. While the labourer's services are worth 30s. he will receive 30s., whatever be the price of corn. To suppose the contrary, is to consider the labourer not as a free agent, but as a slave or domestic animal, fed not according to his value, but his necessities.

" All experience shows that in the case which I have been supposing, the labourer's resource would be, not to raise his wages, but to reduce his expenditure. He must first give up his weekly pittance of animal food. He must drink his tea without sugar, and surrender his pipe, and perhaps his beer. He must sink from wheat to rye, or barley, or oatmeal, and from oatmeal to potatoes. He must look on the wheat which he would raise, as he now does on

the sheep and cattle that he tends, as a luxury beyond his enjoyment. The price of corn is nearly as high in Ireland as in England;
but have the wages of the Irish labourer risen to enable him to consume it? Did the exportation of corn and cattle from Ireland cease
even during the rages of famine, and of pestilence occasioned by
famine ?

" The only mode by which I can account for the phenomena
which I have been describing is, by supposing that the countries
which have the precious metals to dispose of, either as producers,
or as having a temporary superfluity at their own current rate of
prices, are willing to give more than one-fourth more for the exportable commodities produced by the labour of one North American
in a year, assisted by an advance of capital equal in value to his
wages for a given period, than for the commodities produced by the
labour of one Englishman, and more than ten times as much as for
the commodities produced by the labour of one Hindoo, similarly
circumstanced. Or in other words, that the diligence and skill with
which English labour is applied, enables the English labourer to
produce in a year exportable commodities equal in value to those
produced in a year by eight Hindoos; and that the diligence and
skill with which North American labour is applied, inferior as they
are perhaps to our own, yet by the assistance of the fertile soil which
he cultivates, enable the North American labourer to produce exportable commodities more than one-fourth more valuable than those
produced by the Englishman in a given period, and more than ten
times more valuable than those produced by the Hindoo. Or to use
a still more concise expression, that labour in England is eight times
as productive of exportable commodities as in Hindostan, and labour
in North America is one-fourth more productive of exportable commodities than in England."

Having thus taken money wages as the measure
of production, without allowance for the effect produced by the mode of taxation in increasing their
apparent difference, Mr. Senior has fallen into the
error of supposing a much greater difference in the
reward of the labourer than really exists, as I propose to show. By the following statements the reader

will be enabled to compare the rate of *money* wages of England and the United States. I propose, on a future occasion, to examine what is the amount of *real* wages.

The number of persons employed in the cotton manufacture of the United States is thus stated in the memorial of the New York Convention, 1832: —males, 18,539; females, 38,927; children, 4,691; hand weavers, 4,760; in all, 66,917; total wages, $ 10,294,944, equal to $ 3 or 12*s*. 6*d*. per week.

In the History of the Cotton Manufacture, by Mr. Baines, (p. 511) the above amount of wages is taken, but the children and hand weavers are omitted, by which the number of operatives is reduced to 57,466, and the wages are thereby made to appear to be 14*s*. 11*d*. per week. Mr. Baines's reasoning in relation to the comparative wages of the United States and England, is thereby vitiated.

It is to be regretted, that the gentlemen by whom the report was drawn up, did not give the average wages of men, women, and children. As they have not done so, we must endeavour to estimate them.

18,539 men, at $5 per week, would be	$92,695
38,927 women, at $2 per week,	77,854
4,691 children, at $1 75 per week,	8,211
4,760 hand weavers, at $4 per do.	19,040
	$197,800

52 weeks, at $197,800 each, would be $10,285,600, being nearly the amount given in the report.

In the above, it will be observed, that only about

* F

seven per cent. are termed children, and even those
are much above the age at which children are employed in England. At Lowell, the number employed
below 16 is very small, and none below 12. In the
Lawrence Factory at that place, out of 1000 females,
only 129 are below 17, and of the males there are 28
below that age. Deducting those over 16, those below
that age, or who may properly be styled children,
cannot exceed eight per cent. of the whole number
employed, which is 1160.

In a summary of the returns to the questions of
the Factory Commissioners, of 151 owners of cotton
mills, in Lancashire, Cheshire, and Derbyshire, for
five weeks, ending May 1833, it is stated, that out
of 48,645 persons employed, 20,084 are under 18
years of age. The average wages in these mills, are
10s. 5d..*

In an estimate of the number of persons employed
in the cotton mills of England, the total number is
given at at 212,800,† of whom 43,703 are under 14
years of age, and 39,554 between 14 and 18. One
half of the latter being deducted, the total number
employed below 16 years, would be 63,480, or 30
per cent. of the whole quantity. Notwithstanding
the vastly greater quantity of inferior labour thus
used, wages are estimated at 10s. 6d. per week, or
within two shillings of what was paid in the United
States in 1832.

Dr. James Mitchell was employed under the Factory Commissioners, to draw out tables, showing the

---

* Baines, p. 371.   † Ibid. p. 379.

wages, health, &c. of the factory operatives; and the results of some of the principal cotton mills, embracing 7614 operatives, are as follows :—*

1415 males below 16	2355 males above 16
1278 females below 16	2566 females above 16

giving above 35 per cent. below the age at which children are usually employed here. As wages differ very much with age, and as it is to be supposed that the efficiency of the labourer is in proportion to the wages received, the only fair mode of comparing those of the United States and England, is to strike off all whose ages are below that at which they are here employed. The average wages of persons above 16, in those factories, as given by Dr. Mitchell, are as follows :

2355 males, 16s. 3d.
2566 females, 8s.
———
4921—general average 12s.

or within 6d. as much as the average of the estimate furnished by the New York Convention. It may be said, that seven per cent. of the labourers employed in the United States being below 16, there should be some allowance made therefor, but they are generally so little below that age, that any allowance would have small effect upon the result.

The great disproportion that exists between the two countries, in the employment of male and female labour, cannot fail to strike the reader. In England, the females exceed the males by only about 9 per

* Baines. p. 437.

cent., while in the United States they exceeded them, agreeably to the above statement, by above 110 per cent. Since that time, great improvements have taken place in machinery, increasing the proportion of females very greatly, as will hereafter be shown. At first sight, it might be supposed that this should cause wages to be lower here, the labour of men being generally more productive than that of women, and that this would be an offset to the number of children employed in England. Such is not, however, the case, women being employed *here* because every thing is done to render labour productive, while *there* a large portion of the power of the male operatives is wasted.

By the above statement it is shown, that in the United States there were only 4760 hand weavers in the year 1832, and the number can hardly be supposed to have increased. From the great influx of emigrants from Ireland, it is probable that there will be, for a long time to come, an equal number; but the modes of employment are so numerous, that a large number must be annually absorbed. On the 1st January, 1835, there were in the town of Lowell 5051 power looms, or more, by nearly 300, than the whole number of hand looms in this country.

The whole number of power looms in England, in 1820, was 14,150—in 1829 it had risen to 55,500, and is now supposed to be 85,000, which, with 15,000 in Scotland, would give a total of 100,000.* During this time it is supposed that the number of

* Baines, p. 238.

hand looms has rather increased, and it is now estimated at 250,000.

The condition of the weavers is thus described:

" ' The hand-loom weavers,' says Dr. Kay, speaking of those
living in Manchester, ' labour fourteen hours and upwards daily,
and earn only from five to seven or eight shillings per week. They
consist chiefly of Irish, and are affected by all the causes of moral
and physical depression which we have enumerated. Ill-fed, ill-
clothed, half-sheltered, and ignorant—weaving in close, damp cellars, or crowded, ill-ventilated workshops—it only remains that
they should become, as is too frequently the case, demoralized and
reckless, to render perfect the portraiture of savage life.' The statement that the weavers work fourteen or sixteen hours per day, has
been so often made, that it is now generally believed. The fact,
however, is, that they work these long hours only two or three days
in the week, and they generally, notwithstanding their poverty,
spend one or two days in idleness; their week's labour seldom exceeds fifty-six or fifty-eight hours, whilst that of the spinners is
sixty-nine hours. This irregularity on the part of the weavers is
to be ascribed in some degree to the wearisome monotony of their
labour, from which they seek refuge in company and amusement;
and also to their degraded condition, which makes them reckless
and improvident."*

It may be asked, why they should continue in an
employment so degrading.

" These were the occasions and direct causes of the lamentable
fall in weavers' wages; but their effects could not have been so
serious if there had not been permanent causes, belonging to the
nature of the employment itself. Of these, the *first* and grand cause
is, *the easy nature of the employment*. The weaving of calicoes is
one of the simplest of manual operations, understood in a few mo-
ments, and completely learnt in a few weeks. It requires so little
strength or skill, that a child eight or ten years of age may practise it. A man brought up to any other employment may also very
shortly learn to weave. From the facility of learning the trade,

* Baines, p. 485.

* F 2

and from its being carried on under the weaver's own roof, he naturally teaches his children to weave as soon as they can tread the treadles, if he cannot obtain places for them in a factory. Thus they begin at a very early age to add to the earnings of the family, and the wife also toils in the same way to increase their scanty pittance. But it is obvious, that that which is only a child's labour, can be remunerated only by a child's wages. There are large departments of hand-loom weaving, which are almost entirely given up to women and children, and their wages go far to regulate all the rest. The men, where they are able, procure better kinds of work; and where they are not able, they must put up with the most paltry earnings.

The *second* cause for the low wages of weavers is, that their employment is in some respects *more agreeable, as laying them under less restraint than factory labour.* Being carried on in their own cottages, their time is at their own command: they may begin and leave off work at their pleasure: they are not bound punctually to obey the summons of the factory bell: if they are so disposed, they can quit their loom for the public-house, or to lounge in the street, or to accept some other job, and then, when urged by necessity, they may make up for lost time by a great exertion. In short, they are more independent than factory operatives; they are their own masters; they receive their materials, and sometimes do not take back the web for several weeks; and—what is a lamentable, but far too common occurrence—they have the power, in case of urgent necessity or strong temptation, to embezzle a few cops of their employers' weft in order to buy bread or ale. All this makes the weaver's occupation more seductive to men of idle, irregular, and dissipated habits, than other occupations. It is a dear-bought, miserable liberty, but, like poaching or smuggling, it is more congenial to some tastes, than working under precise restrictions for twice the remuneration. The mention of this unquestionable fact by no means implies a charge against the weavers, that they are all of loose habits and morals; but it helps to account for many continuing at the loom, notwithstanding the wretchedness of their circumstances."*

Various estimates have been made of the wages of weavers, as will be seen by the following extract:

* Baines, p. 493.

" The weekly wages of several classes of hand-loom cotton weavers, in each year, from 1810 to 1825, have been given in a table at p. 438; and their wages in 1832 are given in a table at p. 439. The former states the wages of the weavers of calicoes at the astonishingly low rate of 4s. 3d. in the year 1825; but these goods were chiefly woven by women and children. The latter table does not mention the prices paid for calicoes; but it shows that in 1832, the average wages for weaving common checks, common nankeens, and cambrics, all of which are woven principally by women and children, were from 6s. to 6s. 6d., 7s., and 8s.; the wages for fancy checks, woven by men, were 7s. to 7s. 6d.; and for fancy nankeens and quiltings, from 9s. to 12s., 13s., and even 15s. Mr. George Smith, of the firm of James Massey and Son, of Manchester, gave evidence before the Committee of the House of Commons on Manufactures, Commerce, &c., in July, 1833, that the weavers of calicoes in the neighbourhood of Burnley and Colne earned little more than 4s. per week net wages: these, however, were almost all children: of the whole number of hand-loom cotton weavers in the kingdom, which he estimated at 200,000, he supposed that 30,000 earned this low rate of wages; whilst the remaining 170,000 would only earn 6s. or 7s. a week: in the neighbourhood of Manchester he thought the average would be 7s. Mr. John Makin, a manufacturer, of Bolton, stated before the Committee of the Commons on Hand-loom Weavers, in July, 1834, that a weaver of the kind of cambric most commonly produced there, namely, a six-quarter 60-reed cambric, 120 shoots of weft in an inch, could only weave one piece in a week, the gross wages for which were 5s. 6d.—subject to a deduction of about 1s. 4d. Hugh Mackenzie, a hand-loom weaver of Glasgow, informed the same Committee, that the average net wages of the weavers of plain goods in that city and neighbourhood, would scarcely amount to 5s. per week. Mr. William Craig, a manufacturer of handkerchiefs and ginghams at Glasgow, stated the net wages of weavers in that department to be 4s. 6d. to 5s. a week; and Mr. Thomas Davidson, a manufacturer of fancy lappet goods in that city, stated the wages of the plain weavers to be from 5s. to 5s. 6d. net on the average, and that the plain weavers were two-thirds or three-fourths of all the hand-loom weavers in Scotland, whilst the remaining one-third or one-fourth earned on an average about 8s. a week. On the proceedings of the Committee on Hand-loom Weavers, it may be observed, that the selection of the witnesses, and the mode of examining them, show some disposition to make out a case; and the most unfavourable view of the weavers' condition is presented."*

Wages must depend upon production, and the following statement will at once satisfy the reader, that low as are those received by the weavers, they are fully equal to their deserts as producers.

" ' A very good *hand weaver*, 25 or 30 years of age, will weave *two* pieces of 9-8ths shirtings per week, each 24 yards long, containing 100 shoots of weft in an inch; the reed of the cloth being a 44 Bolton count, and the warp and weft 40 hanks to the lb.

" ' In 1833, a steam-loom weaver, from 15 to 20 years of age, assisted by a girl about 12 years of age, attending to four looms, can weave *eighteen* similar pieces in a week; some can weave twenty pieces.' "†

In a description of the cotton goods made in Lancashire, at page 418 of Mr. Baines's work, it is stated, that the only goods that are the product of the power-loom *exclusively*, are stout printing calicoes. Stout calicoes for domestic purposes, as sheetings, coarse shirtings, &c., cotton shirtings, and small wares, are said to be *chiefly* the product of the power-loom. Cotton velvets, velveteens, &c., of power and hand-looms; but all other articles, *including common printing calicoes*, are made at hand-looms.

Hence it will be seen, that hand-looms continue to be used for the manufacture of the commonest articles; and while such is the case—while human labour undertakes to compete with machinery—wages must necessarily be low. In the extract above given, it will be seen that two-thirds or three-fourths of the

* Baines, p. 486.   † Ibid. p. 240.

weavers in Scotland are employed in the production of plain goods.

If one half of the hand-looms, or that portion of them now employed in producing articles that could be made by the power-loom, were set aside, and replaced by the necessary number of power-looms, and females to attend them, the effect upon the average of wages would be very great. There would be 125,000 persons, at the lowest rate of wages, withdrawn, and replaced by a small number, at the highest rate of female wages.

Hence it is evident, that much of the apparent difference in wages arises from the misapplication of labour in the weaving department, and I propose now to show that a similar result is produced in the spinning department.

The following is the account given by Mr. Baines of the throstle, which is the latest improvement in spinning machinery.

" Mr. Bannatyne thus describes this improvement :—' In the throstle, the spinning apparatus is in every respect the same as in Sir Richard Arkwright's frame, but the movement of the parts is different. In place of four or six spindles being coupled together, forming what is called a head, with a separate movement by a pulley and drum, as is the case in the frame, the whole rollers and spindles on both sides of the throstle are connected together, and turned by bands from a tin cylinder lying horizontally under the machine. The merit of the invention chiefly lies in the simplification of the moving apparatus just mentioned. The movement is not only rendered lighter, but greater facility is afforded for increasing the speed of the machine, and consequently, when the nature of the spinning admits it, for obtaining a larger production. The throstle can also, with more ease, and at less expense, be altered to spin the different grists of yarn; only a few movements require to be changed in it to produce this end, while in the spinning-frame there are a great many.'

" Further improvements, which have the effect of increasing the veloci'y of the spindles, and consequently of augmenting the quantity of twist produced, have been made within the last few years by American mechanics; but these machines cause a large quantity of waste, and they are therefore by no means established in general use as real improvements. Owing to these advantages—the greater quantity of twist produced, its consequent cheapness, and its adaptation to the purpose of warps for power-loom cloth of the coarser kinds—it is probable that the throstles will come into use more extensively than at present. For all the finer qualities of yarn the mule is the only machine employed."*

" Some idea may be formed of the proportions which these two machines at present bear to each other in the extent of their adoption, from the statement of mule and throstle spindles in Lanarkshire, in November, 1831, made by Dr. Cleland, in his ' Enumeration of the Inhabitants of Glasgow,' &c. The number of mule spindles is stated to be 591,288, and of throstle spindles 48,900.—p. 151."†

By the above it is seen, that at Glasgow, in 1831, the number of throstles was only about one-twelfth of the mule spindles. In one of the tables above referred to,‡ the whole number of persons employed in mule spinning is given at 65,216, of whom more than one-third are male adults, while the throstle spinners are 7709 in number, and only 793 are male adults. Three-fourths of the mule spinners are males, while nearly three-fourths of the throstle spinners are females.

At Lowell, the mule is not in use in any of the factories. The throstle has been greatly improved, and is now worked to great advantage, and the conse-

---

* Baines, p. 208.   † Ibid. p. 209.—Note.
‡ Ibid. p. 379.

quence is, that female labour here takes the place of the male labour employed in England.

It will be seen by the following passage that the throstle, where it has been introduced in England, has had the effect of superseding the demand for the labour not only of males, but of young children.

"The throstle, which hardly ever requires the operative to deviate from the perpendicular posture, has for a great many years super-seded entirely that machine" [the water frame]. "It is managed by young persons from fifteen years of age and upwards, and does not necessarily involve the employment of children. One girl is adequate to superintend a throstle-frame of 220 spindles. From this great factory department, therefore, children are in a great measure ex-cluded."*

In the carding department, the difference in the proportion of males and females employed is exceed-ingly great.† Of 48,645 persons engaged in the cot-ton manufacture, there were employed in the carding rooms,

2350 male adults.

1328 males under 18 years.

Total, males,   3678

3501 female adults.

2578 females under 18 years.

Total, females, 6079

At Lowell, in the card rooms, are employed 13 or 14 males to 33 females; the latter exceeding the former by 150 per cent., while in England the differ-ence is only 65 per cent.

* Ure. Philosophy of Manufactures, p. 362.
† Baines, p. 372.

The whole number of persons employed in the carding rooms in England, is estimated* at 40,484, of whom there were,

Male adults,	10,361	
Children,	5,522	
		15,883
Female adults,	15,062	
Children,	8,720	
		23,782
Age and sex uncertain,		819
		40,484

In this case the difference is only 50 per cent.

Nearly all the most recent improvements of machinery have been made in the United States. That such should be the case, will not appear extraordinary, when it is recollected, that the best workmen are to be found where the best wages are paid, and as wages are highest in the United States, there is every reason to suppose, that at least as high a degree of intelligence prevails among the labouring classes, as in any other country.†

Reference has before been made to the return of

* Baines, p. 379.

† The following remark, made by a Frenchman in relation to the English workmen, will perhaps apply with greater force to those of the United States.

" M. Roman, delegate from Alsace to the Commission of Inquiry, who has travelled in England to inspect our manufactures, said, with much justice—'Il y a, dans l'ouvrier Anglais, un espéce de croisement du caractère Français et du caractère Allemand, un melange de Saxon et de Normand, qui lui donne, en même temps, l'attention et la vivacité.' "—*Baines*, p. 513.

151 cotton mills, in which it was shown, that of 48,645 there were 13,740 male *adults*, being about 27½ per cent. of the whole.* Of these, 927 are engineers, firemen, &c., and the remainder are employed in the different processes of carding, spinning, reeling, weaving, &c., nearly all of which is here done by women. At Lowell, the proportion of male *adults* does not amount to more than 12½ per cent.

It thus appears, that in every department of the cotton manufacture, there is an economy of labour greatly exceeding that of England, and that although apparently rather more expensive, it is really more productive. The effect of these improvements in the price of female labour, is the most remarkable and the most gratifying. By substituting it for that of males, to the greatest possible extent, it has been rendered so productive, that the wages received by females now average more than the average wages paid to men, women, and children, in the cotton mills of England.

Since the preparation of the report to the New York Convention in 1832, there have been various improvements in cotton machinery, the effect of which has been to increase the rate of wages, by rendering labour more productive. By a statement prepared at Lowell by W. Austin, Esq., superintendent of the Lawrence Factory, there were employed in the manufacture of cotton goods (exclusive of the printing establishments) about 4800 females, and 800 males. The average wages of the former

* Baines, p. 371.

* G

were $3 15, or 13s. 1d. per week, and of the latter
$6 75, or 28s. 1d.—average of the whole, $3 67,
or 15s. 4d. sterling, being considerably more than
the average of the English cotton mills, as given
above.

The factories at Lowell are, however, on the best
footing, and it would not be just to compare the
wages there paid with those of the ordinary mills of
England. I will therefore take some of those selected by Mr. Baines, and enable the reader to make a
comparison between the wages there paid, and those
of Lowell.

Fine cotton spinners, in the employ of Mr. T.
Houldsworth, Manchester, received, in 1833, from
54s. to 65s. per week, out of which they paid their
piecers 21s. to 22s. 6d., leaving them from 33s. to
42s. per week.*

There are 111 spinners at present employed in the
mill; their average net earnings 33s. 3d. per week.†

In the card room, males receive from 15s. to 30s.
per week. Females receive from 8s. 6d. to 12s.
Mechanics' wages, blacksmiths, turners, filers, or
machine makers, and fitters up, are now from 27s.
to 31s. per week.‡

Spinners in the employ of Mr. Thomas Ashton, of
Hyde, earned, in 1832, from 20s. to 35s. Dressers
received 30s. 6d. Weavers, all of whom are employed in attending the power-loom, and are for the most
part young girls, average 12s.§ Deducting the young

---

* Report of Commons Committee, quoted by Baines, p. 443.
† Ibid.   ‡ Ibid. p. 444.   § Ibid. p. 445.

persons, who receive inferior wages, and who would not be employed in this country, there can be little doubt the average of wages paid by Mr. Ashton is nearly as high as that of Lowell.

" The net wages of a cotton spinner have been rarely under 30s. a week, the year round."*

Mr. George Royle stated on oath before the Factory Commissioners, that the whole of his spinners, whose average weekly wages were 53s. 5d., turned out for higher wages †

The average of wages of all persons, *young and old*, at the mills of Messrs. Lees, in Gorton, is 12s. per week.‡

The improvements in machinery since 1832, have materially increased the wages of spinners, as will be seen by the following extract:

" In the year 1834, in two fine spinning-mills at Manchester, a spinner could produce sixteen pounds of yarn, of the fineness of two hundred hanks to the pound, from mules of the productive fertility of three hundred to three hundred and twenty-four spindles, working them sixty-nine hours: and the quantity that he turned off in sixty-nine hours more frequently exceeded sixteen pounds than fell short of it. These very mules being in the same year replaced by others of double power, let us analyze the result. The spinner had been accustomed to produce sixteen pounds of No. 200 yarn from mules of the said extent. From the list of prices, it appears, that in the month of May, he was paid 3s. 6d. per pound; which being multiplied by sixteen, gives 54s. for his gross receipts, out of which he had to pay (at the highest) 13s. for assistants. This leaves him 41s. of net earnings. But soon thereafter his mules have their productive power doubled, being re-mounted with six hundred and

* Ure. Philosophy of Manufactures, p. 280.
† Ure. p. 283.   ‡ Ure. p. 307.

forty-eight spindles. He now is paid 2s. 5d. per pound, instead of
3s. 6d.—that is, two-thirds of his former wages per pound; but he
turns off double weight of work in the same time, namely, thirty-
two pounds, instead of sixteen. His gross receipts are therefore 2s.
5d. multiplied into thirty-two, or 77s. 4d. He now requires however *five* assistants to help him, to whom, averaging their cost at
5s. a-piece per week, he must pay 25s.; or, to avoid the possibility
of cavil, say 27s. Deducting this sum from his gross receipts, he
will retain 50s. 4d. for his net earnings for sixty-nine hours' work,
instead of 41s., being an increase of 9s. 4d. per week. This statement of the spinner's benefit is rather under the mark than above
it, as might be proved by other documents, were it necessary.—
Supplem. Fact. Report.—Preface to Tables by J. W. Cowell, Esq."[*]

A statement of the weekly rates of wages paid in
March and April, 1832, gives, for

Spinners, men,   20s. to 25s.

Spinners, women,   10s. to 15s.

Stretchers, men,   25s. to 26s.

Dressers, men,   28s. to 30s.

Mechanics,   24s. to 26s.[†]

A statement of average net weekly earnings, of
different classes of operatives, in various cotton factories, May 1833, gives the following :

Carders, or overlookers, -   -   23s. 6d.

Spinners, overlookers,   -   -   29s. 3d.

Spinners, male and female, average, 25s. 8d.

Throstle spinners, overlookers,   22s. 4d.

Dressers,   -   -   -   -   27s. 9d.

Engineers, firemen, mechanics, &c. 20s. 6d.

Warpers, weavers, & roller coverers, 10s. 10d. to
12s. 3d.   These are both male and female.[‡]

---

* Ure. p. 323.   † Ibid. p. 439.

‡ Baines, p. 436.

From a statement of daily wages of persons employed in the cotton mills of Glasgow and its vicinity,
April 1832, compiled by Dr. Cleland, it appears that
men on piece work, at spinning, earn from 21*s.* to
27*s.* per week. Lads and girls earn from 12*s.* to 18*s.*
per week.*

" The Glasgow mills are, in productive power,
much in arrear of the Manchester ones, as is proved
by the circumstance of thirty or forty per cent. more
being paid for the same produce of yarn in the former
than in the latter place."† A necessary consequence
of this deficient production, is that the average of
wages is lower in Glasgow than in Manchester.

I am not possessed of information in regard to the
woollen trade, as copious as that furnished by Mr.
Baines's excellent work, but the improvements that
have been made in machinery in the United States
are very important, and have enabled the employers,
in like manner, to employ female labour for many
purposes for which male labour is still required in
England. The following statement will enable us to
see what is the proportion:—" The statistics of the
woollen trade, at present, as far as they can be ascertained, give us the following results: number of
manufactories, 1315—male operatives, 31,360—female operatives, 22,526."‡

At the Middlesex woollen factory, in Lowell, the
number of females is 240, and of males 145, whereas

* Report of Commons Committee, quoted by Baines, p. 442.
† Ure. p. 328.
‡ London Athenæum, July 4, 1835.

* G 2

in England the number of the latter would be **336.**
In the one case, the males exceed the females by **40**
per cent., while in the other they are 40 per cent.
less in number.

The following extract will show the average rate
of wages paid in the woollen manufacture. Were
the children deducted, it cannot be doubted that the
rate would be nearly as high as that given by the
New York Convention, say 12*s.* 6*d.* per week.

" The woollen manufacturers in the neighbourhood of Leeds,
amount to about 20,000, working twelve hours per day, and may be
divided into three classes, viz. weavers, earning 14*s.*—spinners and
slubbers, 21*s.*, and dressers the same—women gain about 6*s.*—children from eight to twelve years, 3*s.* to 5*s.*; from twelve to sixteen
years, 6*s.* to 8*s.* Forty years since, the *average* wages of men, women, and children, in the woollen manufacture, were from 5*s.* to 6*s.*
each per week; they are now from 9*s.* to 10*s.* per week."—*Leeds
Mercury, March* 23*d,* 1833, *quoted in Hist. of Middle and Working
Classes,* p. 572.

The difference in the rate of wages paid in the woollen manufacture is remarkable. At Leeds, according to a table furnished by Dr. Ure,* men between
the ages of 26 and 51 average from 22*s.* to 22*s.* 6*d.*
In Gloucester, men of the same age average from
13*s.* to 1*s.* 3*d.*—in Somerset, 16*s.* 3*d.* to 19*s.* 9*d.*—
in Wiltshire, 13*s.* 7*d.* to 15*s.* 5*d.* The latter counties
are in the south of England, where the abuses of the
poor laws have been carried to the greatest extent.
The following statement will enable the reader to
see how regularly low wages accompany a high
poor's rate.

* Philosophy of Manufactures, p. 476.

	Wages.	Poor's rate per head of population, 1831.
Leeds,	22s. to 22s. 6d.	5s. 7d.
Gloucester,	13s. to 15s. 3d.	8s. 8d.
Somerset,	16s. 9d. to 19s. 9d.	8s. 9d.
Wilts,	13s. 7d. to 15s. 5d.	16s. 6d.

The cause of these extraordinary differences is to be found in the poor laws, which obstruct the circulation of labour, and produce the effects described in the following extract:

" ' Were I to detail the melancholy, degrading, and ruinous system which has been pursued throughout the country, in regard to the unemployed poor, and in the payment of the wages of idleness, I should scarcely be credited beyond its confines. In the generality of parishes, from five to forty labourers have been without employment, loitering about during the day, engaged in idle games, insulting passengers on the road, or else consuming their time in sleep, that they might be more ready and active in the hours of darkness. The weekly allowances cannot supply more than food; how then are clothing, firing, and rent to be provided? *By robbery and plunder;* and those so artfully contrived and effected, that discovery has been almost impossible. Picklocks have readily opened our barns and granaries; the lower orders of artificers, and even, in one or two instances, small farmers, have joined the gang, consisting of from ten to twenty men; and corn has been sold in the market of such mixed qualities by these small farmers, that competent judges have assured me, it must have been stolen from different barns, and could not have been produced from their occupations. Disgraceful as these facts are to a civilized country, I could enumerate many more, but recital would excite disgust.'—*Report of the Poor Law Commissioners, p. 70, 8vo. edit.*"*

The average of carpet and hardware manufacturers, is 22s. 4d., or $5 36 per week.

Carpet Manufacturers, 1st class, 30s.

2d   do.   23s.

3d   do.   20s.

* Ure. p. 355.

Hardware and Metal, 1st do. 25s.
                     2d do. 20s.
                     3d do. 16s.

I think it must be evident to the reader, that any difference in wages that may exist between England and the United States, must arise out of its better application in the latter. The perfection to which machinery has been brought, enables the proprietor to avail himself much more extensively of female labour than is the case in Europe. The labour of the females, as shown, is much more productive, and they consequently receive higher wages. The males, not being compelled to compete with machinery, are enabled to apply their powers in other ways that are more productive, and as a consequence, when they marry, the necessity for the employment of their wives* and young children in factories is unknown. A further consequence is, that all parents have it in their power to obtain education for their children, and the children have time to receive it. A still further consequence is, that the state of morals at Lowell, Dover, Providence, and other places where extensive factories exist, is such as is almost utterly unknown in any other parts of the world, and constitutes a phenomenon in the moral, equal to that of Niagara in the natural world.†

---

* Of one thousand females in the Lawrence Factory at Lowell, there are but *eleven* who are married. There are nineteen widows.

† The following passage from a statement furnished by a gentleman who has charge of one of the principal establishments in Lowell, shows a very gratifying state of things. "There have only occurred three instances in which any apparently improper connexion or inti-

The necessity for the passage of "Factory Bills," does not exist in this country. In England, by interferences of all kinds, the parents are oppressed and reduced to the necessity of sending their children to work at the earliest possible age, and then it becomes necessary to interfere anew, to prevent the children from bearing too much of the burthen. In the United States, on the contrary, it is so desirable to have efficient hands, that the owners are not disposed to employ children at too young an age, and thus,

---

macy had taken place, and in all those cases the parties were married on the discovery, and several months prior to the birth of their children; so that, in a legal point of view, no illegitimate birth has taken place among the females employed in the mills under my direction. Nor have I known of but one case among all the females employed in Lowell. I have said known—I should say heard of one case. I am just informed that that was a case where the female had been employed but a few days in any mill, and was forthwith rejected from the corporation, and sent to her friends. In point of female chastity, I believe that Lowell is as free from reproach as any place of an equal population in the United States or the world."

At the great establishment at Dover, New Hampshire, I have been assured there has never been a case of bastardy.

Let this be compared with the statements of the Poor Law Commissioners, and it will go far to show that the means which tend to promote the increase of wealth, tend also to the promotion of morality, and, as a necessary consequence, of happiness. There can be no doubt, that with a different system, there would in time arise, in the factories of England, a similar state of things. There are, even now, some similar cases to be found in England, proving how much good may be done where the owners are disposed to do what is in their power to promote the cause of morality.

" Amongst the great numbers of factory operatives employed under this gentleman, [William Grant Esq., at Rumsbottom,] only one case of female misconduct has occurred in the space of twenty years, and that was a farmer's daughter."—*Ure, p.* 416.—*Note.*

while the excellent situation of the labourer renders it unnecessary, the interest of the employer would tend to prevent it, should idleness or dissipation lead the parent to desire it.*

Owing to the system of making up wages out of the poor rates, it is exceedingly difficult to ascertain what is usually paid to the agricultural labourer, but I find in the *Report of the Poor Laws Commissioners,* that in 1832, wages at Eastborne were 2s. per day; at Brede 2s. 3d. per day, *winter and summer;* at Northian and Ewhurst the same.

The following extract will show the wages paid to common labourers at the Docks in London.

" What are the wages of permanent and extra? The wages of a permanent labourer are 16s. per week; extra labourers 2s. 6d. per day, the latter being only employed according to the demands of the service.

" Is there ever any insufficiency felt of *English* labourers? There

---

* The following passage from a late English journal, serves to show the inefficacy of legislative interferences. In the endeavour to avoid Scylla, they are sure to fall upon Charybdis.

" Mr. Brotherton has brought before Parliament a grievance which ought to obtain an immediate cure. The public are scarcely aware that children under eleven are required to produce a certificate of their age from a surgeon; still less do they know that this surgeon is empowered to exact sixpence for each certificate; or that when the child, as is frequently the case, is transferred from one factory to another, a fresh certificate is necessary. The children of Manchester alone have thus been taxed, within a twelvemonth, to the extent of 520l. In two districts, the sum of 4000l. has been thus wrung from the wages of the children within eleven months! These harsh, these monstrous truths are contained in returns laid before the House of Commons. Will that House close its labours for the year, without terminating a system of spoliation that amounts to sacrilege?"

is; without the aid of the Irish and some Germans, the business of the docks would at times be impeded."—*Evidence of John Hall, Secretary of St. Katherine's Dock, &c., before the Poor Laws Commissioners.*

Two shillings and three pence per day is equal to $170 per annum. An agricultural labourer in the United States receives nine dollars per month, equal to $108 per annum, and his board, estimated at $65, making $173. In the immediate vicinity of the principal cities, wages are somewhat higher, being frequently ten, and sometimes eleven dollars per month. The cost of boarding is also somewhat higher. The price given above would be considered a fair one at the distance of twenty or thirty miles from those cities. At greater distances they frequently do not exceed $8, so that nine dollars may be considered as a fair average price.

The following is given in the History of the Middle and Working Classes, as an evidence that wages are " *still lower in Scotland than in Lancashire.*" It will be recollected, that Lancashire is the head quarters of the hand weavers, whose situation has been described.

"At Dumfries hiring market, on Wednesday, healthy, unmarried men, who understood their business, commanded readily £6 for the half year, with board and lodging, and, in some instances, the pounds were made guineas. Dairy maids and others were hired at from 50s. to 55s., according to character, capability, and experience; but the former was most common." Here we find wages from 56 to 60 dollars per annum, with board and lodging, while the

same labourer would obtain here $ 108, with board
and lodging, making a difference of $ 50 per annum,
or about 96 cents per week, between this country
and Scotland, in a case that is adduced as an evidence of the extremely low rate of wages, and *where
the taxes on consumption must be paid by the employer.* When those taxes are added, it will be found
that the cost of labourers is not probably 50 cents
per week less than in the United States. The female
servant has from £ 5 to £ 5 10*s.*, being an average
of $ 25 40, or about 50 cents per week. In this case,
the difference is considerable, although but a few
years since good female servants could readily be
had at 75 cents. Adding to the wages of the Scot-
tish lass, the taxes on consumption, the difference
will be very much lessened.

The average of the wages of carpenters, brick-
layers, masons, and plasterers, as given in the contract prices of Greenwich Hospital, by Mr. M'Culloch, has been, *for many years*, 5*s.* 6*d.* per day, equal
to $ 1 32. The wages of similar persons in Phila-
delphia, as already given, (p. 26,) average about the
same sum.

The wages of domestic servants, I believe, are
higher in London than in any city of this country.
By the following extract it will be seen that £ 15 is
given as the wages of female servants. This is much
above the average here.

"There are, perhaps, no services which, in England, are more
amply remunerated than those of domestic servants. While all other
classes have suffered a great depreciation during the last twenty
years, the wages paid to domestic servants have undoubtedly increased. The ordinary items of the expenditure of this class have

also very considerably diminished; the cost of clothing, which, we presume, constitutes the chief disbursement of female domestic servants has diminished, since the peace, at least 80 per cent. Hence the £15 now paid as yearly wages, is equivalent to £27 twenty years since. The number of female servants in Britain is upwards of 700,000 ; and if their ages were calculated, we do not doubt it would be found that two-thirds of all the British damsels between the ages of fifteen and twenty-five, are domestic servants ; yet, notwithstanding this immense supply of female labourers, the demand is superior to it; their wages rise and their prosperity is strikingly evinced by their elegant garments and costly decorations. Male servants are not so numerous, yet the demand is superior to the supply; and the services of a footman, gratuitously educated at the parish school, already command an equal remuneration, and promise to command a higher price than the services of a curate, who has expended large sums in the acquirement of classic lore at the universities."*

From the above it is evident that there is not the difference that has been supposed in the amount of *money wages* received by the labourers of England and the United States. At page 63 it will be seen that Mr. Senior estimates wages in Great Britain at an average of £35 per annum, and in the United States and Canada at £46 13s. per annum. The lowest weekly wages in the former he puts at 10s. per week, the highest 17s., and the average 13s. 6d. In the United States and Canada, the lowest is 13s. 6d., the highest 22s. 6d., and the average 18s. By the statements given above it has been seen that the average wages of males and females above 16 in a cotton factory, in which more than half are females, are 12s., nearly equal to his average of *men's* wages.

* Browning's Political and Domestic Condition of Great Britain, p. 413.

* H

It has also been shown that the wages of agricultural labour in some parts of England, are 2*s*. 3*d*. per day, equal to the average wages stated by Mr. Senior. It is very true that in a large portion of England not more than 10*s*. are paid as wages, but *to that must be added the parish allowance*, which would make it equal to what is paid elsewhere.* Even in Scotland, where wages are exceedingly low, it is shown that from six pounds to six guineas the half year is paid, and if to that be added 6*s*. per week for board, the whole will exceed 10*s*. In Wade's History of the Middle and Working classes (p. 538,) the average of husbandry wages is stated at 12*s.* If this be correct, the whole average must certainly very much exceed 13*s*. 6*d*.

The average of carpet and hardware manufacturers is 22*s*. 4*d*. per week—of carpenters, bricklayers, masons, &c., 33*s*. per week. Is it possible that such wages could be obtained when the average of men's wages was only 13*s*. 6*d*.? I believe it is not.

It is probable that a much nearer average of wages will be found at 18*s*. per week, or 72 cents per day.

---

* Judging from the following statement, we might suppose the rate of agricultural wages fully equal to the deserts of the labourers.

"Good ploughmen are not to be found. The labourers say they do not care to plough, because that is a kind of work which, if neglected, will subject them to punishment, and if properly done requires constant attention; and the lads do not even wish to learn. Nine able-bodied young men were in the workhouse last winter; such was their character, that they were not to be trusted with threshing."—*Report of Poor Laws Commissioners, p*. 70.

That of the United States is perhaps a little higher, but the difference cannot, I think, exceed 8 or 10 per cent., and arises entirely out of the superior application of labour.*

* The following statements, omitted in their proper places, give a view of the operations of two factories of the highest character, *south of New England*, and show a nearer approach to the condition of the average English factories, than is to be found at Lowell.

		Average wages.
The first is a *cotton* mill, employing	65 men,	$ 7 70
	148 females,	2 81
	98 children,	1 50

Average wages $ 3 41, or 14s. 2d. Here it will be observed, that the proportion of men is nearly 20 per cent.; about 30 per cent. are children; and less than one half are women. In the English mills referred to at page 71, 31 per cent. are men, 36 per cent. children, and about one-third women.

		Average wages.
The second is a *woollen* mill, employing	44 men,	$6 25
	57 females,	2 50
	39 children,	1 25

Average wages $3 33, or 13s. 10d. If the children be equally divided between the sexes, there will be 64 males, and 76 females. At Lowell, in the woollen manufacture, 64 males would give 106 females, while in England there would be only 39.

It is probable that the machinery in these mills is not so perfect as that of the Lowell mills, which will account for difference of production and difference of wages. The improvements of the present times, tend very much to reducing the demand for children and men, and increasing that for young women, a change that cannot be otherwise than advantageous.

CHAPTER VII.

IF Mr. Senior is in error as to the *amount*, he is not less so, I think, as to the *causes*, of difference. He admits himself to be unable to account for it, except by ascribing it to British superiority in industry and skill. There is here a want of precision in the use of the word " skill." It is well known that it is not want of skill in the management of the miserable tools he possesses, that affects the Hindoo. On this head, Bishop Heber says:—

" Nor is it true that in the mechanic arts they are inferior to the general run of the European nations. Where they fall short of us, which is chiefly in agricultural implements, and the mechanics of common life, they are not, so far as I have understood of Italy and the South of France, surpassed in any degree by the people of those countries. Their goldsmiths and weavers produce as beautiful fabrics as our own, and it is so far from true that they are obstinately wedded to their old patterns, that they show an anxiety to imitate our models, and do imitate them successfully. The ships built by native artists at Bombay are notoriously as good as any which sail from London or Liverpool. The carriages or gigs which they supply at Calcutta are as handsome, though not as durable as those of Longacre. In the little town of Monghyr, three hundred miles from Calcutta, I had pistols, double-barreled guns, and different pieces of cabinet work, brought down to my boat for sale, which in outward form, for I know no further, nobody but perhaps Mr. —— could detect to be of Hindoo origin, and at Delhi in the shop of a native jeweller, I found broaches, ear-rings, snuff-boxes, &c., of the latest models, (so far as I am a judge,) and ornamented with French devices and mottos."

From this it will be seen that it is not skill, but *capital*, in the form of improved tools, and other aids to industry, that is wanting, and if the Hindoo did not possess very considerable skill in the management of such as he has, it would not be possible for him to pay the enormous assessments of the Company.

Labour is said to be dearer in America than in England, because of the superior capital in land; but if such be the case, why would it not be as correct to say that it is cheaper in Hindostan because of the inferior capital in land, as well as of tools with which it is to be wrought? If superior capital give superior wages, we may well believe that inferior capital will give inferior wages. Superior capital in land is deemed sufficient to make amends for deficient skill in the American, enabling him to earn even higher wages than the Englishman; but if it produce so much effect, why should not a similar effect be produced in Russia, which, with an *European* population of forty-two millions, has twelve times as much *European* territory as Great Britain and Ireland, with a population of twenty-two millions? Or why are not wages as high in Brazil, with its immense territory and limited population? Or why should not the abundance of capital in other shapes, existing in England, have an equal effect? Her lands are in a high state of cultivation; the amount of capital invested in turnpikes, and railroads, and canals, is immense; and steam, with its mighty power, is used to an extent almost incredible. Her mines of iron, lead, tin, copper, and coal, are abundant, and highly productive; mills and machinery of every description abound, and are of the first order, and circulating capital, with which to work them, is abundant, at a low rate of interest. In this country,

land, and mines of iron, gold, lead, and coal are abundant; but circulating capital is scarce, and while it
remains so, much of this important machinery is of no
more use for present purposes than the mill to the man
who has used his whole credit and capital in erecting
it, and is unable to command the means with which to
put it in operation, as has not unfrequently occurred.
So scarce is this description of capital in many parts
of this country, that it is not unfrequently worth from
twelve to twenty-four per cent. per annum, and in
some of the states, the legal rate of interest is ten
per cent. Mr. S. has certainly erred in supposing
the difference of wages to arise from this cause, and
if there be inferiority in point of skill, it must be com-
pensated in some other way.

I say *if there be* inferiority of skill, not being at all
prepared to admit such to be the case. On the contrary, my impression, as stated at the close of the
last chapter, is that labour is more advantageously
applied in the United States than in England. In
making a comparison between two countries, it is
necessary to take some pursuit in which both are
fairly engaged, as it would not do to compare a flutist
and violin player, and attribute superior skill to the
latter, because the former could not handle the bow;
nor to the native of Hindostan, because he displayed
more ability in the management of a rice plantation,
than an Englishman who had but recently seen one.

In what does this superior skill consist? Is it in
agriculture? The farmer of the United States would
be most unwilling to exchange his implements for
those of England; all that he uses are calculated to

save labour in a much greater degree, and he would lose much by relinquishing the cradle for the reaping hook, or the horse-rake for the hand-rake.*

Is it in the manufacture of flour? Oliver Evans is the first authority in the world on this subject, and his book is studied in England, while it has been translated on the continent, and is adopted every where. Is it in the manufacture of cotton goods? The English journalists tell us that all the recent improvements have been sent from this country to England. Is it in navigation? Compare the number of English vessels engaged in the trade between the two countries, and the question will be answered; or compare the number of vessels engaged in the whale fishery, when it will be found that the American ships triple those of England. Or remark the fact, that with her immense trade with all the world, with her great empire in India, there is nothing in England to compare with the lines of packet ships between the United States and Europe. Is it in steam navigation? Compare the steam vessels of the several countries, and it will not long be a matter of question.

I am disposed to believe that Mr. Senior himself

---

* The following extract will show the difficulty that exists in introducing into England improvements in agricultural machinery.

"Instances, nevertheless, have been frequent, of farmers being obliged to use the scythe instead of the sickle.—Though the resorting to this instrument has, on all occasions, excited the ill will of the labourers to a very dangerous extent, for the scythe is a most powerful and efficient instrument, and it is thought that if brought into use would extinguish the usual harvest earnings."—*Report Poor Laws Commissioners.—Evidence of Mr. Chadwick.*

would withdraw the claim of superior skill, and admit that in every pursuit in which the people of the United States have been, or are, fairly and fully engaged, there is no deficiency such as he has supposed, requiring superior capital in land to make amends for it.

The question now arises: what is the cause of the difference in the productive powers of the nations to which we have referred? Why is it that a man labouring on the shores of the Ganges cannot obtain an equal amount of the comforts of life with another labouring on the banks of the Thames or the Delaware? Why is the labourer in the vicinity of Calcutta barely able to exist, while another in the neighbourhood of Philadelphia or New York can accumulate capital? Why is it that when the labourer of Calcutta is content with a handful of rice per day, he does not drive the American labourer out of the markets of South America, open to both, upon equal terms, and with little difference of freight? Why is it that he cannot even hold his own market for the sale of his cottons?

The answer is, that the system of government of Hindostan tends to prevent the growth of capital, while that of England, and still more, that of the United States, tends to promote it. Upon capital depends production; upon production depends wages. Where production is small, wages cannot be otherwise than low.

If capital increase more rapidly than population, the ratio of production, or revenue, to population, will increase, and wages will rise; but if population increase more rapidly than capital, the contrary effect must be produced, and wages must fall. The experience of the United States shows how much more rapidly capital may increase than population, when security of person and property are obtained at moderate cost of government, while that of Great Britain, the Netherlands, and France, shows that the tendency so to do, is too great to be prevented, even by the lavish expenditure of those nations. In Spain and Turkey, mis-government has been carried so far as to prevent it; but it is doubtful, if in any other part of Europe such is the case. With these exceptions, Europe, and certainly the United States and Canada, may be cited in proof of the assertion, that *capital has a tendency to increase more rapidly than population, and that it will do so, when not prevented by disturbing causes,* the most important of which are,

First. Insecurity of person and property.

Second. Heavy taxation.

Third. Restrictions upon the freedom of action, or of trade.

All tending to produce the

Fourth. Want of industry.

All of which it is proposed to consider, with reference particularly to England, the United States, and Hindostan.

In his Lectures on Wages, Mr. Senior adverts to two of the above disturbing causes, restraints upon commerce and difference of industry, but he does not notice the others, which are of the utmost importance.

CHAPTER VIII.

Fɪʀsᴛ among these causes is insecurity of person or property, or both, as where these exist improvement can hardly be hoped for. The beneficial effect of security is well described by Mr. M'Culloch in the following passage, and he does not attach to it more importance than it merits.

" The immediate cause of the rapid increase and vast amount of the commerce of Great Britain, is doubtless to be found in the extraordinary extension of our manufactures during the last half century. To inquire into the various circumstances that have contributed to the astonishing development of the powers and resources of industry that has been witnessed in this country since Arkwright and Watt began their memorable career, would be alike inconsistent with our object and limits. There can be no question, however, that *freedom* and *security*—freedom to engage in every employment, and to pursue our own interest in our own way, coupled with an intimate conviction that acquisitions, when made, might be securely enjoyed or disposed of,—have been the most copious sources of our wealth and power. There have only been two countries, Holland and the United States, which have, in these respects, been placed under nearly similar circumstances as England: and, notwithstanding the disadvantages of their situation, the Dutch have long been, and still continue to be, the most industrious and opulent people of the continent—while the Americans, whose situation is more favourable, are advancing in the career of improvement with a rapidity hitherto unknown. In Great Britain we have been exempted for a lengthened period from foreign aggression and intestine commotion; the pernicious influence of the feudal system has long been at an end; the same equal burdens have been laid on all classes; we have enjoyed the advantage of liberal institutions, without any material alloy of popular licentiousness or violence; our intercourse with foreign states has, indeed, been subjected to many vexations and oppressive regulations; but full scope has been given to the competition of the home producers; and, on the whole, the natural order of things has been less disturbed amongst us by artificial restraints, than in most other countries. But without security, no degree of freedom could have been of any material importance. Happily, however, every man has felt satisfied, not only of the temporary, but of the *permanent* tranquillity of the country, and the stability of its institutions. The plans and combinations of the capitalists have not been affected by any misgivings as to what might take place in future.

" Moneyed fortunes have not been amassed, because they might be more easily sent abroad in periods of confusion and disorder; but all individuals have unhesitatingly engaged, whenever an opportunity offered, in undertakings of which a remote posterity was alone to reap the benefit. No one can look at the immense sums expended upon the permanent improvement of the land, on docks, warehouses, canals, &c., or reflect for a moment on the settlement of property in the funds, and the extent of our system of life insurance, without being impressed with a deep sense of the vast importance of that confidence which the public have placed in the security of property, and, consequently, in the endurance of the present order of things, and the good faith of government. Had this confidence been imperfect, industry and invention would have been paralyzed; and much of that capital, which clothes and feeds the industrious classes, would never have existed. The maintenance of this security entire, both in fact and in opinion, is essential to the public welfare. If it be anywise impaired, the colossal fabric of our prosperity will crumble into dust; and the commerce of London, like that of Carthage, Palmyra, and Venice, will, at not a very remote period, be famous only in history. It is, therefore, of the utmost consequence, that in introducing the changes which the wants and altered circumstances of society require should be made in the frame of our polity, nothing be done to impair; but every thing to strengthen, that confidence and security to which we are mainly indebted for the high and conspicuous place we have long occupied among the nations of the earth."

In the United States equal security has existed. Their course has been peaceful, and they have known nothing of the calamities of war since the peace of 1783, except for a short period, and even then it was confined to a very small portion of the country. Confiding in the protection of the laws, capitalists have invested their fortunes in mills and machinery; in canals and rail roads. The most gigantic projects have been started; many of them have been commenced, and several completed. No enterprise seems too great, and capital is always to be found when it can be shown that the investment will be profitable. The capitalists of Europe, feeling the same confidence, make investments in the stocks of our canals, rail roads, and banks, thus aiding in giving employment to the population, which ignorance of the true principles of political economy drives to our shores.

In India, on the contrary, security of person or property has never been known. Since the Mahommedan Conquest the country has at all times been desolated by the march of immense armies. At one time by the invading hosts of a Tamerlane; at others by those of a Baber or Nadir; at all times by the contending forces of opposite factions, always existing in a country where the succession to the throne is irregular, and its possession uncertain; and where it is constantly the object of contention among fathers and children; brothers and cousins; sovereign and subject.—The history of India is a long scene of horrors, marked only by the " incessant plunder and devastation of provinces: the perpetual marching and counter-marching of armies, and their lawless predatory habits." Nothing more fully illustrates the state of society, than the fact of the existence in their language, of two such terms as " Wulsa" and " Joar," describing, in single words, scenes so unusual in other countries, that no term has been invented for them. The following account of them is from Rickards's India.*

" Illustrations of the manners and immemorial habits of a people are sometimes unexpectedly derived from a careful attention to the elements or structure of their language. On the approach of a hostile army, the unfortunate inhabitants of India bury under ground their most cumbrous effects, and each individual, man, woman, and child above six years of age, (the infant children being carried by their mothers,) with a load of grain proportioned to their strength, issue from their beloved homes, and take the direction of a country, (if such can be found,) exempt from the miseries of war: sometimes a strong fortress; but more generally of the most unfrequented hills and woods, where they prolong a miserable existence, until the departure of the enemy; and if this should be protracted beyond the time for which they had provided food, a large portion necessarily dies of hunger. The people of a district thus deserting their homes, are called the Wulsa of the district. A state of habitual misery, involving precautions against incessant war, and unpitying depredations of so peculiar a description, as to require in any of the languages of Europe a circumlocution, is expressed in all the languages of the Deccan and the south of India, by a single word.

" The second fact is, the shocking ceremony of the Joar, of which some instances have been above given. We have seen that the Hindoos, when driven to despair by the Mussulman arms, were in the habit of sacrificing their own wives and children, by burning alive, or otherwise destroying them, to avoid the barbarities and pollutions they would have to endure, by falling into the hands of their conquerors. From facts like these it is to conceive how dreadful must have been the fate of the sufferers; whilst the name or appellation it obtained throughout India, proves the cruelty to have been of no

* India; or Facts submitted to illustrate the Character and Condition of the Native Inhabitants. By R. Rickards, Esq. 2 vols. 8vo. London: 1832.

unfrequent occurrence. Even the horrors of the Inquisition in the west, are not to be compared with those of an eastern Joar. In the former, individuals only suffered, and generally under the consolatory hope that their temporary pangs would be rewarded by a happy eternity; but in the latter, thousands at a time were sacrificed, and with no other feeling at the moment than the conviction that the sparing of their lives would only be to expose them to greater cruelties."

The last century was marked by the invasion of Nadir Shah, attended with an extraordinary destruction of life and of property. Independently of all that was destroyed, it was estimated that he carried with him into Persia, gold and silver and jewels to the almost incredible amount of thirty-two millions of pounds sterling. Shortly previous to that invasion, Sevajee had laid the foundation of the Mahratta power, which continued, during the whole of that century, and until its final overthrow by the Marquis of Hastings, to spread havoc and desolation throughout India. Some idea may be formed of the effect of the operations of such a body from the following:—

" The characters of the Mahrattas throughout all these transactions, have been that of the most rapacious plunderers. Their predatory habits are quite proverbial, and their conquests were in a great measure effected by laying waste the countries through which they passed. When, therefore, it is considered, that in their first triumphs over the Moguls, they demanded and exacted, where they could, a *chout*, or fourth, of the revenues; that they obtained from the Emperor, as before mentioned, a formal grant of this tribute, with power themselves to levy it on the disaffected provinces; that is, the vice royalties which had shaken off the imperial authority; the reader may judge of the state of misery and oppression to which the inhabitants of these devoted countries must have been reduced, who were thus subject to threefold plunder and extortion; first, of the imperial armies from Delhi, who still continued to carry off vast contributions from the Deccan; secondly, of their local Mussulman governors; and thirdly, of their equally insatiate Mahratta invaders. The march of a Mahratta army is generally described as desolating the country through which it passes, on either side of its route, which may thus easily be traced by ruined villages and destroyed cultivation. They plunder as they move along, seizing by violence or by treachery, on all that is valuable, or any way conducive to their present security or ulterior views. Sevajee's depredations in this way were excessive; so that at his death his treasuries and arsenals were stocked even to exuberance. Among other acts of the kind, he plundered the rich city of Surat three different times; on one of which occasions only, his booty was estimated at one million sterling. In his celebrated incursion into Drauveda, now called the Carnatic, he is said to have carried off vast wealth; but the best proof, as well as the most characteristic trait of his unbounded and indiscriminate depredations is, that he was at length distinguished by the appellation of " The Robber," which was applied to him as an exclusive and appropriate title."—*Rickards, Vol.* i. 236.

The Pindarees were another description of plunderers, thus described:—

" It is a remarkable proof of the anarchy and tyranny long prevalent in India, and of the deplorable state of its inhabitants, that a power like that of the Pindarees should have grown into such formidable dimensions in the very heart of the country; and spreading terror through all the neighbouring states, should require for its suppression one of the largest British armies that was ever called into the field. There are authentic records of the existence of Pindarees, as a marauding body, for upwards of a century. * * * Their ranks were constantly replenished with vagrants of all castes, and from every quarter of India; men driven from their homes by oppression, despair, or famine, to seek a precarious subsistence by plunder. * * *

" Their incursions into the British territories were so frequent, and their devastations so extensive, as to require a military force to be annually employed against them. Their progress was generally marked by smoking ruins, and the most inhuman barbarities to persons of both sexes.

" Marquis Hastings observes of the Pindarees,—' When it is re-collected that the association in question consisted of above 30,000 mounted men, all professedly subsisting by plunder, the extent of theatre necessary to furnish an adequate prey may be well conceived. The whole of the Nizam's subjects, as well as the inhabitants of the northern circars of the Madras presidency, were constantly exposed to devastation. It was not rapine alone, but unexampled barbarity, that marked the course of the spoilers. Their violation of the women, with circumstances of peculiar indignity, which made multitudes of the victims throw themselves into wells, or burn themselves together in straw huts, was invariable; and they subjected the male villagers to refined tortures, in order to extract disclosure where their little hoards of money were buried.' "— *Rickards*, i. 260.

The French and English nations were also contending for the sovereignty of that vast country, stirring up wars among the natives, that they might profit thereby. The native princes themselves, among the most distinguished of whom were Hyder and his son Tippoo, were plundering their subjects to obtain the means of waging war with their neighbours, either for the purpose of retaining or extending their dominions. In short, war, pestilence, and famine stalked abroad, with poverty, and misery, and wretchedness in their train.

On a smaller scale, for where all are plunderers, there must be some of an inferior order, was what is called Decoity, or gang robbery, another of the inflictions upon this unfortunate country. Recruits were never wanting for the Decoits, or the Pindarees, or any other robbers, for misery and want were constantly driving the people from the homes of their fathers, to seek by plundering others, to make amends for having been plundered. " Murder, robbery, rape and torture in the most barbarous shapes, were the constant practice of these Decoits. Nothing was more usual with them than to bind up persons in straw, hemp, or quilts moistened with oil, and to burn them alive to force a discovery of hidden treasures."—*Rickards*, ii. 207. The judge of the Calcutta Circuit says, June 13, 1808, " If its vast extent were known, if the scenes of horror, the murders, the burnings, the excessive cruelties which are continually perpetrated here, were properly represented to Government, I am convinced some measures would be adopted to remedy the evil. * * * It cannot be denied that there is in fact no protection for persons or property." This too was in Bengal, in the vicinity of Calcutta, the earliest and most important possession of the Company!

The police were little better, if we may judge from an extract from a letter of Mr. Secretary Dowdeswell, (1809), quoted by Mr. Rickards. He says they are an actual " pest to the country from their avarice, and addiction to every species of extortion."

Since that time the Mahrattas and Pindarees have been subdued, but gang robbery still exists, although to a much more limited extent. During the existence of such a state of things, all that could be hoped for by the unfortunate cultivator, would be sufficient to secure him and his family from starvation. Not only capital could not accumulate, but it was destroyed much more rapidly than it could be reproduced, and the people were retrograding towards barbarism. Immense tracts of land were depopulated and soon became Jungle, inhabited only by lions and tigers,

H

who now roam unmolested where the Hindoo had for ages cultivated the arts of peace.

During the period of comparative security that has followed, population has again begun to extend itself slowly, and part of those lands that had been abandoned, have again been brought under cultivation; but a long time will be necessary to recover from the effects of such a state of things as has been described.

We have seen the calamitous effects produced by the revolution of 1830 in France. Paris was deserted; workmen were discharged and left to starve; merchants were ruined; and the agriculturist was without a market for his products. Yet compare all the tumults of France in the last five years, with a single hour of the presence of Nadir Shah in Delhi, and they sink into insignificance.

In the organization of the Courts of Justice there are also defects which tend to increase insecurity. "The delay in the administration of justice is, of course, enormous and increasing. Under the Bengal presidency, the causes in arrear were, in 1819, 81,000; and in 1829, they had crept up to 140,000, or in ten years sustained an increase of 75 per cent." —*W. Rev. Vol.* xix. p. 142.

The traveller through England sees the country dotted over with farm houses and cottages, as is the case in the United States; but crossing the channel and entering France, he is immediately struck with the difference in the landscape. Instead of neat cottages, each with its little piece of land, he sees here and there a dirty village, and finds that is the residence of all the cultivators of the surrounding country. Living here, they are compelled to *walk daily one or two or three miles to their patches of land*, and with a view to save expense and trouble of transportation, they occupy that which is nearest, whether fitted or not, for raising their heavy crops, while those of a lighter kind are reserved for the more distant land. A slight knowledge of history, with a little reflection, will satisfy him that this is the result of the insecurity that has prevailed in that country, as well as in most countries of Europe. Exposed at all times to the violence of contending factions; robbed alternately by the soldiers of Valois and of the League; by the Catholic and the Hugonot; the labourer could look for protection only to union with his neighbours, and deemed a residence in a dirty village, with security, preferable to purer air, with the risk of being daily plundered by friend and foe. The injurious effect of this is described by Mr. Jacob, thus :—

" The residences of the peasants are generally near together, in villages so distant from the extremities of the parish, as to make those extremities very expensive to cultivate. The barns and other buildings are near them; these are, upon a scale regulated by the nature of the climate, much more expensive to construct than in our own, more agreeable, country. At present the lands, divided to each occupier in scattered fragments over the whole common fields, receive crops according to their vicinity to the village, and that part appropriated to wheat, which is manured, is generally near to it. If those lands were parcelled out in separate farms, some allotments must be at a great distance from the village. The shares in such situations might be, and in justice should be, comparatively large. The expense of carrying manure, and of bringing the produce to them, would make the houses and erections in the villages, nuisances and incumbrances on the land, rather than beneficial property."— *Second Report,* p. 144.

To the same cause may be attributed the indisposition of the people of the continent to engage in great public improvements, and the necessity for their being undertaken, if at all, by the government; while in England they are made entirely, and in the United States in a great degree, by individual capital and exertion. Who would be willing to invest his capital in the building of a bridge liable to be blown up during the next war, by either friends or invaders? or in making canals, the right to collect tolls upon which would probably cease at the next war, and which, at the ensuing peace, would perhaps be transferred to an adjoining State? Even in France, where such events are least likely to occur, the people have been so long accustomed to look to the government for all improvements of this description, that they can with difficulty accustom themselves to the idea of such investments of capital, and the most important communications remain unimproved.

"The want of canals and navigable rivers in most parts of the kingdom, compels the inhabitants generally to have recourse to the roads for the conveyance even of the most bulky articles of merchandise. The raw cotton is transported by land from Havre to Alsace, a distance of 440 miles, and the manufactured article is sent in caravans to Paris, upwards of 400 miles. * * * Though rich in minerals and vegetable productions, all industry is checked for want of means of export, and by reason of its small internal consumption. * * * This state of things is strikingly portrayed by M. Cordier, one of the most skilful of French engineers, in his able work, 'Sur les ponts et Chaussées.' After expatiating upon the superior advantages of England, derived from the enterprising spirit and real patriotism of its inhabitants, and then upon her internal communications, he says, ' Je parcours apres une longue absence les departemens du Jura, de l'Ain, du Saone et Loire, du Rhone, et les provinces intérieures du Royaume; je trouve les chemins vicinaux, les rivieres, les fleuves, dans l'ancien état de nature; on n'arrive d'une contrée à l'autre que par des directions forcées et difficiles. En s'écartant des grandes routes entretenues, on entre dans des espèces de déserts; on ne découvre plus que quelques traces des familles qui ont illustré ou enrichi la France; on n'apperçoit que les ruines de leur demeures, ou des débris de domaines qui passent sans cesse de main en main, ou s'exploitent par procuration, au détriment du maitre et de la contrée. J'ai traversé plusieurs fois dans differens départemens vingt lieues carrées, sans rencontrer un canal, une route, une manufacture, et surtout une terre habitée. La campagne semble un exil abandonné aux malheureux; ses interets et ses besoins sont meconnus, et sa détresse toujours croissante par le bas prix des produits et la difficulté des transports.' "—*Quarterly Review*, Vol. xxxi., p. 412.

For many years it has been in contemplation to make a canal or rail-road from Havre to Paris, and thence to the Rhine; but it is not yet commenced, although offering greater advantages than almost any other route in Europe. With a capital like Paris and similarly situated, the people of the United States would, before this time, have made some half dozen communications with the ocean, and most probably have reached the Rhine in two or three places. Already there are two communications between the ocean and the western waters completed, and several others are in progress, and likely to be completed sooner than that between the Rhine and the ocean, although the latter would afford facilities of intercourse to a population at least twenty times greater than can benefit by any one of the others. At Amsterdam, capital may often be had at two per cent. per annum, but it is not wanted for such purposes, and the bankers find a market for it here at a much higher price than can be obtained at home.

The same causes have prevented the construction of roads or canals in Spain, the consequence of which is, that "all means of transport are dear, and in the neighbourhood of Salamanca it has been known, after a succession of abundant harvests, that the wheat has actually been *left to rot upon the ground*, because it would not repay the cost of carriage."—*Ed. Rev.* Vol. LV., 448.

CHAPTER IX.

THE second great disturbing cause is the unproductive expenditure by government of the enormous sums collected by taxation.

In the United States, taxation has been at all times light. With a government comparatively cheap, and abstaining from war, it has never been necessary, except for a short period after its establishment, and again during the war of 1812, to seek for subjects of taxation elsewhere than at the custom house. The state governments have had to support themselves by other taxes, chiefly those on land, but the whole amount of taxation has been comparatively small, and the absence of the other great drawbacks has rendered it very easy to meet these demands. False ideas of the effect of legislation upon the price of labour have induced the extension of the duties on imports so far as to compel the people to pay considerable sums for the protection of domestic manufactures, but the effect has not been heavily felt, and it is to be hoped that the more correct views that now obtain will, at no very distant period, with the present tariff law, put the matter on a proper footing.

There is still too much disposition on the part of Congress and the state legislatures to legislate away money, without due consideration, and particularly for what are called internal improvements; without reflecting that if those improvements were really necessary, they would be made by private enterprise, and that, even if they be necessary, there does not

seem to be any good reason why the money of **A.**
B. and C. should be expended to improve the property
of D. E. and F., particularly when it at the same
time probably reduces the value of that of the former.
The people of Maryland, and the District of Colum-
bia, have been very urgent with Congress to complete
the Chesapeake and Ohio Canal. If done, it must be
done with the money of New York and Pennsylvania, both of which states have made canals for the
same purpose at their own expense. There can be
no doubt there will be ample business for all, but is
it right to require the people of New York to make
a canal in opposition to their own, or the people of
New Orleans to contribute to a great work, the chief
object of which is to draw trade from the Gulf of
Mexico to the Atlantic sea-board?

Legislators would do well to recollect the following sound remarks of Sir Henry Parnell:—

"Taxation is the price we pay for government; and every parti-
cle of expense that is incurred beyond what necessity absolutely requires for the preservation of social order, and for the protection
against foreign attack, is waste, and an unjust and oppressive imposition upon the public. Every minister, and every member of Parliament who has the power to spend or save the public money,
should do his best to prevent the wants of the state from depriving
the people of the means of providing for their wants, and therefore
economy and frugality, which are virtues in a private station, for
their vast influence upon national happiness in public stations, become the most pressing of duties." p. 107.

Since the revolution of 1688, England has deemed
it necessary to take a part in all the wars of Europe,
but all previous exertions were trivial, compared with
those which she made under the pretence of "*fighting
for the liberties of Europe*," the true object of which

was to prevent the spread of the revolutionary spirit at home, and check the demand for a reform, that would have a tendency to distribute more equally the burthen of government. These extraordinary efforts for the *freedom of the world*, caused enormous expenditure, enormous debts, and their associate, enormous taxation. In collecting these large sums, the interests of the land owners required to be considered, as they were the makers of laws, and thus the taxes on land are light, while almost the whole revenue is raised by taxes on consumption, and levied upon articles used chiefly by the labouring classes. Mr. Pitt said, that "three-fifths of the price of labour are said to come into the Exchequer."* Sir Henry Parnell estimates that the higher classes do not pay more than six millions out of fifty. Mr. Bulwer says, "By indisputable calculation it can be shown that every working-man is now taxed to the amount of one-third of his weekly wages; supposing the operator to obtain twelve shillings a week, he is taxed therefore to the amount of four shillings per week; and at the end of six years, (the supposed duration of Parliament,) he will consequently have contributed to the revenue, from his poor energies, the almost incredible sum of £ 62 3s."† The Metropolitan for July, 1833, gives the following "amount of taxes paid by a citizen of London, having, we will suppose, an income of £200 a year, out of which he is necessitated to support himself, his wife, three children, and a servant maid!" showing that out of that sum, above eighty pounds are paid to government.

* Quarterly Review, Vol. XLIII.
† England, Vol. I., p. 187, London edition.

Articles Taxed and Used.	Rate of Taxation demanded.	Amount of Taxes levied by Government.		
		£.	s.	d.
Tea—½ lb. a week, at from 5s. to 6s. per lb. - - - -	100l. per cent.	3	5	0
Sugar—6 lbs. a week - - -	2½d. per lb.	2	14	2
Coffee—1 lb. per week - -	6d. per lb.	1	6	0
Porter and ale—2 pots per diem (malt and hop tax) - - - -	2d. per pot.	3	0	10
Spirits—1 pint per week (lowest average taxation on Foreign and British)	10s. per gall.	3	10	0
Wine—1 quart per week, on a yearly average - - - - -	5s. 6d. per gall.	3	11	6
Soap—3 lbs. per week - - -	3d. per lb.	1	19	0
Pepper—5 lbs. a year at least -	1s. per lb.		5	0
Other spices—viz. ginger, cinnamon, cloves, &c. - - - -	at least		6	6
Paper—for the family, or boys at school, 1 lb. weekly - - -	3d. per lb.		13	0
Starch—12 lbs. yearly - -	3½d. per lb.		3	6
Newspaper to read only—daily 1d.	¼th of sta.	1	10	5
Currants dried—25 lbs. a year -	5d. per lb.		10	5
Raisins, oranges, lemons, prunes, nuts, &c.	various rates.		10	0
Occasional use of an omnibus, cab, hackney, or stage-coach - -	ditto.	1	5	0
Sundries—such as taxes on medicines, books, glass, silver-spoons, small items, and luxuries, &c. - -	ditto.	2	10	0
House, window, and land tax -	ditto.	10	10	0
Poor, church, highway, water, gas, police, &c.	ditto.	10	0	0
Taxes on house materials which are included in the rent—viz. on bricks, timber, glass, &c. - - -	ditto.	12	0	0
Taxes paid to butcher, baker, tailor, milliner, shoemaker, hatter, and all persons employed, who being themselves taxed on the preceding articles, proportionably enhance their demand for goods rendered or services done - - - -	at least	21	0	0
Total taxes paid by a person with 200l. per annum - - - -		80	10	4

Of the whole sum collected for the support of government, fifty-two millions sterling, less than one third is raised by taxes on lands, stamps, insurances, wood, wine, servants, carriages and horses, probates and legacies, and by the Post Office, leaving the remainder to be paid chiefly by the articles used by the labouring classes, as malt, hops, sugar, spirits, tea, tobacco, coffee, corn, soap, newspapers, &c., &c.

The land tax which affected the aristocracy, was made permanent in 1798, upon an assessment then more than a century old, and produces now little more than a million of pounds, notwithstanding the immensely augmented value of landed property. The income tax was repealed immediately after the close of the war, because it affected the pockets of the law makers. The house tax is assessed in a manner that secures that class from the payment of their share of the public burthens almost as effectually as the same class were secured in France before the revolution. The following are specimens.

	Sworn annual value.	Land tax.
A shop in Regent street, 21 feet by 75, *owned and occupied by a tradesman,*	£ 400	£ 56 13 4
Stowe palace, *owned by the Duke of Buckingham*—a regal mansion, principal front 916 feet; Corinthian columns, pilasters, saloon paved with marble; tower, obelisks, temples, &c., woods and groves, - - - -	300	42 10 0
Blenheim, *owned by the Duke of Marlborough*, 348 feet from wing to wing, park 2,700 acres, - - ▪	300	42 10 0
Eaton Hall, *Marquis of Westminster*, - ▪ - ▪ - ▪ -	300	42 10 0

Alnwick Castle, *Duke of Northumberland,* - - - - -	£ 200	£ 28 6 8
Nottingham Castle, *Duke of Newcastle,* - - - - - - -	100	14 3 4

Northumberland House, in London, pays 4½*d.* per square foot, and the grocer's shop next door, 7 *shillings!*

Nottingham Castle, being injured some time since by a mob, the Duke received TWENTY THOUSAND pounds sterling for the *damage to a property valued at* £100 *sterling per annum.* " Let it be supposed, however, that Nottingham Castle is worth a quarter of a million sterling, which is probably much nearer its price. His Grace's mansion ought, in this case, to be rated at £16,250 per annum, while his house tax ought to be £2,301 1*s.* 8*d.* per annum." * * * " Farm houses are wholly exempted from taxation, which farm houses are as much the property of the landed aristocracy as the hedges and the ditches and the very fields which compose their estate."*

A house with eight windows pays a tax of 2*s.* each —sixteen windows 4*s.* 11*d.* each—thirty-two windows, 6*s.* 8*d.* each—and the scale rises gradually, until at thirty-nine windows the charge is about 7*s.* each. Having thus arranged to include all the middle and working classes, a provision is now to be made to let off as easily as possible what Captain Hall calls the money-spending classes. Accordingly, forty-four windows are 6*s.* 6¾*d.* each, and gradually reducing, one hundred are 5*s.* 10½*d.* each, and after one hundred and eighty the charge is but

---

* **Westminster Review, No. 41, p. 87—***American edition.*

one and sixpence. The labouring man who has eight
windows, and wants a ninth, must pay 4s. 6d. for it;
but the Duke of Northumberland may have the same
permission for his one hundred and eighty-first for
one-third of the money. Some mansions are said to
contain a window for every day in the year, and
would be charged at 3s. 3¾d. per window, which
is less than half the rate of charge to the middle
classes.

Real estates, or lands, are wholly exempted from
legacy or probate duty. Thus lands are not only
almost free from tax, but they are the only species
of property that can be inherited without the payment of an enormous duty. The landholders have
well understood the mode of making laws which
shall exempt them, in a great degree, from contributions, while every one is made to contribute to *them.*
A more atrocious system of plunder does not prevail
in India, although done more openly.

" In Germany, France, Belgium, and Italy, the land tax never
constitutes less than one fourth part of the public income, nor is its
rate in any of these countries estimated at less than one fifth of the
actual rental. This last has generally been its rate in England. In
Great Britain (Ireland is exempted from it altogether), instead of
forming a fourth part of the public income, it forms about one
twenty-fifth part. The total rental of Great Britain at present, including tenements and mines, as well as lands, or what would be
subject on the continent to what has been called by the French, the
contribution foncière, is commonly estimated at fifty millions. If,
therefore, the English proprietors of real property were to contribute
an equal share of their rents with the continental nations, and indeed what the rate was generally fixed at in early times in England
itself—they ought to contribute, not two millions, but twelve millions, which would then constitute, as is the case with their neigh-

I

bours, about a fourth part of the public income. By having had the making of laws in their own hands, they have in fact contrived to add ten millions to their own property, and of course rob the public to the same extent. It is curious to contrast the difference of their conduct when they make laws for themselves and when they are called upon to make them for other people. A very few years before the British Parliament enacted a law fixing their own land tax in perpetuity at 4s. in the pound, on a careless and imperfect assessment made one hundred years before, they had passed a law fixing the land tax of British subjects in India at 18s., on a modern and inquisitorial assessment. This they called creating an Indian landed aristocracy."—*West. Rev.* xli. p. 85.

As an evidence that this exemption of landed property from taxation has not arisen out of any desire peculiar to the present generation, it may be mentioned, that in 1731–2 the land tax was reduced to *one shilling in the pound*, or *five per cent.*, at the expense of taking two and a half millions from the sinking fund.*

While the landholders are, as has been shown, exempt from the payment of taxes, they have taken care that nothing they produce shall be lessened in price by foreign competition. Not only is the importation of corn prevented by prohibitory duties, but every article of agricultural produce is in the same way subject to duties that are almost, if not entirely prohibitory. The high prices thus caused, must be paid out of the wages of the labourer, while his wages are diminished by the reduced demand for his labour, produced by the prohibitory system, which forbids the exchange of woollens, cottons, and hardware for corn. "The makers of laws have contrived

* Stewart's Political Economy. Vol. iv. p 57.

to throw the great burden of taxation, first, by their selection of the taxes imposed, and secondly, by their selection of the taxes repealed, from off their shoulders, upon the industrious classes, so that out of the 50,000,000*l.* of annual revenue, not more than six millions fall upon the landlords."—*Parnell*, p. 67.

The amount of taxation for the support of the church, in the form of tithes, is enormous. It is, however, asserted that it is borne by the landholders, constituting a deduction from their rents, and that the price of grain is not enhanced by it. In support of this assertion is adduced the case of lay-improprietors, who receive as much in rent as is elsewhere paid in rent and tithes. Such must continue to be the case so long as the corn laws shut out the competition of tithe-free land abroad, and the tithe system forbids the cultivation of any lands that cannot pay one-tenth of their produce to the church before paying rent. Were the system abolished, it would soon be found that lands that are now of no value, would be rendered productive, paying to the owners a rent of two, three, or five per cent. of the produce, and gradually increasing as they should be improved, until it would probably amount to a tenth, or as much as would have been claimed by the church at the outset. The effect of this extension of cultivation, would be to reduce the price of grain so as to prevent the landholder from adding the tithe to his rents, and the consumers would be thereby relieved from a heavy tax. The landholders would, however, benefit by the change, as those who own lands that are now unproductive, would be able to obtain a small rent from them, and those whose lands are now productive, would find that the improved cultivation that would be the result of relief from the interference of tithe proctors, would speedily enable their tenants to pay higher rents. Reduction of price would cause increased consumption, while the extension of cultivation, and improved methods, would cause production to keep pace with it, and the tenant would find that the increased product would enable him to pay a high rent even while the price of grain was low. The low price of grain would enable the government to do away with all restriction on the trade in corn, and its price would thenceforward be steady, as has been the case in this country during periods of peace. (See page 27.) This would relieve both landlord and tenant from the vexatious changes that have for years impoverished both parties, and thus, while the labourer would be supplied with corn at a lower rate than heretofore, the situation of both landowner and tenant would be improved.

The following extract will show the extraordinary growth of indirect taxation, payable by the labourer, while direct taxation, or that payable by the landlord, has been stationary.*

Expenses of the family of an agricultural labourer in 1762, from London Magazine for 1762.

					Per week.	Per annum.		
Bread, flour, oatmeal,	-	-	-	-	2s. 6d.	£6	10s.	0
Roots, greens, leaves, fruit,	-	-	-		5	1	1	8
		Amount carried forward,				£7	11	8

* History of the Middle and Working Classes, by J. Wade, London, 1833, p. 545.

	Per week.	Per annum.
Amount brought forward,		£7 11 8
Firing 6d. candles 3d. soap 2½d. - -	11½	2 9 10
Milk 1¾d. butter 1¾d. cheese 5d. - -	8½	1 16 10
Flesh 6d. rent 6d. pins, worsted thread, &c.1d. 1	1	2 16 4
Clothes, repairs, bedding, shoes, - -	1	2 12 0
Salt, beer, exotics, vinegar and spices, -	8½	1 16 10
Medicines, churching, lying in, - -		16 6
		£20 00 0

Taxes on the above consumption—on malt 4s. 2d.—salt 1s. 8d.—soap and candles 3s.—leather 2s.—sundries 2d.—total 11s. *Total about* 1·36.—Page 540.

Proper food for the able bodied labourer, with a wife and four children, per week, with the proportion of the price of each article of provision occasioned by tax or monopoly. 1833.

	Price.	Tax and monopoly.
5 gallons of bread, - -	7s. 6d.	2s. 6d.
3 lbs. of bacon at 7d. -	1 9	7
2 lbs. of butter at 10d. -	1 8	6½
2 lbs. of cheese at 6d. -	1	3
Tea, - - - -	9	6
Sugar, - - - -	7	3½
Beer, 7 quarts, at 2d. -	1 2	7
1 bushel of coals, - -	1 2	¼
3 faggots, - - -	9	
½ lb. of soap, - - -	4	2¼
¼ lb. of candles, - -	4	
	17s.	5s. 5½d.

By the above it will be seen that in 1762 the tax upon the consumption of the labourer was only one-thirty-sixth, while in 1833 it is almost one-third. It will be observed that a very considerable portion of this arises out of the monopoly of tea granted to the East India Company, and of corn to the land owners. At the time of the first statement, corn was in general

cheaper in England than on the continent, and with
a view to raise its price the labouring classes were
taxed for the payment of bounties on exportation,
while importation was prevented by high duties.
When, however, the increased population engaged
in manufactures enhanced the price so as to make it
unnecessary to look abroad for a market, it was
deemed proper to keep up the prohibitory duties, because corn was cheaper abroad.   Thus in 1762 importation was prevented, because corn was too cheap
at home, and in 1834, because it is too cheap abroad.

Mr. M'Culloch estimates the difference in cost
produced by the corn laws at about 20 per cent.,
while the above statement makes it 33⅓ per cent.,
but I am disposed to believe that a repeal of those
laws would be attended with very small reduction
of price, because the countries to which a supply
could be looked for, and where it is now low, are
totally destitute of the capital necessary for its *cheap*
production, on a large scale, in the general market
of the world.

Mr. M'Culloch asserts that corn is cheap in Poland,
because produced by low priced labour. Cheapness
of production is dependent, on that gentleman's own
principles, on the quantity of labour that enters into
it. The wages of a labourer, on the Vistula, midway
between Warsaw and Cracow,* are 4*d.* per day, and

---

* From a statistical account of the Lordship of Pulaway and
Kouskowola, in the province of Lublin, in Poland. " The subjects,
when called to work *with their teams* on the estate, beyond the days
of stipulated service, receive six pence a day for agricultural labour,
(ploughing and sowing,) and three pence for other manual work.

the average price of wheat at Cracow, for a period of 10 years, (Jacob, 1st Rep. p. 94,) 25s. sterling, while at Warsaw it was higher. It required, then, 75 days' labour to produce a quarter of wheat, which is obtained in Ohio by the labour of 9 or 10 days. Where is wheat cheapest, at Cracow or in Ohio? Again, we must take, not its cost in Cracow, or in the heart of Ohio, but the cost of producing it in the general market of the world; at Dantzic, or Hamburgh; at New York, or New Orleans. To do otherwise, would be equivalent to comparing the observations of half a dozen astronomers in different parts of the world, without an allowance for parallax. Its average value at Cracow was 25s., but the cost of transportation, and loss before reaching Dantzic, were 11s. 6d., making 36s. 6d. per quarter, or 4s. 7d. per bushel, nearly as much as the ordinary price in the United States. The labour of the producer being aided by capital, as much is thus accomplished by one man in the United States, as by 8 or 10 in Poland. As that country depends for the value of its products on the foreign demand through Dantzic, the land that is cultivated in the vicinity of Cracow, is, in relation to that near the former city, in the situation of an inferior soil, to the extent of the expense of transportation and loss; or 11s. 6d. per quarter; an enormous rent, which must be calculated as a part of the cost of production.

If they do not work on the estate, but are employed elsewhere, they are paid from eight to twelve pence for agricultural labour *with their team*, and from *three pence to six pence for their own work.—Jacob, First Report*, p. 171.

Such is the poverty of the people of those countries, that they are totally unable to make the improvements in their implements, or in their modes of cultivation, that are necessary. The consequence is, that the product does not usually exceed three, four, or five times the amount of seed sown, as may be seen by the following statements, taken from Mr. Jacob's reports.

In Pomerania, in 1804, the poverty of the people was such that they were unable to keep a sufficiency of stock to supply their lands with manure, and consequently the returns were little more than treble the seed, as follows :*—

Wheat sown,	155,936	tchetwerts.	Produce,	996,224
Rye sown,	1,254,960	do.	do.	4,383,584
Barley sown,	619,992	do.	do.	2,757,688
Oats sown,	1,245,704	do.	do.	2,975,880
	3,276,592			11,113,376

At page 103 he states, that although Volhynia is represented as a district of extraordinary fecundity, he finds, by the official harvest returns of the Russian Empire, the return was little more than four times the seed sown.

Sowed 635,700 tchetwerts; reaped 2,626,832.

Podolia, also represented as very fertile, yielded only 3,067,846 from 644,803 tchetwerts of seed.

"The greater part of France, a still much greater portion of Germany, and nearly the whole of Prussia, Austria, Poland, and Russia, present a wretched uniformity of system. It is called the three-course husbandry, consisting of, 1st, one year's clean fallow; 2d,

* Jacob, First Report, p. 34.

winter corn, chiefly rye, with a proportion of wheat commensurate to the manure that can be applied; 3d, summer corn, or barley and oats. There are occasional and small deviations from this system. In some few cases potatoes, in others, peas are grown, in the fallow year; but they are only minute exceptions to the generally established system. It is not surprising that under such a system the produce should not be much more than *four times the seed*, at which rate it is calculated, it appears to me rightly, by Baron Alexander Humboldt."*

It must be evident, that when production exceeds by so small a quantity what must be retained for seed, the chief part must be absorbed by the consumption of the producers, leaving but a very small quantity to be sold. If the demand should be considerable, it could not be supplied except from a very extensive tract of country. Having neither canals nor rail roads, the cost of transportation would be enormous.† Capital is as necessary for the production of wheat or cotton as of cotton goods, and the nations best supplied with the one will produce the other to the greatest advantage. No better evidence of this need be adduced than the present state of the trade in cotton wool. The two chief competitors for the supply of the world, are Hindostan, where labour is lowest, and the United States, where it is highest; but the latter having the aid of capital, are enabled almost to monopolise the trade. It is not at all improbable that a few years will see this country among the first in regard to the production of silk, and pos-

---

* Jacob, Second Report, p. 140.

† Mr. Jacob states that the cost of transportation in Mechlenburgh is so great that a distance of 240 miles would be equal to the whole value of the corn.—*Second Report*, p. 9.

sibly absolutely the first. In that it will be necessary to compete with Hindostan, China, Italy, and France, the cheapest countries, as to the price of labour, in the world, but the United States possess advantages that enable them to compete with any country whatever in the production of those articles for which their soil and climate are fitted, and they need fear no competition.

The benefit to the labourer from the repeal of the corn laws, would be not so much in the reduction in the price of corn, as in the increased amount of commodities obtainable for his labour, arising out of the increased demand for it that would be produced by a free intercourse with corn-growing countries. That benefit would be obtained without any sacrifice on the part of the land owner, whose lands would probably rent as high as at present. Notwithstanding the enormous deductions from the product of his toil, the labourer receives a constantly increasing quantity of the usual articles of consumption, showing an augmentation of the fund out of which he is to be paid; but how great would be the increase were he at liberty to exchange the products of his labour, without the intervention of custom houses, excise offices, or corn laws! Had the true interests of the nation been consulted, taxation would not now be as great as in 1762, and the reward of labour would be as great as in the United States, if not greater.

————

In Hindostan the Mahommedan Sovereigns claimed to be owners of the land, and to demand as rent such amount as they might judge expedient,

The Company succeeded to all their rights and privileges, and has not failed to avail itself of them to the full extent, and not unfrequently has gone far, very far, beyond the demands of the most oppressive of the native princes. It would occupy too much space to give an account of the several modes of collection adopted in that country, and distinguished by the names of Zemindary, Ryotwar and Mouzawar settlements. The meaning and intent of all are the same, which is to take from the unfortunate cultivator every farthing that can be squeezed out of him, leaving him in no case more than is necessary to support life. In the first the collector is the Zemindar, a farmer general, responsible for the amount assessed; in the second the collection is made directly from the Ryot or labourer, and in the third the settlement is made with the village collectively. In order that the reader may understand the mode of assessing taxes in that country, the following instructions to the assessors under the Ryotwar settlement are given:

" The cultivated lands were ordered to be classed into dry, wet, and garden lands; each was then to be measured field by field, and marked 1, 2, 3, &c. Each field to consist of as much land as could be cultivated by one plough, and the boundaries thereof to be marked and fixed by the surveyors. No deduction was to be allowed for land in a field shaded by *productive* trees; but for the land shaded by *unproductive* trees, a deduction was made. Forts, suburbs, open villages, court-yards of houses, with the number and species of trees in each, banks of tanks, rivers, nullahs, ravines, hillocks, roads, barren lands, wells, salt mounds, and topes or groves, with the number and species of trees in each, were all required to be particularized. In Palmira topes or groves, the trees were ordered to be classed into male and female, young, productive, and old or past bearing. The same was to be done in garden lands generally, taking care to notice the number of plants of young trees, and to specify whether they are cocoa nut, soopari, tamarind, jamoon, lime, orange, &c., and likewise to enter all plantations of betel, sugar-cane, tobacco, red pepper, &c."—*Rickards*, I. 454.

Under the Zemindary settlement, in the division of the produce of estates assigned to them, it is fixed, or rather estimated, that after deducting the expense of collecting, *one-half or two-fifths of the gross produce should be left to the Ryots*, the remainder constituting the rent of the state, except one-eleventh to the Zemindars. That settlement is permanent, and some improvement having taken place in the condition of the country, the taxes in Bengal, where it exists, are collected generally in full, but in the commencement the assessments were so high, that nearly all the Zemindars were ruined. Some idea may be formed of the enormous amount of taxes, and the consequent low value of property, from the fact that in 1799, ten years after the settlement, lands were sold in every province, the taxes upon which amounted to 777,965 rupees, and produced at the sale 654,215 rupees, *not even one year's purchase of the taxes*. The Zemindars having been ruined, and their property in those estates sold, the present proprietors, who purchased at reduced prices, are enabled to live. Under the other settlements the Company are not bound by any fixed rent, *the only limit being the possibility of collection.*

" In the despatches of the Court of Directors to their governments abroad, anxiety is uniformly expressed, lest their right to participate, according to usage, in the annual produce of the lands, should be either limited or infringed. From the commencement of the present century, more especially, it has constituted their main objections to the Zemindary settlement. Looking, as they naturally do, to the land revenues of India as the only source from whence the public exigencies can be supplied, they have always dreaded a fixed Jumma in perpetuity, as debarring them from the means of increased supply, in the event of future exigencies requiring it. The Ryotwar system has accordingly been preferred, because no bounds are unalterably affixed to the amount of the land tax; and because (as they say,) it provides for their moderate participation with the proprietors at stated intervals in the growing improvement, or extended cultivation'of the country."—*Rickards*, I. p. 609.

Any improvement in cultivation produces an immediate increase of taxation, so that any exertion on the part of the cultivator would benefit the company, and not himself. One-half the *gross produce* may be assumed as the average annual rent, although in many cases it greatly exceeds that proportion. The Madras Revenue Board, May 17th, 1817, stated that "the conversion of the government share of the produce (of lands) is in some districts as high as 60 or 70 per cent. of the whole."—*Rickards*, Vol. I. p. 288.

" The following statement is extracted from Colebrook's Treatise on the Husbandry of Bengal, to show the average gain of a Ryot from agriculture in the lower province.

16 Anas, 1 Seer—40 Seers, 1 Maund, or 74 lbs.

" Ten Maunds of rice are a large produce from one Bigha, and a return of fifteen for one.

	M. S. A.	M. S. A.
"Cultivators share, - - -		5 0 0
"Seed which the proprietor of the land had advanced, and which is repaid to him with 100 per cent. by way of interest, -	0 26 10¼	
"Labour of reaping ditto, at the rate of a sixth of the whole crop, - -	1 26 10¼	
"Ditto weeding, at 20 days, at 2¼ seer,	1 10 0	
		3 23 5
		1 16 11
"Ditto husking, with the wastage of 3-8ths,		0 21 4
		0 35 7

K

" Thirty-five seers and seven-sixteenths of clear rice, at the average rate of twelve Anas for the Maund, are worth eleven Anas, (eleven-sixteenths of a rupee,) nearly; and this does not pay the labour of ploughing at two Anas, (6 cents,) per diem for eight days. It appears then that the peasant, cultivating for half produce, is not so well rewarded for his toil as hired labourers; and it must be further noticed that he is under the necessity of anticipating his crop for seed and subsistence, and of borrowing for both, as well as for his cattle, and for the implements of husbandry, at the usurious advance of a quarter, if the loan be repaid at the succeeding harvest, and of half, if repaid later. We cannot then wonder at the scenes of distress which this class of cultivators exhibits, nor that they are often compelled by accumulating debts, to emigrate from province to province."—*Rickards*, I. 568.

It might be supposed, that having taken one-half of the gross produce, the cultivator would be permitted to exist on the remainder, but not so. At page **218**, Vol. II., Mr. Rickards gives a list of sixty other taxes, invented by the Sovereigns, or their agents, many of which he states to exist at the present day. If they have any other occupation, in addition to the cultivation of their patches of land, as is very commonly the case, they are subject to the following taxes, the principle of which is described as *excellent* by one of the collectors, December 1st, 1812.

" The Veesabuddy, or tax on merchants, traders, and shopkeepers; Mohturfa, or tax on weavers, cotton-cleaners, shepherds, goldsmiths, braziers, iron-smiths, carpenters, stone-cutters, &c., and Bazeebab, consisting of a number of smaller taxes annually rented out to the highest bidder. The renter was thus constituted a petty chieftain, with power to exact fees at marriages, religious ceremonies, *to inquire into, and fine the misconduct of females in families,* and other misdemeanours, and in the exercise of their privileges, would often urge the plea of engagements to the Cirkar, (government,) to justify extortion. The details of these taxes are too long to be given in this place. The reader, however, may judge of the operation and character of all, by the following selection of one, as described in the collector's report: 'The mode of settling the Mohturfa on looms hitherto has been very minute; *every circumstance of the weaver's family is considered, the number of days which he devotes to his loom, the number of his children, the assistance which he receives from them, and the number and quality of the pieces which he can turn out in a month or year, so that let him exert himself as he will, his industry will always be taxed to the highest degree.*' This mode always leads to such details, that the government servants cannot enter into it, and the assessment of the tax is, in consequence, left a great deal too much to the Curnums of the villages. No weaver can possibly know what he is to pay to the Cirkar, till the demand come to be made for his having exerted himself through the year; and having turned out one or two pieces of cloth more than he did the year before, though his family and looms have remained the same, is made a ground for his being charged a higher Mohturfa, and at last, instead of a professional, it becomes a real income tax."—*Rickards*, I. 500.

The following will show that nothing is allowed to escape the notice of the tax gatherer.

" The reader will, perhaps, better judge of the inquisitorial nature of one of these surveys, or pymashees, as they are termed in Malabar, by knowing that upwards of seventy different kinds of buildings —the houses, shops, or ware-houses of different castes and professions —were ordered to be entered in the survey accounts; besides the following ' implements of professions' which were usually assessed to the public revenue, viz:

" Oil-mills, iron manufactory, toddy-drawer's stills, potter's-kiln, washerman's stone, gold-smith's tools, sawyer's saw, toddy-drawer's knives, fishing-nets, barber's hone, blacksmith's anvils, pack bullocks, cocoa-nut safe, small fishing-boats, cotton-beater's bow, carpenter's tools, large fishing-boats, looms, salt storehouse."—*Rickards*, I. 559.

" If the landlord objected to the assessment on trees, as old and past bearing, they were, one and all, ordered to be cut down, *nothing being allowed to stand that did not pay revenue to the state.* To judge of this order, it should be mentioned that the trees are valuable, and commonly used for building, in Malabar. To fell all the timber of a man's estate when no demand existed for it in the market, and merely because its stream of revenue had been drained, is an odd way of conferring benefits and protecting property."—*Rickards*, I. 558.

"Having myself, been principal collector of Malabar, and made, during my residence in the province, minute inquiries into the produce and assessments of lands, I was enabled to ascertain beyond all doubt, and to satisfy the revenue board at Madras, that in the former survey of the province which led to the rebellion, lands and produce were inserted in the pretended survey account, which absolutely did not exist, while other lands were *assessed to the revenue, at more than their actual produce.*"—I. 557.

At page 561, Vol. I., is given a detailed statement of the produce of an estate in Malabar, for a period of ten years, from 1815 to 1824, for the correctness of which Mr. Rickards vouches:

							Rupees.		
The total produce was,	-	-	-	-	-	-	8167	1	4
Revenue,	-	-	-	-	-	-	6423	4	10
Landlord's share, *and expenses of cultivation,*						-	1743	1	94
In 1824 there was a new assessment upon the betel and cocoa-nuts, and jack trees, amounting to							680	1	44
While the *gross produce* was	-	-	-	-			599	0	74
The assessment *exceeded the produce* by	-	-					81	0	74

By the following remarks, extracted from *letters of the Revenue Board at Madras,* it will be seen that in the Ryotwar settlement, where every cultivator is separately liable for his own taxes, he is also bound for the payment of those of his neighbour, in case of failure. It would really appear, that the object of those who devised such a system of revenue was to deprive man of every possible inducement to exertion. "*Lasciate ogni speranza, o voi ch'entrate!*"—

would be as appropriate an inscription over India as over the gates of hell, and an Indian Dante would perhaps so apply it.

" This last mentioned rule of the Ryotwar system, which is to make good the failure of unsuccessful Ryots, imposing an extra as-sessment, not exceeding ten per cent. upon their more fortunate neighbours in the same village, and even occasionally upon those of the villages in the vicinity, was found to be indispensable to the security of the revenue under that system. *The little profit accruing to the industrious Ryots was thus taken by the state, to remunerate it for the losses it sustained from the failure of the less fortunate or more extravagant,* and while the Ryotwar system dissolved the unity of interest, and the joint partnership in profit and loss, which for-merly existed in each village community in all the provinces east of the Ghauts, and was so beneficial both to the members of its own municipal body, and to the government, it, in fact, admitted that their joint responsibility was necessary for the security of the public revenue, and precluding the Ryots from an equal participation of the profit, most unjustly obliged them to share jointly the loss."— *Rickards.*

To this system is very properly attributed by the Board, the decline of Agriculture.

" To the practice of loading the lowly assessed or industrious Ryot with the tax of his less fortunate or more improvident neigh-bour, (condemned by the very officer who adopted it, as both impo-litic and unjust,) to the *consumption of a maximum standard of assessment much beyond the capability of the country, even at the period of its greatest prosperity,* to the gradual approximation made to this high standard in the actual demand on more than half the landed property in Canara, and to the annual variation and conse-quent uncertainty in the amount of this assessment on individual Ryots, as much as to any temporary reduced value of produce, or the imposition of new indirect taxes, are to be ascribed the *decline in agriculture, the poverty among the Ryots, the increased sale of landed property by the landlords, the difficulty of realizing the col-lections, and the necessity, before unknown, of disposing of defaulters' lands, in satisfaction of revenue demands, which, after fourteen years residence in Canara, at length constrained the late collector to*

*record his conviction, that the present assessment is beyond the re-
sources of the province."—Rickards, Vol. II. 263.*

In the enforcement of such an extraordinary system of revenue, it must be evident that the number
of persons " dressed in a little brief authority" must
be almost endless, and that the unfortuate cultivator
must be almost entirely at their mercy. The Zemindars have not failed to do their share towards the
destruction of the rights of all those under them, as
will be seen by the following extract from Lord
Moira, afterwards Marquis of Hastings, September,
1815.

" Within the circle of the perpetual settlement, the situation of
this unfortunate class is yet more desperate; and though their cries
for redress may have been stifled in many districts, by perceiving a
uniform indisposition to attempt relieving them, which results from
the difficulty of the operation, their sufferings on that account have
not been less acute. In Burdwan, in Behar, in Cawnpore, and indeed wherever there may have existed extensive landed property at
the mercy of individuals, (whether in farm or Jaghire, in Talook,
or in Zemindary,) of the higher class, complaints of the village Zemindars have crowded in upon me without number, and I had only
the mortification of finding that the existing system established by
the legislature, left me without the means of pointing out to the
complainants any mode in which they might hope to obtain redress.
In all these towns, from what I could observe, the class of village
proprietors appeared to be in a train of annihilation, and unless a
remedy is speedily applied, the class will soon be extinct. Indeed,
I fear, that any remedy that would be proposed, would, even now,
come too late to be of any effect in the states of Bengal, for the license of 20 years, which has been left to the Zemindars of that province, will have given them the power, and they never wanted the
inclination, to extinguish the rights of this class, so that no remnants
of them will soon be discoverable."—*Rickards, Vol. I. p. 564.*

In 1769, Governor Verelst wrote, that in addition
to the enormous taxes for government, the people

were taxed by the collectors "for every extravagance that avarice and ambition, pride, vanity, and intemperance can lead them into." Annexed are extracts from his account of affairs at that period, and from several others, that will show the continuance of the same system to the present time.

"Governor Verelst's account, indeed, in 1769, of the conduct of Zemindars, is one which subsequent investigations have fully confirmed. He adds, 'the truth cannot be doubted, that the poor and industrious tenant is taxed by the Zemindar or collector, for every extravagance that avarice and ambition, pride, vanity, or intemperance may lead him into, over and above what is generally deemed the established rent of his lands. If he is to be married, a child born, honours conferred, luxury indulged, nuzzeranas, (presents,) or fines exacted, even for his own misconduct; all must be paid by the Ryot, and what heightens the distressful scene, the more opulent, who can better obtain redress for imposition, escape, while the weaker are obliged to submit."—*Rickards, Vol. II. p.* 59.

In a report by the Judge of Moorshedabad, dated 1st August, 1810, it is stated, that—

"The Zemindar, his farmers, and Amlah, (officers of government collectively), of all denominations, abuse the powers with which they are vested, to exact from the Ryot to the utmost extent of his ability. He is thus often deprived of the means of complaint; and this system, carried on from year to year, reduces the Ryot to the extremes of poverty, frequently the cause of the commission of crimes; *not, it is to be hoped, from any inherent depravity, but driven thereto by necessity,* to obtain a precarious and insecure subsistence."
—*Rickards, Vol. II. p.* 64.

The magistrate of Dinagepore, under date of July 24th, 1810, describes the state of affairs as

"A general system of rack-renting, hard-heartedness, and exactions, through farmers, under farmers, Kutkeenadars, (under tenants,) and the whole host of Zemindary Amlah. Even this rack-renting is unfairly managed. We have no regular leases executed between the Zemindar and his tenants. We do not find a mutual consent, and unrestrained negotiation in their bargains. Nothing like it; but instead, we hear of nothing but arbitrary demands enforced by stocks, duress of all sorts, and battery of their persons."— *Vol. II. p.* 65.

The collector of Rajeshahye, August, 1811, says:

"The Zemindar's only security for the possession of his estate being the punctual discharge of the government revenue, to screw this out of the wretched cultivators is his first consideration. With his miserable pittance of one-eleventh, the under-tenants, farmers, Ryots, and all the Amlah together, are then left to fight and scramble for the remainder of the produce."—*Vol. II. p.* 68.

The following statements are furnished by the magistrate of Rungpore:—

"One of them, Rajchunder Chowdry, bought a house at Rungpore, which cost 4100 rupees, (£512). It is a notorious fact, that Rajchunder Chowdry collected from the Ryots of his estate, to defray this expense, no less a sum than 11,000 rupees, (£1375,) under the bold item of Delan Khurchu, (house or hall money.) The same Zemindar expended 1200 rupees, (£150) on the ceremonies attending the birth of his grandson, and collected from his Ryots 5000 rupees (£625) on this account. Another Zemindar, Sudasheb Raee, had his house burnt down. He imposed an addition on the rent-roll of his estate to defray the expenses of rebuilding it; but having once established the exaction, it outlived the case, and became a permanent addition to the former rent, under the title of Ghur Bunace, (house-building.")—*Vol. II. p.* 72.

"Sudasheb Raee celebrated a festival, which lasted three months, and cost him 20,000 rupees, (£2,500); all of which fell on the tenantry of his estate.

"Jyram Baboo, a man of boundless extravagance, used to visit in great pomp, annually, the villages of his estate, levying contributions as he went along, under the name of Mangun or Bhukha, which literally means begging. 'I am unprepared, (says the Judge,) to state the amount of the collections thus made; the mode in which they are levied bids defiance to all inquiry. Lest, however, it should be thought that this practice is confined to one instance, I beg to observe, that this is the most general of all the modes of illegal exactions practised in Rungpore.' "—*Vol. II. p.* 73.

" Moonshee Himayutoollah, once Serishtadar of the judge's court, and late Dewan of the collectorship, bought a very large estate in Dinagepore. In a visit of ceremony to his new tenants, he collected from them in Mangun contributions, a full moiety of the purchase money. Himayutoollah had also occasion to buy an elephant, and exacted the cost, 500 rupees, (£62 10s.) from his Ryots, it being ' as essential to their respectability as his own, that he should no longer mount the back of so mean a quadruped as a horse.'

" Another Zemindar, Raee Danishnund Niteeanund, has very extensive estates in Rungpore, Dinagepore, and Moorshedabad. On his Rungpore estate alone he pays revenue to government of 69,742 rupees, (£8,742,) and collects a cess on his tenants of one Anna in the rupee, or 4,358 rupees per annum, (£544,) to defray the expense of daily offerings to his idol, or household god, Bunwaree.

" The above, (adds the judge,) are but a few of the many practical proofs which may be adduced, in support of what I have advanced relative to the state of the Ryot in Rungpore." Every extra expense, and every religious or superstitious ceremony, is paid for by the defenceless Ryot. ' Not a child can be born, not a head religiously shaved, not a son married, not a daughter given in marriage, not even one of the tyrannical fraternity dies, without an immediate visitation of calamity upon the Ryot. Whether the occasion be joyful or sad, in its effects, it is, to the cultivator, alike mournful and calamitous.' "—*Rickards, Vol. II.* 74.

Under such an oppressive weight it cannot be matter of surprise, that vast quantities of land are relinquished, from the absolute impossibility of paying taxes: the land not being worth a single year's assessment. The following are extracts from a Revenue letter to Bengal, from the Court of Directors, dated August 1, 1821, quoted by Mr. Rickards, Vol. II. p. 149.

" The present assessment, he affirms, is not too high; yet he says, that the ' *Jumma (tax) of estates resigned (that is which their owners have relinquished rather than undertake to pay this assessment,) amounts to nearly six lacs,* (£600,000,) *or more than one-fifth of the whole.*' "

" *The resignations in Bareilly are upon a similar scale, amount-ing to near five lacs, (£500,000,) of rupees. In Shahjehanpore, the proportion of estates resigned appears to be much the same as in Ba-reilly, and for the same reasons.*"

The favour of superiors being always to be con-ciliated by any *improvement* of revenue, the collectors are always prepared to avail themselves of any op-portunity to increase the assessment. In 1813–14, to 1817–18, a large increase of jumma was made in Rohilcund, Bareilly, and Shahjehanpore, but in at-tempting to collect it, "It is officially certified that the owners of estates, the annual jumma of which amounted to 1,500,000 rupees, (750,000 dollars,) had, in despair, *abandoned their property, from utter in-ability to pay their over assessment.*"—*Rickards, Vol. II. p.* 146.

It is a common saying of the Ryots, that "their skins only are left them," and the reader may per-haps be already disposed to believe it, but he has by no means reached the end of the oppressions of this unfortunate people. Thus far we have dealt only with *direct* taxation, but that has been carried so far, that it would appear almost impossible to find any means of collecting *indirect* taxes, which, neverthe-less, is done. The following extract from the fifth report of the Select Committee of the House of Com-mons, will show the nature of the indirect taxation, uniting all that is detestable in the French octroi, and the Spanish alcabala.

" In addition to the assessment on the lands, or the shares of their produce received from the inhabitants, they were subject to the du-ties levied on the inland trade, which were collected by the renters under the Zemindars. *These duties, which went by the name of*

Sayer, as they extended to grain, cattle, salt, and all the other neces-
saries of life passing through the country, and were collected by
corrupt, partial, and extortionate agents, produced the worst effects
on the state of society, by not only checking the progress of industry, oppressing the manufacturer, and causing him to debase his
manufacture, but also by clogging the beneficial operations of commerce in general, and abridging the comforts of the people at large.
This latter description of imposts was originally considered as a
branch of revenue too much exposed to abuses to be intrusted to
persons not liable to restraint and punishment.   It was therefore
retained under the immediate management of the government. The
first rates were easy, and the custom houses few ; but in the general
relaxation of authority, this mode of raising revenue for the support
of the government was scandalously abused.   In the course of a little
time, new duties were introduced, under the pretence of charitable
and religious donations, as fees to the Chokeydars, or account
keepers' guards, and other officers at the stations, as protection
money to a Zemindar; or as a present to those who framed the
duties. Not only had the duties been from time to time raised in
their amount, and multiplied in their number, at the discretion of
the Zemindars and the renters under them, but they were at length
levied at almost every stage, and *on every successive transfer of*
property—uniformity in the principles of collection was completely
wanting; a different mode of taxation prevailing in every district,
in respect to all the varieties of goods, and other articles, subject to
impost. *This consuming system of oppression had, in some instances,*
been aggravated by the Company's government, which, when possessed of a few factories, with a small extent of territory around
them, adopted the measure of placing Chokies, or custom stations,
in the vicinity of each, for the purpose of ascertaining the state of
trade within their own limits, as well as to afford them a source of
revenue.   Under the head of Sayer revenue, was also included a
variety of taxes, indefinite in their amount, and vexatious in their
nature, called Moturpha; they consisted of imposts upon houses, on
the implements of agriculture, on looms, on merchants, on artificers,
and other professions and castes.

"Again, speaking of the Company's administration in reference
to the Nunjah, Punjab, and Baghayut lands above described, the
select committee observe—' The demand on the cultivator was,

however, by no means confined to the established rates of land tax or rent; for beside the Sayer duties and taxes, personal and professional, the Ryot was subject to extraordinary aids, additional assessments, and to the private exactions of the officers of government, or renters, and their people; so that *what was left to the Ryot was little more than what he was able to secure by evasion and concealment.*"
—*Rickards, Vol. I. 414.*

The manufacture of salt is a strict monopoly, which produced in Bengal alone, in the years 1822–3 to 1825–6, an average revenue of 15,785,376 rupees, or nearly eight millions of dollars. The total revenue in the three presidencies from this source, was 18,000,000 of rupees per annum. Mr. Rickards says, "comparing the revenue with the cost and charges in each year, it appears that the former is more than $3\frac{1}{2}$ times the latter." This extravagant charge is necessarily augmented by the profits of the retailers, and the salt which is sold by government at 3 rupees per maund, (equal to a dollar per bushel,) is re-sold in Calcutta at 5 rupees, ($1 67 per bushel,) after being adulterated with ten or fifteen per cent. of dirt. No one not conversant with the revenue system of India, after being informed that one-half of the whole produce of their patches of land had been taken to meet the demands of government, could have conceived the possibility of such an assessment upon an article like salt, by which it should be quadrupled in price for *the payment of dividends on India stock!* Another of the effects of this oppressive tax, is to increase the risk of famine, to which this unfortunate people are always liable. "The great impediment," says Mr. M'Culloch, "to the intercourse between the Bengal and Madras provinces

is the salt monopoly; the quantity of salt annually
taken being restricted by the government of Bengal. This limits the consumption of salt in Bengal,
where it is actually dear, and by compelling the
inhabitants of Madras to grow corn on poor lands,
precludes the export of the cheap rice of Bengal.
The India government, instead of having improved
of late years in liberality, have actually drawn tighter
the cords of monopoly. The effect of this upon the
export of corn from Bengal to Madras has been remarkable. In 1806–7, when the salt of Madras was
admitted into Calcutta with some liberality, their export of grain to the Coromandel coast, amounted to
2,635,658 maunds, (74 lbs. each.) or about 470,000
quarters; whereas in 1823–4, a year of scarcity, it
amounted to 1,591,326 maunds, or about 284,000
quarters."

In 1804, Lord Wellesley writes, that the " main
and avowed object of the Company's system is an
exclusive appropriation of the labour of the weavers,
and the establishment of a control over that labour,
to enable the commercial officers to obtain the proportion of goods required for the Company *at prices
to be regulated by the officers themselves.*"—*Rickards,
Vol. I.* 84.

Tobacco was monopolised, and the Ryots were
prohibited from cultivating any smaller quantity than
ten maunds, to the injury of those who had been accustomed to discharge part of their rent by the help
of a small plantation of one or two maunds.—*Rickards, I.* 91.

Opium is also a monopoly. The average of the

L

gross receipts from this source for fourteen years, ending with 1821-2, was 9,382,263 rupees, and the cost and charges 990,738 rupees, giving a profit of 850 per cent.! Since the introduction of Malwa opium, which the company has been unable to monopolise, the profits of this department of trade have very much diminished.

By the monopoly of the sale of salt to, and the purchase of opium from, this unfortunate people, the Company realized a profit of thirteen millions of dollars, a sum almost equal to the whole expenses of the government of the United States.

The following extract will give a general view of the state of India under all these exactions:—

"Let us suppose England to be divided into small tenures, not much bigger than Irish potato gardens; the produce of the soil a great variety of articles, of which some one or more, come to maturity in almost every month in the year; the present landlords forced to emigrate, or reduced to cultivate their own lands, or perhaps converted into Zemindars, with power to exact, flog, fine and imprison *ab libitum;* the land tax fixed at one-half the gross produce, to be ascertained by admeasurement of every acre, and by valuation, or by weighing the produce; or, in the event of difference of opinion with the cultivators of any village or district, by calling in the farmers of a neighbouring district to settle the dispute. From the oppressive, as well as vexatious nature of this tax, let us also suppose the fears and jealousies of government occasion the appointment of hosts of revenue servants, armed and unarmed, some to make, others to check the collections; that accounts and check accounts be also multiplied, to guard against imposition; and that servants required for these various purposes, be authorized to collect additional imposts from the cultivators, or to have land assigned to them, as a remuneration for their own services; and that, under colour of their privileges and grants, excessive exactions are enforced, leaving but a bare subsistence to the farmers; that this system of taxation should be liable to increase with every increase of cultivation; that the defalcations of one farmer, or one village, should be made good from the surplus produce of others; that the spirit of the people should be so broken by the rigour of despotic power, as to suffer the government with impunity to step forward, and declare itself sole proprietor of all the lands in the country; and that its avarice and cravings had so multiplied imposts as to inspire cultivators with the utmost alarm and dread, whenever changes or reforms were projected in the revenue administration, lest further additions should be made to their almost intolerable burdens. Let the reader, I say, consider these things, and then ask himself if a government assessor, with every soul in the country thus opposed to his research, is likely to obtain the requisite information for justly valuing every acre of cultivated land, including every variety of soil, and of products; or if it could be justly valued, whether the collectors of such a government were likely to be guided by any better rule, than to extract from the contributors all that could with safety be drawn into their own and the public purse. This, however, is but a sketch of the state of society in Hindostan, of which demoralization was the inevitable result; where laws, regulations, and even official instructions, are but a name: where power is really uncontrolled, and usage affords abundant openings for its arbitrary exercise, the holders of power, with their numerous hangers-on, will be arrayed on one side as instruments of oppression, to which the Ryots, or the mass of people, have naught to oppose but evasion, falsehood, artifice and cunning. Some of the worst passions of the human mind, thus called into constant action, become settled habits; and every rising generation being of necessity, and from infancy, driven to the practice of these habits, a character of slavish submission, and moral degradation, is generated, which it is most illiberal and unjust to impute to this oppressed people, as inherent and incorrigible depravity."—*Rickards*, Vol. II., 43.

Notwithstanding the horrible picture that is here presented, the Quarterly Review, for August, 1834, says, " It is to be hoped that no further encroachments will be made on the authorities who have so long and so ably administered the government of India, and whose *successful endeavours in diffusing*

*happiness among countless millions of a quiet and in-
nocent people, are universally allowed.* Placed, as
these natives are, under the immediate rule of able,
upright, and honourable men, taught from an early
age to respect their prejudices and to treat them with
kindness and humanity, *no change of the present system,* we are quite satisfied, *could tend to better their
condition,* or to promote the tranquillity of this extensive empire." p. 368.

I have made these very copious extracts, believing
that a very large portion of my readers cannot be
familiar with the revenue system of British India, and
that its importance, affecting, as it does, the happiness
of a nation of above one hundred millions, is a sufficient excuse for so doing. Copious as they are,
they give but a faint idea of the abuses to which it
has given rise, and which can only be understood
by a perusal of the excellent work of Mr. Rickards,
of whom Mr. M'Culloch says, " his opinion, from the
high station he filled in India, his intelligence, can-
dour, and experience in commercial affairs, is entitled to great weight."

Having perused them, the reader can have little
doubt as to the difficulty in obtaining commodities
to exchange for silver, by the people of India, as
compared with the United States or England—nor
can he have much doubt of the fact that the fund
out of which the labourer is to be supported, must
be very small, when an individual cultivator of some
half dozen acres, the whole produce of which would
not support an American, is compelled to pay one-
half for rent; then to meet a succession of demands

from those who are placed over him; then to pay
duties on the transport of all he has to sell; and
finally, to sell and buy at prices fixed by the Company; selling always at the lowest, and buying always at the highest. That a people so situated, should
be " poor and miserable," is not matter of surprise,
but that they are able to exist at all is wonderful!

The effects of excessive taxation upon a nation are
well described by Mr. M'Culloch—" The effect of
exorbitant taxes is not to stimulate its industry, but
to destroy it. No man will ever be really and per-
severingly industrious, whose industry does not yield
him a visible increase of comforts and enjoyments.
If taxation be carried so high as to swallow the
whole, or even the greater part of the produce of
industry above what is required to furnish us with
mere necessaries, it must, by destroying the hope
and means of rising in the world, take away the most
powerful motive to industry and frugality, and, instead of producing increased exertion, will produce
only *despair.* The stimulus given, by excessive taxation, to industry, has not been unaptly compared to
the stimulus given by the lash to the *slave*—a stimulus, which the experience of all ages and nations has
proved to be as ineffectual as it is inhuman, when
compared to that which the expectation of improving
his condition and enjoying the fruits of his industry
without molestation, gives to the productive energies
of the citizen of the free state."—*Sup. Ency. Brit. art.
Taxation.*

CHAPTER X.

The third great disturbing cause is restraint upon freedom of action and of commerce.

Freedom of action has never been interfered with in the United States. Every man may travel from North to South, from East to West, without a passport, and without the necessity of visiting police offices, so annoying to those who travel on the continent of Europe. Every man who finds business unprofitable, or employment scarce, may change his residence until he finds himself suited, without incurring the risk of being sent back to his parish, as would be the case in England. There, a constant strife exists as to the right of settlement, and immense sums are squandered in law proceedings, to determine whether parish No. 1 or No. 2 shall support the unfortunate pauper; and even when a demand for labour exists, so much apprehension is there of permitting a settlement to be gained, that engagements are made for eleven months, in order that, before the expiration of the year, the man may be returned to his parish to take up a new departure in quest of employment.

" The enterprising man who has fled from the tyranny and pauperism of his parish, to some place where there is a demand and a reward for his services, is driven from a situation which suits him, and an employer to whom he is attached, by a labour rate, or some other device against non-parishioners, and forced back to his settlement to receive as alms a portion only of what he was earning by his own exertions. He is driven from a place where he was earning, as a free labourer, 12*s.* or 14*s.* a week, and is offered road work as a pauper at 6*d.* a day, or perhaps to be put up by the parish authorities at auction, and sold to the farmer who will take him at the lowest allowance."—*Rep. Poor-Laws Com.* p. 86.

" The Rev. R. R. Bailey, chaplain to the Tower, who has had extensive opportunities of observing the operation of the poor-laws in the rural districts, states, ' I consider that the present law of settlement renders the peasant, to all intents and purposes, a bondsman! he is chained to the soil by the operation of the system. Very frequent instances have occurred to me of one parish being full of labourers, and suffering greatly from want of employment, whilst in another adjacent parish, there is a demand for labour. I have no doubt that if the labourers were freed from their present trammels, there would be such a circulation of labour as would relieve the agricultural districts.' "—*Mr. Chadwick's Report.*

If he has devised any improvements, he incurs the risk of interfering with the vested rights of some corporate body, as in the following instance:—

" At the Thames police office on Wednesday, the captain of the steam boat Adelaide, which has recently been running between Hungerford market and Greenwich, for the conveyance of passengers, *to the great injury and annoyance of the Thames watermen, was fined £5* under a law of the Watermen's Company, for acting as master of the steam boat, without being duly approved and licensed by the Watermen's Company. It is further understood that this verdict will go to *put a stop to any further steam conveyance to Greenwich*, as it is the intention of the Watermen's Company not to grant a license to any steam boat which shall only run to Greenwich."—*Westminster Review, July,* 1834.

The following extract will serve to show the effect produced upon the price of labour by the settlement laws:—*West. Rev.* No. xlii. p. 40.

" If higher wages were offered from a distant parish to the labourers in your parish than they now get there, do you not think they would move out of it ?—No, I am quite sure they would not, because, in addition to the usual parish relief, they have a very large charity there: it is some lands bequeathed in Edward the Sixth's time, for the repairs of the church, the roads, and the use of the poor. We expend that portion with relation to the poor in clothing, and coals and rents, and some in educating their children. At times it occasions desperate swearing to get settlements in the parish, and at all times it is a very great hindrance to people going out of the parish. I do not blame them for remaining in the parish, and sticking to their settlements; I should do so myself, if I were in their place."

In the United States, there are no apprentice laws, and a man may change his trade as often as he thinks proper; nor is he compelled to pay for making himself free of the "Worshipful Company of Merchant Tailors," or any other company, before he can exercise his skill in any one of our cities. Mr. Gallatin says:—

"No cause has, perhaps, more promoted, in every respect, the general improvement of the United States, than the absence of those systems of internal restriction and monopoly which continue to disfigure the state of society in other countries. No laws exist here, directly or indirectly, confining men to a particular occupation or place, or excluding any citizen from any branch he may, at any time, think proper to pursue. Industry is, in every respect, free and unfettered; every species of trade, commerce, and professions, and manufacture, being equally open to all, *without requiring any regular apprenticeship, admission, or license.* Hence the improvement of America has led not only to the improvement of her agriculture, and to the rapid formation and settlement of new states in the wilderness; but her citizens have extended their commerce to every part of the globe, and carry on with complete success even those branches for which a monopoly had heretofore been considered essentially necessary."

This absence of interference with the affairs of individuals, produces a state of things so different from that usually met in Europe, that it is perfectly incomprehensible to most of foreigners who write upon the affairs of the United States. Thus in Blackwood's Magazine for March 1835, in an able article on Mr. Pitt and his policy, is the following passage:—

" It is remarkable as a national distinction, and still more remarkable as a public advantage, that in England all the great principles of the life of nations, are in a state of perpetual inquiry. In the continental kingdoms, the sole object of public interest is the conduct of the monarch or the minister. In France a new era has lately begun, but it is still in the infancy of legislation, and may never reach the manhood. Even in America, we hear of little more than the tricks of elections transferred to the tricks of Congress; quarrels, among obscure *coteries* in the villages, expanded into interminable speeches in the legislature; and the whole annual labour of American wisdom, compiled for the world in the speech of the president, whose whole labour seems to be that of lucky finance, and whose financial triumphs, in the midst of a new world, demanding the largest liberality of government to foster the growing powers of the people, seem to be limited to the saving of so many dollars this year, within the narrowest scale of national penury the year before. But in England we have topics of a more deliberate, manly, and majestic order."

Misconception of the true object of government was never more clearly displayed than in the above passage. It is claimed as a national distinction and advantage, that the great principles of government are matters of debate, and such it certainly is when compared with those nations of the continent whose absolute monarchs forbid inquiry; but it would be equally proper for the people of Baden, or Bavaria, or Hesse, to boast their superiority over those of England, because the great question of the freedom of the press, or the right of habeas corpus, happened to be under debate at this time. Should such a claim be made, the Briton would feel towards the German precisely as an American must feel towards the writer of an article like the above. All the important principles of government are settled in this country, and have ceased to be matters of discussion; and notwithstanding the departure therefrom in the case of the tariff, it is now so fully understood that the true policy of the United States is abstinence from meddling with the affairs of individuals; or in other words, freedom of trade and of action; that there will be every day less disposition to interfere with it. It never occurs to any one on the floor of Congress to doubt the expediency of abolishing all restrictions upon navigation, and thus the reciprocity treaties are deemed by all an improvement upon the old and barbarous system, while in England they are as often discussed as the question of tithes! The true object for which government was instituted, is understood to be to give to every man security of person and property, at the smallest cost, and with the least possible interference with his freedom of action; a very simple theory, but apparently very difficult of comprehension to one brought up in the habit of contemplating the very complicated machinery of an European government. His view of the object of government is found in the idea contained in the above, of "fostering the growing powers of the people"—or, in other words, plundering A. to enrich B.; for such must be the result of all such attempts to "foster the growing powers of the people." When the object of government shall be as well understood in Great Britain as it is in the United States, the idea will be exploded, and many of the discussions referred to as being of that "deliberate and majestic order," will be deemed as absurd and

unnecessary as would be a repétition of those in relation to tonnage and poundage. Two centuries since,
many very important questions were discussed in the
most "manly and deliberate" manner, but a reference
to those discussions would now excite little other feeling in the mind of the above writer, than that of surprise that the object of government should have been
so little understood.   Precisely such is the condition
of the people of the United States.   They see the
bar, the press, and both houses of parliament, engaged in the discussion of tithes, corporations, marriage
acts, the union of church and state, the right of dis-
senters to take degrees, the right of Roman Catholics
and Jews to the enjoyment of certain privileges, the
right of exporting machinery, and numberless other
questions, which appear to them absurd and ridiculous, and totally unworthy the period in which we
live. All such matters are settled, and can never be
revived in the United States. There are important
questions peculiar to this form of government, such
as the constitutionality of the tariff—the powers of
the states—and the executive power—that have been
within a few years brought into discussion, and it
may be safely said that some of the debates upon
them are of as " deliberate and majestic" a character
as those of any deliberative body in the world.

CHAPTER XI.

RESTRAINTS upon the *freedom* of commerce are next in order, and to them and to the colonial system has been owing a large portion of the wars of Great Britain and France of the last century. Even previous to that time, during the administration of Colbert, they had produced the same effect between France and Holland.

" Before his time, Holland supplied all Europe with manufactures, and received in payment for them the raw produce of her poor neighbours. M. Colbert, overlooking the facts, that manufactures cannot be established in a country until it has acquired a considerable capital, and until the people of it have become rich enough to buy them, sought to force the growth of manufactures in France merely by issuing his famous tariff of 1667, by which the importation of all manufactures into France was prohibited. * * * Immediately after the appearance of the tariff of 1667, the Dutch retaliated by prohibiting the importation of the wines, brandies, and other productions of France. This commercial warfare produced open hostilities in 1672, and a war that lasted six years; and it is to commercial prohibitions and retaliations that most of the wars of Europe, since 1667, are to attributed."—*Parnell*, p. 74.

The internal trade of the United States is perfectly free, except that flour, tobacco, staves, and a few other things are required to be inspected, a species of regulation which will, doubtless, soon disappear.

Their foreign trade has always been comparatively free, and even with the tariff at its highest rate, it was vastly more so than that of England. In the early part of their existence as a nation, all duties were very moderate, but the war of 1812 produced the necessity of increasing them, and the system of protection continued it. At present, however, with the exception of cottons and woollens, paper, sugar, lead, hardware, and a few other articles, duties are very light, and in many cases importations are absolutely free, so that the grower of cotton may now exchange for coffee or tea, without paying a farthing to the government for the privilege. This country was the first to propose the abolition of all restrictions upon navigation, and the equalization of duties upon domestic and foreign vessels; a measure to which Great Britain assented only when it could not be avoided, and *even to this hour,* as has before been stated, *the advantages and disadvantages of "the reciprocity system" are matters of discussion in the House of Commons, and in the newspapers and magazines of Great Britain!*

The necessity of raising a large revenue in England, compels the government to impose taxes upon many of the exchanges that take place, by the aid of excise laws, which prevent the shoemaker from exchanging his products for those of the paper maker or glass blower, unless he will pay the government for permission so to do. Nor is this the only disadvantage. To secure the collection of the revenue, it has been found necessary to prescribe the modes of operation in various branches of manufacture, and thus the brewer, the paper maker, the glass blower, &c. are prohibited by law from making improve-

M

ments, lest the collection of the revenue should be endangered.

"By the excise laws prescribing the processes of fabrication, the manufacturer cannot manage his trade in the way his skill and experience point out as the best; but he is compelled to conform to such methods of pursuing his art as he finds taught in the acts of Parliament. Thus the unseen injury arising from excise taxation, by its interference with the free course of manufactures, is much greater than is suspected by the public. The consequence of the activity and invention of the manufacturers being repressed, is, that the consumers of goods pay increased prices, not only for the duties imposed on them, but for the additional expense incurred by absurd and vexatious regulations; and in addition to this, the goods are generally very inferior in quality to what they would be if no duties existed." p. 29, "In the act of Parliament for the collection of these duties, (on glass,) there are no less than thirty-two clauses of regulations, penalties, and prohibitions; all great obstacles in the way of introducing improvements, vexatious in the highest degree to the manufacturer, and necessarily obliging him to sell his goods at much higher prices than what the mere amount of the duty occasions."—*Parnell, p.* 31.

"The zeal for securing revenue has so kept down the trade of malting, as to have made the consumption stationary for the last forty years; whereas, there can be no doubt, that if the trade had not been so harassed by excise rules, checks and penalties, the consumption would have increased with increased population and wealth, and consequently the revenue derived from it."—*Ibid. p.* 176.

The following extract from a speech of Mr. Powlett Thompson, will show the effect of duties on glass:

"It appears, therefore, that notwithstanding the increase of population and general luxury, the consumption has been kept down by your improvident system, and is actually now less than it was five and thirty years ago. But here again the duty is far from being the greatest evil. Let any one turn to the act: he will find thirty-two clauses of regulations, penalties, prohibitions, all vexatious to the manufacturer, and all to be paid for by the public. I have said that the duty on flint glass is 6*d.* per pound; the glass, when made, selling for 1*s.* But the excise officer has the power of imposing the duty, either when the glass is in the pot, 3d. per pound, or after it has been turned out, at 6d.; the glass, when turned out, gaining 100 per cent. It is found more advantageous to the revenue, to exact the duty on glass in the pot, at 3d.; and in this way the duty is raised to 7d. Nor is this all. The manufacturer is driven by this method into the necessity of producing frequently an article which he does not want. He makes the fine glass from the middle; the coarser from the top and bottom of the pot. He frequently wants only fine glass, and he would remelt the flux of the coarser parts, if he had not paid duty upon it; but of course he is unable to do so. All the glass manufacturers whom I have consulted, agree that the whole cost of the excise, to the consumer, besides the duty, which is 100 per cent., is 25 per cent.; and besides, there is great inconvenience and oppression from the frauds that are daily taking place. And observe the effect which is produced upon your trade, both at home and abroad. A manufacturer who has lately travelled through France, the Netherlands, and Germany, has assured me that our manufacturers could advantageously cope with foreigners, were it not for the duties imposed by the government. Labour is as cheap in this country, our ingenuity greater, and the materials are also as cheap: it is, then, the vexatious onerous duty alone that gives the foreign manufacturer the advantage over the English. But the effect of the duty goes further; it operates to prevent all improvement in the article, because to improve experiments must be made; but a man with a duty of 125 per cent. over his head, is not very likely to make many experiments. This argument applies especially with respect to colours. A manufacturer has assured me, that he has never been able to produce a beautiful red, because the duties have prevented his trying the necessary experiments, without his incurring a great risk or loss. Thus a miserable duty, amounting to only £ 500,000, and upon which a charge of 10 per cent. is made for collecting, is allowed to impede our native industry, and to put a stop to all improvements, and be a source of endless oppression and fraud. I really cannot believe that the legislature will resist such an appeal as the manufacturers of this article could make to them, or refuse to relieve them from the gratuitous injury which is inflicted on them."

———

Great Britain retains a host of colonies for no con-

ceivable purpose but to act as drains of her capital.
Canada alone costs her £600,000, or three millions
of dollars per annum, in addition to the enormous
sums paid in bounties on Canadian timber used in
Great Britain. Canadian wheat is admitted at a
duty of 6d. per quarter, while that of the United
States, Prussia, and Poland, is shut out by prohibitory
duties.

The West India Islands are compelled to supply
themselves from Canada at prices much higher than
they would pay to the United States, and to make
amends therefor, West India sugar is allowed a
bounty in the home market over that of British subjects resident in India. Millions of pounds are expended in the protection of colonies, for no purpose
but to enable the colonists to supply their fellow subjects with wheat, lumber, &c., at greatly higher prices
than other persons would gladly sell at. In the report of the Poor-Laws Commissioners, are statements
in regard to the number of persons who are born and
brought up to be paupers, in consequence of the injudicious nature of the system, but they have given it
on a very small scale. They might have included in
the same category the whole mass of the colonists, all
of whom are supported at the expense of the labouring
classes of Great Britain. "The history of the colonies
for many years, is that of a series of loss, and of the
destruction of capital; and if to the many millions of
private capital which have been thus wasted, were
added some hundred millions that have been raised
by British taxes, and spent on account of the colonies,
the total loss to the British public of wealth which

the colonies have occasioned, would appear to be quite enormous."—*Parnell*, 247.

No exchange for any foreign product can take place without the payment of a heavy duty, except in the case of certain raw materials indispensable to her manufacturers. With a limited territory at home, incapable of supplying her population with food, she refuses to avail herself of the advantages of her position as a manufacturing nation, to obtain it on the best terms, and deprives her mechanics of the vast business that would arise therefrom. Thus by internal and external regulations, every thing is done to prevent freedom of action and of trade; to prevent her population from employing themselves either at home or abroad, where they would be best paid; and to prevent, by this means, any increase in the fund for the support of the labourer, while the chief part of the expenses of the estate is borne by that fund; and then great astonishment is expressed at the increase of pauperism, the remedy for which is to discourage matrimony! and that too in a country in which it has been recently declared by high authority, that "female chastity among the labouring class is a virtue almost unknown!"* The time is not

---

* Extracts from the Reports of the Poor-Laws Commissioners:
"Swaffham Norfolk. A woman in a neighbouring parish had five illegitimate children, for which she was allowed 10s. per week, and 6s. for herself." Remonstrating with another, she replies, 'I am not going to be disappointed in my company with men, to save the parish.' This woman now receives 14s. a week for her seven bastards. Had she been *a widow with five legitimate children, she would not have received so much by four or five shillings.*" "It is

remote, when it will be altogether unknown, unless
the burthens of the labouring classes are alleviated,

considered a good speculation to marry a woman who can bring a
fortune of one or two bastards to her husband." p. 171.

" An unmarried girl, upon leaving the work-house, after her
fourth confinement, said to the master, ' Well, if I can have the
good luck to have another child, I shall draw a good round sum
from the parish, and with what I can earn myself, I shall be better
off than any married woman in the parish.' " p. 172.

" At Bulkington, the clergyman of the parish, who was interro-
gated as to the proportion of pregnant women 'among the poor
whom he married, replied, ' not less than nineteen out of twenty.' "

" At Mantua, ' seventeen out of every twenty of the female poor
who went there to be married, were far advanced in pregnancy.' "
p. 173.

" Several clergymen told me, that four-fifths of the women are
with child, and frequently near the time of their confinement at the
time of their marriage." p. 174.

" I know of many instances in which the mothers have themselves been instrumental in having their daughters seduced, for the
express purpose of getting rid of the *onus* of supporting her." p. 176.

" They are almost always with child when they come to church."
p. 173.

" One day," said one of the witnesses examined by Mr. Chadwick,
" I went into the house of one of the people who work at the chalk
quarries at Northfleet, to buy fossils, and a young woman came in
for a few minutes, whose appearance clearly showed approach to
maternity. When she went out, I said to the woman of the house,
' Poor girl, she has been unfortunate.' She replied, ' Indeed she has,
poor girl, and a virtuous good girl she is too. The fellow has be-
trayed her, and gone to sea.' I said, ' She should not have trusted
him until they had been at church.' To this observation the woman replied, and, let me observe, *her own children were all about
her*, ' What could she do, poor girl! if she did not do as other girls
do, she would never get a husband. Girls are often deceived, and
how can they help it?' "

" The causes why illegitimate children are less numerous in manufacturing towns, are manifold; of these I shall allude but to two

and the Malthusian doctrines which lead men away from the true cause of distress are abandoned.

" If once men were allowed to take their own way, they would very soon, to the great advantage of society, undeceive the world of the error of restricting trade, and show that the passage of merchandise from one estate to another, ought to be as free as air and water. Every country should be as a general and common fair for the sale of goods, and the individual or nation which makes the best commodity, should find the greatest advantage. The distance and expense of carriage are sufficient reasons for any nation's preferring its own goods to those of others, and when these obstacles cease, the stranger is preferable to our own countrymen, otherwise domestic trade is injured instead of being favoured. For these reasons, trade claims liberty, instead of those protections by which it has been discouraged."—*Parnell, p.* 292.

After the view given of the taxation of India, it can hardly be necessary to say, that no freedom of any kind exists there; nor has existed, except to

—the inferior health of the women, and the desperate remedy of destroying the burden prematurely in the womb. The existence of these facts will be acknowledged by any one who has seen with inquiring eye, the *actual* state of the manufacturing population."— *England, Vol. I. p.* 204.

" I requested," says Mr. Brereton, of Norfolk, " the governor of a neighbouring hundred-house to furnish me with the number of children born within a certain period, distinguishing the legitimate from the illegitimate. The account was 77 born—23 legitimate, 54 *illegitimate."—Bulwer, England, Vol. I. p.* 227.

In Mr. Cunningham's work on New South Wales, is a statement given to him by an English clergyman, " that he considered the women in his parish more moral than they had been, in consequence of the increased number of bastards that were born. Before that time, they had been so promiscuous in their intercourse, that very few births took place."

plunder wherever it was possible to do so. The Hindoo may not sell where he pleases—nor buy where he pleases—he may not decide how much land he will cultivate, nor what he will raise—he may not cultivate tobacco, except under restrictions, nor, since 1797, might he cultivate the poppy, except in Bahar or Benares, until the recent territorial additions have made it necessary to permit its continuance in Malwa. His fellow subjects in England refuse to receive any of his productions, (cotton excepted,) unless burthened with excessive duties, while they require that all their productions, used chiefly by the rich, shall be admitted at a duty of five per cent., and that he shall out of his miserable patch of land contribute more than one-half of the gross proceeds to the support of the State, *and to the payment of his absentee landlords!*

The following extract from the minutes of the Madras Revenue Board, may be taken as evidence of the extent of freedom allowed to the Hindoo.

" The amount levied on each Ryot was in fact left to be determined at the discretion of the European or native revenue officers, for it was the practice to *compel* the Ryot to occupy as much land, and consequently to pay as much revenue, as they deemed proportional to his circumstances ; he was not allowed, on payment even of the high survey assessment fixed on each field, to cultivate only those fields to which he gave the preference ; his task was assigned to him ; *he was constrained to occupy all such fields as were allotted to him by the revenue officers ;* and whether he cultivated them or not, he was, as Mr. Thackery emphatically terms it, *saddled* with the rent of each." Mr. Rickards adds, " that if the Ryot was driven by these oppressions to fly, and seek a subsistence elsewhere, he was followed wherever he went, and oppressed at discretion, or deprived of the advantages he might expect from a change of residence."—Vol. I. p. 476,

CHAPTER XII.

HABITS OF INDUSTRY constitute a very important item in the consideration of the causes which tend to increase or diminish the product of labour, and, of course, the fund out of which it is to be paid.

In the United States every inducement is held out to industry. The people have the confidence that they will have the enjoyment of almost the whole product of their labour undiminished by taxation, and that moderate exertion, with economy, will lead to independence. As no people ever had stronger inducements, so none ever pursued their avocations with more earnestness.

Unfortunately the English System of poor-laws has been introduced, and from the great temptation held out to idleness, there is cause to fear that it will produce most injurious effects, unless carefully watched. There is also a vast increase of charitable societies, whose object is to teach people that they can be supported without labour, and that will be productive of serious injury. The following remarks of Mr. E. L. Bulwer are in the highest degree judicious.

"The system of public charities, however honourable to the humanity of a nation, requires the wisest legislative principles not to conspire with the poor-laws to be destructive of its morals. Nothing so nurtures virtue as the spirit of independence. The poor should be assisted undoubtedly—but in what—*in providing for themselves*.

Hence the wisdom of the institution of Savings Banks.   Taught to bear upon others, they are only a burden upon industry."*

Next in order are the people of Great Britain, who have great reason for exertion, but not the same confidence that they will have the enjoyment of its products, or that it will lead them to independence. Too large a portion of them feel that they must drag on existence without improvement, and that by availing themselves of the temptations held out to idleness by the poor-laws, they place themselves little lower in the scale than the position they must necessarily occupy, exert themselves as they may.

High duties, prohibitions, excise regulations, and game laws, offer the strongest inducement to engage in pursuits that are destructive of industry, and lead to crime.

" It has been well observed, that to create by high duties, an overwhelming temptation to indulge in crime, and then to punish men for indulging in it, is a proceeding wholly and completely subversive of every principle of justice.   It revolts the natural feelings of the people, and teaches them to feel an interest in the worst characters, to espouse their cause, and to avenge their wrongs.   A punishment which is not apportioned in the offence, and which does not carry the sanction of society along with it, can never be productive of any good effect; the true way to put down smuggling is to render it unprofitable, by reducing the duties on the smuggled commodities."†

When such inducements to pauperism and crime are held out, it is extraordinary that the poor-rates and criminal calendar have not increased more

* England and the English, *Vol. I. p.* 231.
† Ed. Rev. *Vol. XXXI. p.* 536,

rapidly than they have done. It is estimated that
the quantity of solid food that can be obtained by

The independent agricultural labourer is - 122 oz.
The soldier has - - - - - - - - - 168 "
The able bodied pauper has vegetables and 151 "
The suspected thief has - - - 181 to 203 "
The convicted thief has - - - - - - 239 "
The transported thief has - - - - - - 330 "

The Poor-Laws Commissioners, (page 228,) state
that " the diet of the work-house almost always exceeds that of the cottage, and the diet of the gaol is
almost always more profuse than that of the work-
house." The following extracts from their Report
will give some idea of the effect of the pauper system upon the labourer and the land owner.

" In Colesbury, the expense of maintaining the poor, has not
merely swallowed up the *whole value of the land;* it requires even
the assistance of two years rates in aid, from other parishes, to enable the *able bodied, after the land has been given up to them, to support themselves;* and the aged and impotent must even then remain
a burden on the neighbouring parishes."

" Our evidence exhibits no other instance of the abandonment of
a parish, but it contains many in which the pressure of the poor
rate has reduced the rent to one-half, or less than half of what it
would have been, if the land had been situated in an unpauperised
district, and some in which it has been impossible for the owner to
find a tenant."—*Report Poor-Law Commissioners, p.* 65.

" In the neighbourhood of Aylesbury there were 42 farms unte-
nanted at Michaelmas last, most of them are still on the proprietors'
hands; and on some no acts of husbandry have been done ever since,
in order to avoid the payment of the poor rate."

" In the parish of Thornborough, Bucks, there are at this time
600 acres of land unoccupied, and the greater part of the other tenants have given notice of their intention to quit their farms, owing
entirely to the increasing burthen of the poor's rate."—*Ib. p.* 66.

" The constant war which the pauper has to wage with all who
employ or pay him, is destructive to his honesty and his temper;
as his subsistence does not depend upon his exertions, he loses all
that sweetens labour, its association with reward, and gets through
his work, such as it is, with the reluctance of a slave. His pay,
earned by importunity and fraud, or even violence, is not husbanded
with the carefulness which would be given to the results of industry, but wasted in the intemperance to which his ample leisure in-
vites him. The ground on which relief is ordered to the idle and
dissolute is, that the wife and family must not suffer for the vices
of the head of the family; but as the relief is almost always given
into the hands of the vicious husband or parent, the excuse is obviously absurd. Wherever, says Mr. Laurence, of Herefield, the
labourers are unemployed, the beer shops of the parish are fre-
quented by them." p. 87.

" Applications to the petty session had been made by some labourers who had been refused relief by the overseer, after they had
rejected work at Wrotham Hill, twelve miles off. This hill was
lowered a short time ago, and the work was let out by contract;
fourteen or fifteen men of this parish might have found employment
at 2s. 6d. per day, or 15s. a week—high pay for winter wages. The
labourers, however, one and all, refused to go, unless the parish
would agree to allow them two days pay, one for going, and one
for returning; in other words, would enable the men to make eight
days of the six, and so raise their wages from 15s, to £1 per week."
Rev. H. Bishop's Report.

That pauperism leads to crime, there is abundant
evidence to be found in the excellent Report to which
we have already referred. I shall, however, quote
only a single passage from the evidence of Mr. Gre-
gory, treasurer of Spitalfields Parish.

" Are we to understand, as the result of your experience, that the
great mass of crime in your neighbourhood has always arisen from
idleness and vice, rather than from the want of employment? Yes,
and *this idleness and vicious habits are increased and fostered by
pauperism, and by the readiness with which the able-bodied can obtain from parishes allowances and food without labour.*"

In Lamb's admirable essays of Elia, is a description of the two races into which mankind is said to be divided: the lenders and the borrowers. It applies so well to the situation of the able-bodied pauper and the miserable workman that toils all day for the support of his family, and is obliged to *contribute a part of his earnings for the support of the Falstaffs and the Sheridans of the poor house*, that I am tempted to extract the following :—

" The human species, according to the best theory I can form of it, is composed of two distinct races, *the men who borrow, and the men who lend;*" (*the men who live by the labour of others, and the men who live by their own labour;*) "the infinite superiority of the former, which I choose to designate as the *great* race, is discernible in their figure, port, and a certain instinctive sovereignty. The latter are born degraded. ' He shall serve his brethren.' There is something in the air of one of this caste, lean and suspicious; contrasting with the open, generous manner of the other. Observe who have been the greatest borrowers of all ages—Alcibiades and Falstaff—Sir Richard Steele—our late incomparable Brinsley—what a family likeness in all four. What a careless, even, deportment hath your borrower! What rosy gills! What a beautiful reliance in Providence doth he manifest—taking no more thought than lilies! What contempt for money—accounting it, (yours and mine especially,) no better than dross! What a liberal confounding of those pedantic distinctions of *meum* and *tuum;* or rather what a noble simplification of language, (beyond Tooke,) resolving these supposed opposites into one clear, intelligible pronoun adjective! What near approaches doth he make to the primitive *community!* to the extent of one half of the principle at least!"

Other causes in other countries produce similar effects. Mr. Senior says:

" The established annual holidays in Protestant countries, are between fifty and sixty. In many Catholic countries they exceed one hundred. Among the Hindoos, they are said to occupy nearly

N

half the year. But these holidays are confined to a certain portion of the population; the labour of a sailor, or a soldier, or a menial servant, admits of scarcely any distinction of days.

" Many of the witnesses examined by the Committee on Artisans and Machinery, (Session of 1824,) were English manufacturers, who had worked in France. They agree as to the comparative indolence of the French labourer, even during his hours of employment. One of the witnesses, Adam Young, had been two years in one of the best manufactories in Alsace. He is asked, ' Did you find the spinners there as industrious as the spinners in England?' and replies, ' No; a spinner in England will do twice as much as a Frenchman. They get up at four in the morning, and work till ten at night; but our spinners will do as much in six hours as they will in ten.'

" ' Had you any Frenchmen employed under you?'—' Yes; eight, at two francs a day.'

" ' What had you a day?'—' Twelve francs.'

" ' Supposing you had had eight English carders under you, how much wore work could you have done?'—' With one Englishman, I could have done more than I did with those eight Frenchmen. It cannot be called work they do: it is only looking at it, and wishing it done.'

" ' Do the French make their yarn at a greater expense?'—' Yes; though they have their hands for much less wages than in England.'

" The average annual wages of labour in England, are three times as high as in Ireland; but as the labourer in Ireland is said not to do more than one-third of what is done by the labourer in England, the price of labour may in both countries, be about equal."*

I doubt much the correctness of this statement in regard to the Hindoos. There is no doubt that their religion leads to enormous waste of time; that mendicity is promoted by it; and that their various pilgrimages and observances are of a most injurious character; but I doubt the correctness of the assertion, that half their time is thus bestowed. Were

* Lectures on Wages, p. 11.

such the case, would it be possible for them to live, and meet the enormous demands upon them? A very important portion of the people of India, are mussulmen, whose religion does not require these observances, yet there is no very material difference in their situation. Mr. Hamilton says, "It may safely be asserted, that with so vast an extent of fertile soil, peopled by so many millions of tractable and *industrious* inhabitants, Hindostan is capable of supplying the whole world with any species of tropical merchandise; the production being in fact, only limited by the demand."

Mr. Rickards says:—

"They are decidedly by nature, a mild, pleasing, and intelligent race; sober, parsimonious, and, *where an object is held out to them, most industrious and persevering.* But they are men of high and gallant courage, courteous, intelligent, and eager after knowledge and improvement, with a remarkable aptitude for the abstract sciences, geometry, astronomy, &c.; and for the imitative arts, painting and sculpture."

Since the above was in type, I have received the Quarterly Review for April, 1835, containing the address of the Assistant Commissioner for the county of Kent, under the new poor-laws, giving so excellent a view of the effects of the poor-law system, as heretofore pursued, that I cannot omit making the following extract:—

"In old times, the English law punished a vagrant by cutting off his ear; and, said the ancient law, '*if he have no ears*' (which means, if the law should have robbed him of both), ' then he shall be branded with a hot iron; his city, town, or village being moreover authorized to punish him, according to its discretion, with chaining, beating, or otherwise.' The legislature, driven by the progress of civilization from this cruel extreme, most unfortunately fell into an. opposite one, wearing the mask of charity.   Instead of mutilating individuals, it inflicted its cruelty on the whole fabric of society, by the simple and apparently harmless act *of raising the pauper a degree or two above the honest, hard-working, hard-earning, and hardfaring peasant.*   The change, for a moment, seemed a benevolent one, but the prescription soon began to undermine the sound constitution of the labourer—it induced him to look behind him at the workhouse, instead of before him at his plough.

" The poison, having paralyzed the lowest extremity of society, next made its appearance in the form of out-door relief, and it thus sickened from their work those who were too proud to wear the livery of the pauper.   In the form of labour-rate, the farmers next began to feel that there was a profitable, but unhealthy, mode of cultivating their land by the money levied for the support of the poor.   He who nobly scorned to avail himself of this bribe, became every day poorer than his neighbour who accepted it; until, out of this distempered system, there grew up in every parish, petty laws and customs, which, partly from ignorance, and partly from self-interest, actually threatened with punishment those who were still uncontaminated by the disease.

" To the provident labourer they exclaimed, ' You shall have no work, for your dress and decent appearance show that you have been guilty of saving money from your labour ; subsist, therefore, upon what you have saved, until you have sunk to the level of those who, by having been careless of the future, have become entitled more than you to our relief!'

" ' You have no family,' they said to the prudent labourer, who had refrained from marrying because he had not the means of providing for children—' you have no family, and the farmer therefore must not employ you until we have found occupation for those who have children.   Marry without means !—prove to us that you have been improvident !—satisfy us that you have created children you have not power to support !—and the more children you produce, the more you shall receive !'

" To those who felt disposed to set the laws of their country at defiance,—' Why fear the laws ?—the English *pauper* is better fed than the independent labourer—the *suspected thief* receives in jail considerably more food than *the pauper*—the *convicted thief* receives still more—and the *transported felon* receives every day *very nearly three times as much food as the honest, independent peasant!*'

" While this dreadful system was thus corrupting the principles of the English labourer, it was working still harder to effect the demoralization of the weaker sex. On returning home from his work, vain was it for the peasant to spend his evening in instilling into the mind of his child that old-fashioned doctrine, that if she ceased to be virtuous she would cease to be respected—that if she ceased to be respected she would be abandoned by the world—that her days would pass in shame and indigence, and that she would bring her father's gray hairs in sorrow to the grave.

" ' No such cruelty shall befall you,' whispered the poor-laws in her ear: ' abandoned, indeed! you shall *not* be abandoned—concede, and you shall be married; and even if your seducer should refuse to go with you to the altar, he or your parish shall make you such an allowance, that if you will but repeat and repeat the offence, you will at last, by dint of illegitimate children, establish an income which will make you a marketable and marriageable commodity. With these advantages before you, do not wait for a seducer—be one yourself!'

" To the young female who recoiled with horror from this advice, the following arguments were used:—' If you do insist on following your parents' precepts instead of ours—don't wait till you can provide for a family, but marry!—the parish shall support you; and remember that the law says, the more children you bring into the world, without the means of providing for them, the richer you shall be !—'

" To the most depraved portion of the sex—'Swear!—we insist upon your swearing—who is the father of your child. Never mind how irregular your conduct may have been; fix it upon a father; for the words, ' *Thou shalt not bear false witness against thy neighbour*,' are not parish law—what's *wrong* before the altar, we have decreed *right* in the vestry! Swear, therefore; and though you swear ever so falsely, you shall immediately be rewarded !'

" I have now endeavoured to explain to you the two extremes of error under which the English poor-laws have hitherto existed; the ancient error having proceeded from the vice called cruelty, the modern one from false virtues assuming the name of charity. Of these two extremes, there can be little doubt that the latter was the worst. However, it is useless to argue—both are now at an end. The new act reigns in their stead, and we have therefore now only to consider what this really is. . . . Those who are enemies to its mechanism, tell you that this new act has a grinding propensity; but so has the mill which gives us our bread. The act truly enough *does* grind; but before we condemn it, let us clearly understand who and what it is that will be ground by it.

" The act rests upon that principle, which, whether admitted or not by law, is indelibly imprinted in the head and heart of every honest person in this country, that no individual, *whether able-bodied, impotent, or vicious, should be left to suffer from absolute want.* To this principle of common social justice, there is attached a liberal feeling almost as universal, namely, that the poor of this wealthy country should not only be barely supported, but totally regardless of expense, they should receive as many comforts and as much alleviation, as can, by any man's ingenuity, possibly be invented for them, *without injuring, corrupting, or demoralizing other members of society.*"

The same Article gives an excellent view of the effect of Foundling Hospitals. That of London has long since been compelled, while retaining its name, to resolve that foundlings should not be accepted, and that " henceforward from none but their mothers should babies be received. All honest women are now denied admittance, on the ground that ' the design of the foundation was to hide the shame of the mothers;' but those who happen to have children without husband, are rigidly examined by the committee, and *if they can succeed in showing that they are really guilty*, a day is appointed on which they are doomed painfully to produce and abandon their offspring,—to be re-christened, to be re-named, and, so long as they remain in the institution, never by their mothers to be seen again."

It contains also some admirable remarks upon that
provision in the new poor-law which relieves the
father from the necessity of providing for illegitimate children. That clause has excited great feeling,
and " It has not only been argued but preached, not
only senators but divines have boisterously contend-
ed, that in cases of bastardy, to relieve the man from
punishment, and to leave his unhappy victim to shame,
infamy, and distress, is a law discreditable to our
national character,—impious, cruel, ungenerous, un-
manly, and unjust."

Upon this head the Assistant Commissioner remarks,—

" We confess that we feel very deeply the force of these observations; at the same time it must be evident that we should have
dreaded (we hope we may say so fairly) to have stated one side of
the question, unless we felt convinced that there was something to
be said on the other. That the virtues of the weaker sex are the
purest blessings which this world affords us,—that they were so
intended to be by nature,—and that, like all her works, they have
not been created in vain, it is not even necessary to admit. From
our cradle to our grave,—in our infancy, our boyhood,—our zenith
and our decline,—rejoicing in our prosperity, ever smiling in our
adversity, there is, we all know, a satellite attending our orbit,
which, like our shadow, never leaves us, and which too often becomes itself a shadow when we are gone; but as the satellite shines
with borrowed lustre, so does the character of a woman much depend upon the conduct of him whose fate she follows;—and if this
be true, how deeply important it is for a nation to take especial care
lest, by too much human legislation, it may (as ours has too often
done) interfere with the wise arrangements of nature, whose motto,
with all her kindness, has ever been, *Nemo me impunè lacessit!*

" Universally adored as woman is, yet it is an anomalous fact,
which no one can deny, that in every climate under the sun man
appears as her open, avowed enemy—and strange as it may sound,

the more he admires the treasure she possesses, the more anxious he
is to deprive her of it:

> ' The lovely toy, so keenly sought,
>   Has lost its charms by being caught;
>   And every touch that wooed its stay,
>   Has brush'd its brightest hues away!'

Now, if this arrangement were totally incomprehensible to us, yet
surely it would not be altogether discreditable, were we to feel
assured that the mysterious dispensation was benevolent and just.

" We have already observed, that with all her kindness, the punishments by which nature preserves her laws are irrevocably severe.
Bestowing on us, with one hand, the enjoyment of health, with what
severity does she, with the other, punish every intemperance which
would destroy it—what human castigation, we beg leave to ask of
some of our opponents, is equal to a fit of their gout?   Compare a
healthy peasant's cheeks with the livid countenance of a gin-drinker,
and who can say that a magistrate's fine for drunkenness is as severe
as hers?   What admonition of a preacher is equal to the reproof of
a guilty conscience?   Even the sentence of death is what the meanest
among us has fortitude enough in silence to endure, but the first
murderer's punishment was 'greater than he could bear!' and after
all, what was this punishment but simply a voice crying to him in
the wilderness of his paradise—' *Cain! Cain! where is thy brother?*'
If abstinence be necessary for the recovery of our health, can any
physician enforce it like the fever which robs us of our appetite?
Can the surgeon explain to the man who has broken a limb the necessity of rest, in order that the bone may knit, as sternly as the
excruciating pain which punishes him if he moves it?   What would
be our sufferings if one man were to have the gout for another man's
intemperance?   Or if the effects of gin-drinking were to be borne
equally by all mankind?   Leaving justice out of the case, would it
be a wise arrangement to divide responsibility, and partially at the
expense of the community to absolve an individual for neglecting
the particular duty he has to perform?   Now, if in these cases it
be admitted, that Nature, though her lips be motionless, maintains
our real welfare by a judicious system of rewards and punishments,
surely it would follow, that it is probable she would consistently
pursue a similar course in protecting female virtue, on which the
happiness of all individuals, as well as of all nations, mainly depends.

Would it be prudent to intrust it to any but her own keeping? If she alone receives the reward which adorns its preservation, is it not a sensible arrangement that she should likewise be the sole sufferer for its loss? Could any better arrangement be invented? In common affairs of life, do we not invariably act on the same principle? Have we not one officer to command our army in the field, on purpose to ensure a responsibility which would not practically exist, were it to be subdivided? But it is loudly argued—'Nature is wrong: a woman ought not to be the sole guardian of her own honour; let us, therefore, make it, by English law, the joint-stock property of the sexes—let the man be punished for its loss as much as herself, and under this clever and superior arrangement, which will make it the interest of both parties to preserve the treasure, it will remain inviolate; depend upon it, no bankruptcy will take place!'

" Well—this theory has long been reduced to practice, and what, we ask, has been the result? Have the lower orders, to whom it has been *exclusively* applied, become more or less moral than their superiors in station? Has the fear of punishment *had* its promised effect? Has it intimidated the enemy? Has it strengthened or ruined the fortress? Has it preserved the citadel? Is there now, as there used to be, but one seducer, or are there two? Has it become the interest of the woman, instead of opposing, to go over to the enemy? For consenting to do so, has not the law almost invariably rewarded her with a husband? Has it not forcibly provided for her? Has not the oath it has extorted from her been frequently productive of perjury? Before the altar, do the ceremonies of marriage, churching, and christening, respectfully follow each other at awful intervals, or are they not now all jumbled together in a bag? Are the peasantry of England a more moral people in this respect than the Irish, among whom no poor-laws exist? Has it not been indisputably proved, that our domestic servants are, as to this matter, by far the most moral among our lower classes; and has not this been produced by our own unrelenting rule of turning them out of our houses, in short, like Nature, abandoning those who misbehave? Has not that severity had a most beneficial effect? Can there be any harm in our acting nationally as we conscientiously act in our own homes?

" If," argues the Assistant Commissioner, " it should be impossible for the defenders of the old law, and the revilers of the Poor-Law Amendment Act, satisfactorily to answer these questions, surely it must follow, that our theory, having been unsuccessful, is false; and standing before the world as we do, convicted of being incapable, on so delicate a subject, to legislate for ourselves, surely we ought, in penitence and submission, to fall back upon that simple law of nature, which has most sensibly decreed, that a woman after all is the best guardian of her own honour, and that the high rewards and severe punishments which naturally attend its preservation and its loss, are the beneficent means of securing our happiness, and of maintaining the moral character of our country. That we have erred from a mistaken theory of charity and benevolence—that we have demoralized society, kindly desirous to improve it—that, in scrubbing our morality we never meant to destroy its polish—that, by our old bastardy laws, we nobly intended to protect pretty women, just as we once thought how kind it would be to nurse infants for them in our national baby-house the Foundling Hospital—and just as we thought how benevolent it would be to raise the pauper above the independent labourer—it is highly consoling to reflect;—but the day of such follies has past. This country has no longer the apology of youth and inexperience—it is deeply stricken in years—age has brought with it experience, and by experience most dearly purchased, it enacted, in the Poor-Law Amendment Bill, the clause to which so much obloquy has attached, but which we humbly conceive, rests on a foundation that cannot now be undermined by the weak tools of mistaken sympathy, or reversed by explosions of popular clamour."

This long extract is given on account of the excellence of the argument and *its applicability to all other cases of regulation.* It is incessantly argued, in relation to the system of free trade, that "Nature is wrong: that man is not the proper guardian of his own interests:" and therefore it is deemed necessary that he should be regulated by law in the manner of pursuing them. If the able writer of the Quarterly Review would apply the Assistant Commissioner's argument to many other questions in political economy, he would speedily be a convert to the doctrine of non-interference.

————

There is no circumstance to which has been attributed more influence upon the industry of a nation than to the character of the relation between the owner of the land and its occupant. As this is a subject of considerable importance, it is proposed to consider it fully in the next chapter.

CHAPTER XIII.

The Rev. Richard Jones of Cambridge, has published the first volume of a series " On the Distribution of Wealth and the Sources of Taxation," in which
he has collected a great body of facts tending to show
the nature of the relation between the owner and occupier of land throughout the world. In his preface,
(page xxv.) he says:—

"I have begun by analysing *rents*, because a small progress in
this subject was sufficient to show, that the greater part of the nations of the earth are still in that state which is properly called
agricultural; that is, in which the bulk of their population depends
wholly on agriculture for subsistence; *and because in this state of
society, the relations between the proprietors of the soil and its occu-
piers, determine the details of the condition of the majority of the
people, and the spirit and forms of their political institutions.*"

The Quarterly Review, Vol. 46, p. 82, noticing the
work, confirms this doctrine in the following terms:

" There is no exaggeration in the assertion that it is *by these circumstances almost alone that the position of any nation in the scale
of civilization is practically determined.* Nor can any one be sur-
prised that the fact is so, when he adverts to the simple consideration that it is from the land, and the land alone, that nations derive
as well the whole of the food on which they are supported, as the
raw materials out of which, by the exertion of their industry and
ingenuity, they elaborate all the other necessaries, comforts, and
luxuries of life; that, therefore, the class who are possessed, no
matter how or why, of the exclusive property of the land, have it in
their power, by the more or less easy and equitable terms upon
which they choose to admit of its cultivation, either to restrain pro-

duction of every kind within the narrowest limits, or to permit its full development to the utmost extent of which human industry is capable."

It is singular that both of these writers should have allowed themselves to be so far misled as to make this relation modify the political institutions of the world, thus mistaking effect for cause. Had they examined it more closely, they could not have failed to see that the political institutions influence that relation, being the reverse of Mr. Jones's proposition. Property is the creature of government, and the object of man in the formation of communities, is to give to each other mutual aid and protection in the enjoyment of the fruits of labour, or property. Having associated themselves together, it becomes necessary to charge some certain person or persons with the maintenance of order, and to give to those persons perpetual succession, either by inheritance or election, as the case may be. Having agreed to maintain each other in the possession of such property as they may obtain, they may resolve that all the *lands* they possess are the property of the community or state, to be held on payment of rent to the state; or, that it shall be the property of a few individuals, who shall be entitled to receive the rents, and shall be liable to the payment of taxes on land; or that it shall be equally divided among all the members of the community, they paying a tax upon it. According to the decision that would be made as to the adoption of one or other of these modes, there might be in such a community, Ryot, labour, cottier, or farmers' rents, and it would then depend upon the subsequent

o

action of those who had the control of the movements
of the political machine thus created, whether, *under
any one of them*, there should be peace and prosperity, or wars, taxation and poverty. If the ruler or
rulers had entire control of its action, they might,
in the first case, demand such rents, or, in the last,
impose such taxes, as would effectually prevent the
improvement of the community, by absorbing nearly
the whole fruits of their labour, as is done in Hindostan, where no more is left to the cultivator than
is sufficient to provide him the most wretched subsistence. Or, if disposed to let the nation enjoy the
benefits of peace, they might content themselves
with a small contribution as in China. The following extracts will show Mr. Jones's views in regard
to those two nations:—

" It has been hitherto the misfortune of that country, (India,) to
see a rapid succession of short lived empires: the convulsions amidst
which they were established, have hardly subsided, before the people
have begun to be harassed by the consequences of their weakness
and decay. While any really efficient general government has existed, it has been the obvious interest, and usually the aim of the
chiefs, to act upon some definite system; to put some limit to their
own exactions; to protect the ryots, and foster cultivation by giving
reasonable security to all the interests concerned in it. The Mogul
emperors acted in this spirit, while exercising a power over the soil,
which had no real bounds, but those which they prescribed to themselves. But as the empire grew feeble, and the subordinate chief-
tains, Mahometan, or Hindoo, began to exercise an uncontrolled
power in their districts, their rapacity and violence seem usually to
have been wholly unchecked by policy or principle. There was at
once an end to all system, moderation, or protection; ruinous rents,
arbitrarily imposed, were collected in frequent military circuits, at
the spear's point; and the resistance often attempted in despair, was
unsparingly punished by fire and slaughter.

"Scenes like these, in the ancient history of India, have been frequently renewed, and succeeded rapidly short intervals of repose. They were of course disastrous. Half the rich territory of that country has never been cultivated, though swarming with a population to whom the permission to make it fruitful in moderate security, would have been happiness; and nothing can well exceed the ordinary poverty of the ryots, and the inefficiency of their means of cultivation."*

In China, " the arts of government are, to a certain extent, understood by the laboriously educated civilians, by whose hands the affairs of the Empire are carried on; the country has, till very lately, been remarkably free from intestine convulsion or serious foreign wars, and the administration has been well organized, pacific and efficient. The whole conduct indeed of the Empire, presents a striking contrast to that of the neighbouring Asiatic monarchies, the people of which, accustomed to see violence and bloodshed the common instruments of government, express great wonder at the spectacle of the Chinese statesmen upholding the authority of the state rather by the pen than the sword. One effect we know to have followed from the public tranquillity: the spread of agriculture, and an increase of people much beyond that of the neighbouring countries. While not one half of India has ever been reclaimed, and less still of Persia, China is as fully cultivated, and more fully peopled than most European monarchies."†

Here we have the *same mode of tenure*, but with the most different results. In the one is a government oppressive almost beyond imagination, and in the other the mildest possible form of absolute monarchy.

The whole land being declared to be the property of the state, it is said by Mr. Jones, [page 140,] that " *The sovereign proprietor has the means of enabling a body of labourers to maintain themselves, who, without the machinery of the earth with which he supplies them, must starve.*" The terms upon which this ma-

---

* Jones on the Distribution of Wealth, p. 116.
† Ibid. p. 133.

chinery will be rented, must depend upon the wants
of the party having it to let, and the extent of those
wants will depend upon the character of the government. If the master be a Cæsar, an Alexander, or a
Napoleon, he will deem his own glory paramount to
the happiness of those who are under him, and will
extract from them the chief part of their earnings, for
the purpose of adding to the number of unfortunates
subject to his control. If, on the contrary, he regard
the happiness of his people as most likely to add to
his glory, he will demand but a small rent, and will
leave the remainder in their possession to become
capital. Of the former character have been most of
the sovereigns of India, and to such an extent has
their oppression been carried, that, although there is
every reason to believe that private property in the
soil*, did, at one time, exist, it has been destroyed,

* Mr. Jones's reasoning in opposition to the existence of any such
rights, is curious.

"Are the Ryots in Rajast'han *practically*, as he (Colonel Tod)
conceives them to be, *freeholders* in any sense in which an English
proprietor is called *the freeholder* of the land he owns? I began in
the text by remarking, that the ryot has very generally a recog-
nized right to the hereditary *occupation* of his plot of ground,
while he pays the rent demanded of him: and the question is,
whether that right in Rajast'han practically amounts to a *proprietary* right or not. Now a distinction before suggested in the text,
seems to afford the only real criterion which can enable us to determine this question fairly. Is the Ryot at rack-rent? has he, or
has he not, a *beneficial* interest in the soil? can he obtain money
for that interest by sale? can he make a landlord's rent of it? To
give a cultivator an hereditary interest at a variable rack-rent, and
then to call his right to till, a freehold right, would clearly be little
better than mockery. To subject such a person to the payment of
more than a rack-rent, to leave him no adequate remuneration for

and the East India Company has declared itself proprietor of the whole land of India.   It will be evident,
upon consideration, that it is now of no importance
whether the Company demands fifty per cent. of the
products as rent, and ten per cent. additional as taxes,

his personal toil, and still to call him a freehold proprietor, would
be something more bitter than mere mockery. To establish by law,
and enforce cruelly in practice, fines and punishments to avenge
his running away from his freehold, and refusing to cultivate it for
the benefit of his hard task master, would be to convert him into a
predial slave: and this, although a very natural consequence of the
mode of establishing such *freehold* rights, would make the names of
proprietor and owner almost ridiculous."*

According to this mode of reasoning, all that is necessary to do
away with private property in land in any part of Europe, is, that
the taxes shall be raised so high as to prevent the owner from having any beneficial interest. In some parts of England the poor tax
has risen so high, that property has been rendered totally valueless;
but Mr. Jones would consider it very extraordinary in any Frenchman or German, who would deny private property therein on the
ground that the owner had no *beneficial* interest in it.

At page [40], Mr. Jones gives the views of Sir Thomas Munro, by
which it will be seen that he considers the Ryot to be the proprietor,
subject to the claim of the state for rent or taxes.

" Yet with all these views of the difficulty of establishing private
property in land, Sir Thomas Munro declares the Ryot to be the
true proprietor, *possessing all that is not claimed by the sovereign as
revenue*. This, he says, while rejecting the proprietary claims of
the Zemindars; which he thinks unduly magnified.—' But the Ryot
is the real proprietor, for whatever land does not belong to the sovereign belongs to him. The demand for public revenue, according
as it is high or low in different places, and at different times, affects
his share: but whether it leaves him only the bare profit of his
stock, or a small surplus beyond it as landlord's rent, he is still the
true proprietor, and possesses all that is not claimed by the sovereign as revenue.'—Vol. III. p. 340."

     * Jones on the Distribution of Wealth. Appendix, p. 36.

or twenty per cent. as rent, and forty per cent. as taxes. In either case, the result must be the same, as the cultivator can only live, and can accumulate no capital.

It is not to be doubted that they would relinquish the claim of ownership of the land, if by doing so there could be a small *increase of revenue* obtained. The contrary is, however, what is required.

"It is the high assessment on the land," the members of the board of revenue observe, "which Colonel Munro justly considers the chief check to population. Were it not for the pressure of this heavy rent, population, he thinks, *ought to increase even faster than in America;* because the climate is more favourable, and there are vast tracts of good land unoccupied, which may be ploughed at once, without the labour or expense of clearing away forests, as there is above three millions of acres of this kind in the ceded districts. He is of opinion, that a great increase of population, and consequently of land revenue, might be expected in the course of twenty-five years, from the operation of the remission."*

By the following passage it will be seen that the Company do not so much object to making changes that *cost them nothing.*

"In India, the Anglo-Indian government have been creditably ready to give more security and more civil rights to their Indian subjects than they before enjoyed; but when it became a question of direct sacrifice of revenue, notwithstanding the clearest conviction in their own minds, that the population would be increased, cultivation improved, and the wealth and resources of their territories rapidly multiplied, still the exigencies of the government would not permit them to remit the actual rents to the amount of 25 per cent., or 15 per cent., even to insure all these confessed ulterior advantages; and therefore they concluded that the state of cultivation, and the poverty of the tenantry, must continue as they were."†

If, instead of making the whole land the property

---

* Jones on the Distribution of Wealth. Appendix, p. 47.

† Jones on the Distribution of Wealth, p. 174.

of the state, it be decided that it shall be the property of a few persons who shall constitute the aristocracy, the effect of this arrangement will depend entirely upon the manner in which the government shall be administered by those who are charged with it. If honestly administered for the good of all, the taxation for the support of the state will be upon property, and as the aristocracy will be the holders of the whole property of the community, it will be to their interest to make it as economical as possible, in order that their rents may not be reduced. Should they chance to have a warlike monarch, his nobles would counsel him that upon the continuance of peace would depend their prosperity, and he would find himself compelled to practise a little restraint. No taxation being imposed upon the labourers, until they should have accumulated some property, they would be at liberty to employ themselves as they might think proper, and many of them would turn their attention to other pursuits than agriculture. *If rents were moderate*, the whole body of the people would find their means improving, and the demand for manufactured articles would increase so rapidly as to absorb a large portion of the new population in their production; and as the quantity of land could not be increased, the rent would rise, in consequence of the general prosperity producing increased demand for its products, by which the landholders would benefit in common with the whole body of the people. *If*, on the contrary, *rents were high*, the expenditure of the landlords would be considerable, and would provide a market for a large amount of the products of labour in other departments than agriculture: or, capital would accumulate in their hands, and they would find it necessary to employ it, in doing which they would increase the demand for, and the reward of, labour. The labourers, free from taxation, would find their wages increase with the demand for their products, and the agriculturist, ceasing to employ his children upon his farm, would send them to the cities that they might participate in the harvest. The effect of this would be to reduce the competition for land, and lower the rent, by which the wages of the cultivator would rise to a level with those of persons otherwise employed.

If, instead of assessing the contributions for the support of government, on property, by which the holders of land would be compelled to furnish the chief part, taxes should be upon consumption, they would not have the same inducement to counsel the continuance of peace. The taxes would not be paid by them, but on the contrary, a heavy expenditure by government would provide places for themselves and their children, where they could be supported out of the moneys paid by the people. The two parties would then compete with each other, which should have the largest share of the spoils, and both would deem it unnecessary to show mercy to the unfortunate producer, because if any thing were left by the one, it would be taken by the other.

Here are two cases in which the tenure of land is precisely the same, and the sole difference is in the spirit with which the government is administered. In the one the expenses of the protection of person and property are fairly divided according to the means of the parties, while in the other the burthens are laid upon the shoulders of those who are incapable of resistance.

The case of Ireland may be adduced as one of a nation governed according to the latter system. There, even the land tax does not exist, and the owners of property, which rents at two, three, and four pounds per acre, are almost totally exempted from contributing to the support of the government. Nearly the whole revenue of Ireland is raised by taxes on consumption, and as a large portion of the landholders are absentees, they escape the payment of them: Various modes have been proposed for the improvement of the condition of the people, among which is the adoption of the English system of poor-laws, but that would only tend to aggravate the disease. Another has been to lay a heavy tax upon the estates of absentee landlords, to compel them either to return, or to pay what will be equivalent to the taxes on consumption that they would pay were they resident. To this there is a very serious objection, that it would be an interference with the rights of person and property. Every man should be equal before the law, and be at liberty to expend the income of his property, whether in land or in the funds, when and where he pleases. In this consists that security which is the first and most important consideration in a state, and should it be interfered with in such a nation as Great Britain,

> " 'T will be recorded for a precedent;
> And many an error by the same example,
> Will rush into the state: it cannot be."—*Merch. of Ven.*

It is of the utmost importance that in the endeavours to remedy an existing evil, we do not make a greater, which would be the consequence of the adoption of either of these plans.

Lord John Russel has another, by which a portion of the revenues of the Irish church is to be appropriated to the education of the people, without distinction of religion. To suppose that this can make any important alteration in the condition of the Irish people, is as absurd as to suppose that a man whose whole system is disordered, is to be cured by the application of a plaster to his little finger.

There is a very simple mode by which the desired change could be effected, and it has the advantage that no man could feel that he had the smallest right to complain of it. The first step should be to transfer the cost of maintaining a government for the protection of property, to the shoulders of those who possess it, relieving those who have none; or in other words, to abolish all taxes on consumption which are paid by the labourer, and not paid by the landlords; and in their place levy a tax on property to the full amount that is now paid by Ireland. This would leave in the possession of the producer a considerable sum now paid in taxes, and much of it would become capital, while the absentee landlord would find that his residence in Ireland would be, under these circumstances, quite as advantageous as his present residence in France, Italy, or Belgium. Second, without interfering in any way with the property in possession of the church, let the tithes be transferred from the clergy to *commissioners for the general improvement of the communications of Ireland*; or, let tithes be abolished, and in lieu thereof a further tax be imposed on land, to be applied as above stated. It would be better if they could be abolished without the necessity of such a measure as that proposed; but the exhaustion of Ireland is such as renders the application of capital in this way absolutely necessary to make some amends for the drain of its resources for so long a period. Without such a provision, the competition for land arising out of the absence of all other means of employment, would enable the landlord to add the tithes to his rent, and thus make amends for the land tax that might be imposed. The application of a sum equal to the tithes of Ireland in its improvement, for the space of twenty years, (to which time it might be limited,) would, in connexion with the measure first above proposed, produce such a change as would now appear utterly incredible. The first effect would be to give employment and wages to all that needed them, and the number would probably be found much smaller than might be anticipated; the second would be to raise wages; the third would be to increase the value of produce, and by so much to lessen the burthen of rent. The cultivator would be enabled to improve his mode, and increase his production. Feeling himself relieved from the burthen that had been imposed upon him for the benefit of his landlord and the church, all cause of agitation would be at an end, and the country would become quiet. Capital would flow in for the purpose of giving employment to the cheap laboure , which would gradually rise, and rents would fall, but the improved modes of cultivation and means of transport, and the extension of cultivation, would place the landholders, as a body, on a very different footing, and one vastly more advantageous, than any they have ever occupied. Should the English people ever feel disposed to do *justice*, they may tranquillize Ireland. Without it they never will do so, and all attempts, such as we have seen and such as are now proposed, will prove fruitless.

According to the doctrine of Mr. Jones, *the nature of this relation regulates the character of the government.* Government is generally (I might almost say always) in the hands of those who hold the property. In China there is no restraint by law upon the will of the Emperor, notwithstanding which, it is deemed highly necessary to conciliate the good feelings of the people, who have, by prescription, acquired a right to hold lands for their own use, or to alienate them for their own benefit, upon payment of a certain fixed rent or tax. In Hindostan, where the people have no rights, and the property belongs to their masters, the action of the Company's agents is uncontrolled. The Autocrat of all the Russias must administer his government in accordance with the wishes and feelings of the nobility. In France, before the revolution, the nobility were masters, as they were almost the sole possessors of property. At present the direction of affairs is in the hands of the higher and middle classes. In Great Britain it has been with the aristocracy, who, until a very recent period, were the great holders of property, but now it is shared with the middle classes. In the United

States it is controlled by the property holders through-out the country, infinitely more numerous there than in any other part of the world. Were the doctrine of Mr. Jones correct, it would follow, that the tenure of land being once fixed, and the character of the government established, no change could take place in the latter, until the holders of property should judge it for their interest to let their lands to their tenants on more liberal terms: or, in other words, the character of the government could not be changed until the government (*i. e.* the holders of property) willed it.

The changes that have taken place in England are thus stated by Mr. Jones:

"Thirteen hundred years have elapsed since the final establish-ment of the Saxons. Eight hundred of these had passed away, and the Normans had been for two centuries settled here, and a very large proportion of the body of cultivators was still precisely in the situation of the Russian serf. During the next three hundred, the unlimited labour rents paid by the villeins for the lands allotted to them were gradually commuted for definite services, still payable in kind; and they had a legal right to the hereditary occupation of their copyholds. Two hundred years have barely elapsed since the change to this extent became quite universal, or since the personal bondage of the villeins ceased to exist among us. The last claim of villenage recorded in our courts was in the 15th of James I. 1618. Instances probably existed some time after this. The ultimate ces-sation of the right to demand their stipulated services in kind has been since brought about, silently and imperceptibly, not by positive law; for, when other personal services were abolished at the restora-tion, those of copyholders were excepted and reserved.

"Throughout Germany similar changes are now taking place, on the land; they are perfected perhaps no where, and in some large districts they exhibit themselves in very backward stages."*

Were the doctrine of Mr. Jones correct, these

* Jones on the Distribution of Wealth, pp. 40, 41.

P

changes could never have taken place, and labour rents once established, they must have continued to the present time. Why have they not? Why did the change in the tenure of land take place earlier than on the continent? Why is it now more complete? Simply because the government was more liberal; because the people of England have always had rights recognised by the law; and because those rights enabled them to obtain property, and thus to influence the action of the government, which was therefore administered more for the general benefit than in other countries. Her insular position secured her against invasion, and the consequence was, that she enjoyed a degree of security unknown to the rest of Europe, and at comparatively moderate cost.

In France, the people were regarded as possessing no rights whatever, and as being of value to their owners only as producers of rent and taxes. They were described as *taillable et corvéeable, a merci et misericorde.* Government was administered for the benefit of the few, who were exempt from taxation, while nearly the whole of the product of labour was absorbed by contributions for the support of the state. These contributions failed to produce security, and the kingdom was torn to pieces by factions among the nobles, too powerful to submit to law. When a momentary calm took place at home, the country was not allowed to profit by it, and it mattered little whether the head of the government was St. Louis, Charles VIII., or Francis the First, as the bigotry of the one produced the same calamitous results for the people as the egotism of the others. Insecurity of property has restrained production, and a long course of war and of heavy expenditure, has prevented accumulation, the consequence of which is seen in the fact that slavery existed in France until the time of Louis XVI., as is shown in the annexed extract; and that a large portion of the kingdom is still in the hands of metayers.

" Besides the serfs thus gradually assimilated to vassals, there were other serfs whose state of slavery was as distinct and undisguised as that of the Russian cultivators is now: they existed for some time in considerable numbers, and continued to exist in several provinces up to the era of the revolution. We will say something of these before we proceed to the metayers. They were found on the estates of the crown, of lay individuals, and of ecclesiastics, under the name of mainmortables, which was used indifferently with that of serf, and appears to have been considered synonymous with it. They were attached to the soil, and if they escaped from it, were restored by the interference of the tribunals to their owners, to whom their persons and those of their posterity belonged. They were incapable of transmitting property: if they acquired any, their owners might seize it at their death: the exercise of this right was in full vigour, and some startling instances led Louis XVI. to make a feeble attempt at a partial emancipation. Proprietors, exercising their *droit de suite*, as it was called, had forced the reluctant tribunals of the king to deliver into their hands the property of deceased citizens who had been long settled as respectable inhabitants in different towns of France, some even in Paris itself; but who were proved to have been originally serfs on the estates of the claimants. The contrast between the condition of these poor people and that of the rest of the population, became then too strong to be endured; but though the naturally kind feelings of Louis appear to have been roused upon the occasion, he ventured no farther, than to give liberty to the serfs or mainmortables on his own domains, and to abolish indirectly the droit de suite, by forbidding his tribunals to seize the person or property of serfs, who had once become domiciled in free districts. In the edict published by the unfortunate monarch on this subject, he declares that this state of slavery exists

in several of his provinces, and includes a great number of his subjects, and lamenting that he is not rich enough to ransom them all,
he states that his respect for the rights of property will not allow
him to interfere between them and their owners, but he expresses
a hope that his example and the love of humanity so peculiar to the
French people, would lead under his reign to the entire emancipation of all his subjects."*

In our own time we have seen the case of a government (Prussia) changing the tenure of land by
a decree. The influence of the land owners was,
however, too great to admit of any very material
change in the distribution of the product. Mr. Jones
says:

"The posterity of the emancipated serfs of eastern Europe are
shut out from the possibility of forming a body of capitalist tenants,
fitted to take charge of the cultivation of the domains of the proprietors. Personal freedom, hereditary possession of their allotments, rights and privileges in abundance, the landlords and sovereigns are willing to grant; and it would be extravagant to say
these grants are worth nothing: but that which is necessary to
enable the peasants to profit by their new position, that is, an *immediate* relaxation of the pressure upon them, an increase of their
revenue, proceeding from a direct sacrifice of income on the part
of either the crown or the landlord, is something much more difficult to be accomplished. In Prussia, the rent charge fixed upon the
serf, now constituted a proprietor, forms, as we have seen, one of
the heaviest rents known in Europe. And among the various
schemes for improving the condition of the peasantry, afloat in the
east of Europe, I know but of one, that of the Livonian nobility, in
which a direct sacrifice of revenue on the part of the landlords is
contemplated as the basis of the expected amelioration."†

This is in direct opposition to the theory previously
advocated. If the character of the government de-

* Jones on the Distribution of Wealth, pp. 89, 90.
† Ibid. 174, 175.

pended upon the tenure of lands, there should be an immediate change in it, consequent upon the alteration of tenure, which should be felt in an improvement in the "details of the condition of the majority of the people." That Mr. Jones does not conceive it to have produced this effect, is shown by the following passage, in which he speaks of the observations of Mr. Jacob.

"He has come to results remarkably similar to those which I had ventured to suggest from a more distant and general knowledge of their circumstances. The still predominant influence of labour rents: the general want of capital among the proprietors: the rapid increase in the numbers of the peasant cultivators which has been taking place since their dependence on the landlords has been less servile: the feeble beneficial effects on agriculture and on the general composition of society which in twenty years have sprung from the strong measures of the Prussian government: the difficulties which every where oppose themselves to all sudden changes in the old system of cultivation: the strong apparent probability that the future progress in the eastern division of Europe will not, with all the efforts that are making, be much more rapid than that of this country when emerging from a similar state of things; all these are points on which I can now refer with very great satisfaction to the local knowledge and authority of Mr. Jacob, in support of the suggestions I have here thrown out. See Second Report passim, but more especially 140 and the following pages."—pp. 71, 72.

Mr. Jones, throughout his work, attributes the condition of the people, and the nature of the government, to the tenure of land, yet the following passage is in direct opposition thereto, and shows that *wherever security is obtained at moderate cost of government,* there is a disposition to change in the relations between the landlord and tenant. "Metayer rents, too, have a constant tendency to spring up and engraft themselves on ryot rents throughout Asia, wherever the moderation and efficiency of the government is such as to ensure protection to the property advanced by the cultivator." p. 137.

There is no nation whatever, in which the tenure of land is, so far as we understand it, more advantageous than that of China, where the government is proprietor, and the cultivator a ryot, whose possession is, however, guarantied upon payment of one-tenth of its produce to the state. In England the church alone would take as much, leaving the cultivator afterwards to the tender mercies of the landlord and the government. Mr. Jones's sympathy, therefore, in regard to a large portion of the ryots of Asia, as shown in the following passage, seems uncalled for.

" An examination into the nature and effects of Ryot rents, receives an almost mournful interest from the conviction, that the political and social institutions of the people of this large division of the earth, are likely for many long ages yet to come, to rest upon them. We cannot unveil the future, but there is little in the character of the Asiatic population, which can tempt us even to speculate upon a time, when that future will essentially differ from the past and the present."—p. 142.

The reader can hardly, I think, hesitate to agree with me, that it is the nature of the government that influences the tenure of land, and not the tenure of land that gives character to the government. If the latter be administered for the general benefit, there will be a steady increase of capital and improvement in the condition of the people. Such improvement will be attended with a change in the tenure of lands, and labour and metayer rents will disappear with the progress of civilization, being replaced by money rents. A further increase of capital will enable the farmer to obtain a longer lease on condition of making improvements, or he will become proprietor of the land he has been accustomed to rent. Were it otherwise—were the doctrines of Mr. Jones correct, the science of political economy would be without fixed principles, and among the most difficult of acquisition, when, on the contrary, it is the simplest of sciences. It teaches that the best system of government is that which gives security of person and property at the lowest cost, either of money or of freedom of action, and its most important maxim is embraced in the words " LET US ALONE." Where that is the rule of action, and where the expenses of protection are fairly distributed, there is a constant tendency to remedy all existing evils, and none more promptly than those which arise out of the nature of the tenure of lands.

CHAPTER XIV.

It has been seen that the United States are comparatively free from those disturbing causes which impede the growth of capital. With a vast body of land; with mines of gold, lead, iron, copper, and coal, abounding in every direction; circulating capital alone was wanting to bring them into activity, and the system has tended to promote its rapid growth. Secure in person and property, comparatively free from taxation, unrestrained in action, comparatively so in all matters of trade, and very industrious, the people of this country, applying their labour in the way which they think will produce the largest reward, find their capital rapidly augment; the consequence of which is, that mines are opened in all directions, new lands are brought into cultivation, rail-roads and canals are constructed, and machinery is applied in every way to increase the produce of labour. Capital flows from all quarters to this country, where it can be best paid for, and, increasing the demand for labour, finds employment not only for the vast natural increase of population, but for great numbers who are led to seek here an improvement of their condition. The fund out of which the labourer is paid is larger, and his wages are consequently greater, than in any other country. It is in a very high degree satisfactory to see that this arises out of circumstances peculiar to the United States, and that there is no reason to believe that any increase which may take place in the extent of their population can make it otherwise, while adhering to the present system.

The following remarks of Mr. Senior on the subject of the high rate of wages in England, as compared with the nations of the continent of Europe, apply with still greater force to this country. In corroboration of them, is the fact that the only competition to be feared by the United States, is that of those nations in which the rate of wages is highest —not that of Hindostan, Italy, or Poland, but that of Great Britain, France, and the Netherlands:—

" The last remark which occurs to me as connected with the present subject, is one which I somewhat anticipated in my first course; namely, *the absurdity of the opinion that the generally high rate of wages in England unfits us for competition with foreign producers. It is obvious that our power of competing with foreigners depends on the efficiency of our labour, and it has appeared that a high rate of wages is a necessary consequence of that efficiency.* It is true, indeed, that if we choose to misemploy a portion of our labourers, we must pay them, not according to the value of what they do produce, but according to the value of what they might produce if their labour were properly directed. If I call in a surgeon to cut my hair, I must pay him as a surgeon. So if I employ in throwing silk, a man who could earn three ounces of silver a week by spinning cotton, I must pay him three ounces of silver a week, though he cannot throw more silk than could be thrown in the same time by an Italian whose wages are only an ounce and a half. And it is true, also, that I can be supported in such a waste by nothing but an artificial monopoly, or, in other words, that I shall be under-sold by the Italian in every market from which I cannot exclude him by violence. But do these circumstances justify me in resorting to that violence? Do they justify me in imploring the legislature to direct that violence against my fellow subjects? If that violence is relaxed, but not discontinued, have I, or has the consumer, the more right to complain? If my estate were water-meadow, I should lose if I were to endeavour to convert it into corn-fields. But surely that is no subject of complaint; surely it is no reason for prohibiting my neighbours from purchasing corn in any adjoining parish. *To complain of our high wages, is to complain that our labour is productive—to complain that our work-people are diligent and skilful.* To act on such complaints is as wise as to enact that all men should labour with only one hand, or stand idle four days in every week."*

It has been shown that in England there is equal security of person, but not equal security of property, because the visits of the tax-gatherer are more numerous, and his demands vastly heavier; that there is less freedom of action, and much less freedom of trade; and that industry is repressed by the allurements of poor-laws, which reward idleness, thus producing some of the effects which superstition produces among the natives of Hindostan. The ratio of capital to population steadily increases, but these disturbing causes not only retard its growth, but prevent the capitalist from employing it at home, and induce him to send it to this country, where the greater freedom of action and of trade enable him to derive from it a larger compensation for its use. All these causes tend to prevent the growth of the fund for the support of the labourer, whose wages are consequently lower than they should be, and he is compelled to emigrate; and thus a large unproductive expenditure by government, while it increases the wants of the nation, tends to lessen its means, by driving abroad its capital and its population. A long course of peace and economy would, and will, retrieve its affairs, and even should

* Lectures on the Mercantile Theory of Wealth, p. 76.

there be no reduction of its debt, the increase of capital and employment that must necess-rily arise out of the improved system that has been adopted, and which without doubt will be extended, *will make its present enormous debt as insignificant, a century hence, as that of* 1750 *would now be deemed.*

The unfortunate Hindoo labours under all these disturbing causes. He is secure in neither his person nor his property; he is taxed to such an extent that scarcely enough is left to support life; confined in all his actions and with all trade repressed by the most grievous monopolies, he finds no inducement to exertion when he knows that it will only produce increased demands upon him. Under such circumstances, capital cannot accumulate, and the aids to labour are of the worst kind. The steam engine, with its wonderful productive power, has hardly been introduced, and the manufacturers are unable with their unassisted exertions, to compete with those of Europe or this country.

The introduction of British capital is prevented, and—

" Down to the present moment, British subjects commonly hold lands in India clandestinely, and no men, nor body of men will be mad enough to embark ten, twenty, or thirty thousand pounds sterling, in stock, machinery, and land, which he can neither openly buy nor sell, and in a country from which, with or without offence, he is liable to be banished forever on the briefest notice."—*W. Review.*

Communications are bad, and rail-roads and canals are yet to be commenced. In short, there is no conceivable obstacle to the improvement of the people

that does not exist in that country, and while they
do exist, there can be no hope of change.

The following passage from Mr. Rickards's book
will show the scarcity of capital, and the enormous
compensation that is required for its use:—

" Of all the effects, too, resulting from this destructive system,
there is none more obvious than its preventing the possibility of accumulating capital, through which alone can the agriculture of the
country be improved. At present the stock of a Ryot consists of a
plough, not capable of cutting deep furrows, and only intended to
scratch the surface of the soil, with two or three pairs of half-starved
oxen. This, a sickle used for a scythe, and a small spade or hoe
for weeding, constitute almost his only implements for husbandry.
Faggots of loose sticks, bound together, serve for a harrow. Carts
are little used in a country where there are no roads, or none but
bad ones. Corn, when reaped, is heaped in a careless pile in the
open air, to wait the Ryot's leisure for threshing, which is performed,
not by manual labour, but by the simple operation of cattle-treading
it out of the ear. A Ryot has no barns for stacking or storing grain,
which is preserved, when required, in jars of unbaked earth, or bas-
kets made of twigs or grass. The cattle are mostly fed in the jungle, or common waste land adjoining his farm, and buffaloes, thus
supported, generally supply him with milk. Horses are altogether
disused in husbandry. The fields have no enclosures. Crops on
the ground are guarded from the depredations of birds and wild
beasts by watchmen, for whose security a temporary stage is erected,
scarcely worth a shilling. Irrigation is performed by means of
reservoirs, intended to retain the water periodically falling from the
heavens, and of dams constructed or placed in convenient situations.
In some places water is raised from wells, either by cattle or by
hand. A rotation of crops on which so much stress is laid in Europe, is unknown in India. A course extending beyond the year,
is never thought of by Indian Ryots. Different articles are often
grown together in the same field, in which the object always is to
obtain the utmost possible produce without the least regard to the
impoverishment of the soil. The dung of cattle is carefully collected
for fuel, after being dried in the sun, and never used for manure.
Oil cake is used for manure in sugar-cane plantations, and for some

other articles; but corn-fields are generally left to their own natural fertility, and often worked to exhaustion without compunction. In some situations near the sea, decayed fish is used as a manure for rice-grounds; but it is seldom permitted where authority can be interposed, as the stench of it is intolerable. In a country like India, where the heat of the climate is great, the construction of tanks or wells, for the purpose of irrigation, is one of the most useful purposes to which agricultural capital can be applied. Wells and tanks are sometimes constructed or repaired by the labour or industry of the Ryots, but most commonly at the expense of government. It has been remarked that where Zemindars have been able to accumulate gains, they never apply them to the improvement of lands subject to public revenue. Where Zemindars have been known to construct works of the above description, they are merely designed to increase the fertility of lands held free. But generally speaking, so entire is the want of capital in India, as well in arts and manufactures as in agriculture, that every mechanic and artisan not only conducts the whole process of his arts, from the formation of his tools to the sale of his production; but, where husbandry is so simple a process, turns cultivator for the support of himself and family. He thus divides his time and labour, between the loom and the plough; thereby multiplying occupations fatal to the improvement of either. In this universal state of poverty, manufacturers always require advances of money to enable them to make up the article in demand; whilst Ryots have frequently been known, sometimes for anticipated payments, and sometimes for their own expenses, to borrow money on the security of growing crops, at 3, 4, and 5 per cent. per annum. No fact is perhaps better established in political economy than that industry cannot, in any of its branches, be promoted without capital. Capital is the result of saving from annual profits. Here there can be none. A dense, or rather redundant population occasions in India, as in Ireland, a competition for land; because in a nation of paupers, land is indispensable as a means of existence. It is therefore at times greedily sought for in India, notwithstanding the exorbitance of the revenue chargeable thereupon, for the same reason that small portions of land in Ireland are occupied under payment of exorbitant rents to landlords; and this extension of cultivation in India is often mistaken for an increase of prosperity, when in fact, it is but the further spreading of pauperism and want.

Q

Hence the acquisition of capital in India, by the cultivators of the soil, is absolutely impossible. Either the revenue absorbs the whole produce of industry, except what is indispensable to preserve the workers of the hive from absolute starvation; or it is engrossed by a Zemindar, or farmer, who will not reapply his gains to the improvement of lands, within a tax-gatherer's grasp. In this view of proceedings, effects are presented to our notice deserving the most serious consideration. It is clear that wherever the wants of government, real or imaginary, may call for increased supplies, recourse will be had to the "*improvement*," or extension of an impost already almost intolerable. It is in fact the only available recourse. Universal poverty leaves no other. Measures will therefore be multiplied for assessing wastes; for resuming rent-free lands; for invalidating former alienations; for disputing rights which had been allowed to lie dormant for half a century; for increasing the aggregate receipts from lands already taxed, or supposed to be taxed at 50 per cent. of the gross produce; in short, for the most harassing, and vexatious interference with private property, and the pursuits of private industry. Every improvement or extension of agriculture is thus sure to be followed, sooner or later, by the graspings of the tax gatherer. Industry, therefore, will be effectually checked, or only prosecuted where the demands of government may chance, through bribery, fraud, or concealment, to be eluded. Or if the necessities of human life, or increased population, should occasion agriculture to be extended to waste lands, to be thereafter taxed at the 'just amount of the public dues,' what is it but the further spread of pauperism and wretchedness."—*Rickards*, Vol. II. p. 196.

Under such circumstances, it is not surprising that the fund for the payment of the labourer is small, and that it does not increase, if it does not even diminish, in its ratio to population. It is evident that the disadvantageous position of the Hindoo does not arise out of any natural defect, as will be seen by the following quotations from Bishop Heber.

"Since my last letter, I have become acquainted with some of the wealthy natives, of whom I spoke, and we are just returned from passing the evening at one of their country houses. This is more like an Italian villa, than what one should have expected as the residence of Baboo Hurree Mohun Thakoor. Nor are his carriages, the furniture of his house, or the style of his conversation, of a character less decidedly European. He is a fine old man, who speaks English well, is well informed on most topics of general discussion, and talks with the appearance of much familiarity on Franklin, chemistry, natural philosophy, &c. His family is brahminical, and of singular purity of descent; but about 400 years ago, during the Mahommedan invasion of India, one of his ancestors having become polluted by the conquerors intruding into his Zenanah, the race is conceived to have lost claim to the knotted cord, and the more rigid brahmins will not eat with them. Being, however, one of the principal landholders in Bengal, and of a family so ancient, they still enjoy to a great degree the veneration of the common people, which the present head of the house appears to value—since I can hardly reconcile in any other manner his philosophical studies and imitation of many European habits, with the daily and austere devotion which he is said to practise towards the Ganges, (in which he bathes three times every twenty-four hours,) and his veneration for all the other duties of his ancestors."[*]

" One of their men of rank has absolutely promised to found a college at Burdwan, with one of our missionaries at its head, and where little children should be clothed and educated under his care. All this is very short indeed of embracing Christianity themselves, but it proves how completely those feelings are gone by, in Bengal at least, which made even the presence of a single missionary the occasion of tumult and alarm."[†]

" I do not by any means assent to the pictures of depravity and general worthlessness which some have drawn of the Hindoos. They are decidedly, by nature, a mild, pleasing, and intelligent race; sober, parsimonious, and, where an object is held out to them, most industrious and persevering."[‡]

" Of the people, so far as their natural character is concerned, I have been led to form, on the whole, a very favourable opinion. They have, unhappily, many of the vices arising from slavery, from an unsettled state of society, and immoral and erroneous systems

* Heber's Travels in India, p. 229.
† Ibid. p. 230.   ‡ Ibid. p. 240.

of religion. But they are men of high and gallant courage; courteous, intelligent, and most eager after knowledge and improvement, with a remarkable aptitude for the abstract sciences, geometry, astronomy, &c.. and for the imitative arts, painting and sculpture. They are sober, industrious, dutiful to their parents, and affectionate to their children, of tempers almost uniformly gentle and patient, and more easily affected by kindness and attention to their wants and feelings than almost any men whom I have met with."[*]

" In the same holy city, I had visited another college, founded lately by a wealthy Hindoo banker, and intrusted by him to the management of the Church Missionary Society, in which, besides a grammatical knowledge of the Hindostanee language, as well as Persian and Arabic, the senior boys could pass a good examination in English grammar, in Hume's History of England, Joyce's Scientific Dialogues, the use of the globes, and the principal facts and moral precepts of the Gospel, most of them writing beautifully in the Persian, and very tolerably in the English character, and excelling most boys I have met with in the accuracy and readiness of their arithmetic."[†]

" I have been passing the last four days in the society of a Hindoo Prince, the Rajah of Tanjore, who quotes Fourcroy, Lavoisier, Linnæus, and Buffon fluently, has formed a more accurate judgment of the poetical merits of Shakspeare than that so felicitously expressed by Lord Byron, and has actually emitted English poetry very superior indeed to Rousseau's epitaph on Shenstone, at the same time that he is much respected by the English officers in his neighbourhood as a real good judge of a horse, and a cool, bold, and deadly shot at a tiger.   The truth is, that he is an extraordinary man, who having in early youth received such an education as old Schwartz, the celebrated missionary, could give him, has ever since continued, in the midst of many disadvantages, to preserve his taste for, and extend his knowledge of European literature, while he has never neglected the active exercises and frank soldierly bearing which become the descendant of the old Mahratta conquerors, and by which only, in the present state of things, he has it in his power

[*] Heber's Travels in India, pp. 285, 286.
[†] Ibid. p. 300.

to gratify the prejudices of his people, and prolong his popularity among them."*

Nothing is wanting but a good system of government, and until that can be obtained, it is useless to send missionaries among them. When they shall have found that the rule of Christians has brought with it peace and prosperity; that they are allowed to live as they should do on the produce of their land; and that their little savings will enable them gradually to improve their mode of operation, and benefit their condition; then, and not till then, will they be disposed to avail themselves of the instruction offered them. They cry for food, and we tender them the gospel; they find in it peace, and good will, and charity, while in their governors, they find nothing but tyranny and oppression.

* Heber's Travels in India, pp. 354, 355.

CHAPTER XV.

A SIMILAR survey of all the countries of Europe would show the same result as that of these three great nations. Where the disturbing causes are in full action, as in Ireland and Spain, we find the population to be "poor and miserable,"* but in other nations, as those causes cease to operate, or diminish in intensity, the condition of the people improves, until at length we arrive at the United States, where the situation of the labouring classes is confessedly better than in any other nation whatever.

The most prosperous country of Europe, after England, was the late kingdom of the Netherlands. In Holland, the truths of Political Economy were first acted upon, and they brought with them a copious harvest of wealth. Security and freedom and economy were looked to as the sources of riches, as may be seen by the following passages from a description of the policy of the republic, written nearly a century since, in answer to inquiries respecting the state of trade, addressed to the merchants of Holland by the stadtholder William IV.

"To sum up all, amongst the moral and political causes of the former flourishing state of trade, may be likewise placed the wisdom and prudence of the administration; the intrepid firmness of the councils; the faithfulness with which treaties and engagements were

* In almost all countries, the condition of the great body of the people is poor and miserable.—*Mill's Political Economy.*

wont to be fulfilled and ratified; and particularly the care and caution practised to preserve tranquillity and peace, and to decline, instead of entering on a scene of war, merely to gratify the ambitious views of gaining fruitless or imaginary conquests.

" By these moral and political maxims was the glory and the reputation of the republic so far spread, and foreigners animated to place so great a confidence in the steady determinations of a state so wisely and prudently conducted, that a concourse of them stocked this country with an augmentation of inhabitants and useful hands, whereby its trade and opulence were from time to time increased."

The following anecdote, given by Lady Morgan, shows that the same correct views are entertained at this time by some of the Belgians. " At Verviers, the King, (Leopold,) observed to the Burgomaster, " qu'il protegerait toujours l'industrie." The Burgomaster replied, " Il n'y a pas besoin; ça va bien comme ca."—*Princess*, Vol. III. 253.

Unfortunately their rulers were not all equally wise, or equally patriotic, and the desire of personal aggrandizement led to war in some instances, while in others it was forced upon them. The consequences were enormous expenditure, heavy debt, and its attendant heavy taxation, carried so far, that it was said that every fish was paid for, once to the fisherman and six times to the state.* This contributed to drive away commerce, and her capital was, and is

---

* " D'autres examineront peut etre si ces taxes out été judicieusement placées; si elles sont perçues avec l'economie convenable. Il suffit ici d'observer que les manufactures de laine, de soie, d'or et d'argent, une foule d'autres ont succombé après avoir lutté longtems contre la progression de l'impot. La Hollande n'a sauvé du naufrage de ses manufactures, que celles que n'ont pas été exposées a la concourence des autres nations."—*La Richesse de la Hollande*, Vol. II. p. 73.

compelled to seek employment abroad. Notwithstanding this, there are so many advantages in their system of public and private economy, that capital accumulates with sufficient rapidity to enable them to lend to all the world, and retain at home sufficient to find employment at wages that are high in comparison with those of the rest of the continent of Europe, for their whole population. Lady Morgan says of the Belgians, " the cheerful, joyous peasantry, so well conditioned, so well dressed, so beyond the miseries and privations of the same classes in other countries."—*Princess*, Vol. III. p. 200.

The proportion of land to population in this kingdom, as it existed prior to 1830, is much smaller than in England and France, there being 9,822 persons to every 10,000 Hectares, while England has 6,930, and France only 5,200. The system of cultivation is, however, admirable, and makes amends in some measure by increased productiveness for the diminished quantity of land, and its population is thereby enabled to bear an equal taxation with that of France; the former paying 14.48 florins, and the latter 14.74 florins per head. That they are able to do this, is owing to the possession of the qualities described by the abbe De Pradt—" voulez vous un peuple bon, franc, hospitalier, laborieux, econome, ami de l'ordre et de la regularité, vous la trouverez dans la Belge."

Taxes are laid chiefly upon land, patents, stamps, &c.; on an average of eleven years, from 1816 to 1826, only 23 millions of florins out of 88 being the produce of import and export duties and excise; the former producing only six millions. Indirect taxes being small in amount, it follows that the quantity of commodities attainable by a given amount of money wages, must be much greater than can be obtained by a similar amount in England. As an evidence of this, it has been ascertained by Baron Keverberg, that the maximum of the actual wants of a labouring man can be supplied at a cost of 20 centimes, (8 cents,) per day, or 73 florins per annum.

The price of labour was ascertained by the government on an average of the ten provinces of Liege, North Holland, North and South Brabant, Friesland, East Flanders, Hainault, Antwerp, Guelderland, and Overyssel, to be 75 centimes, or 30 cents per day. At the coal mines of M. de George, there are 2,000 workmen employed, whose wages are from 70 centimes to 3 francs, (56 cents,) per day. In addition, they have the use of houses and gardens, (of which he has built 260,) at the moderate rent of one to two francs per week, according to size.* These wages enable the workmen to command a larger quantity of commodities than are obtainable by the labourers of the rest of the continent of Europe, and inferior only to those of the United States and Great Britain.

The Netherlands have been the battle ground of Europe; a necessary consequence of which has been insecurity of property, that has prevented the accumulation of capital, and its employment in manufactures. The wars of the French revolution disturbed the commercial arrangements of Holland, and its incorporation with France destroyed its commerce

* For the above facts I am indebted to the Review of M. Quetelet's work, "Recherches Statistiques sur le Royaume des Pays Bas," in the Foreign Quarterly Review, Vol. V.

altogether. Since the return of peace, its system has been comparatively very free, and notwithstanding a rapid increase of population, the rate of wages in commodities was but little inferior to that of Great Britain.

Until within a very recent period, France has known little of the benefit of security, either of person or of property. Constantly engaged in war, her expenses were enormous, and she groaned under an enormous load of taxation, rendered more burthensome by an injudicious mode of collection, and still more so upon the productive classes by the exemption of the nobility. Her commerce has been cramped at all times by monopolies—her internal trade harassed by regulations, to enforce which required an army of *douaniers*—every trade and every occupation the subject of brevets or patents—her manufacturers limited by law in their mode of proceeding, and exposed to the risk of having their goods seized if they departed fr)m the process fixed by law*—in

* " Fettered and oppressed in every way, as France was, under her despotic kings, the spirit of invention and enterprise could never rise to those high conceptions, which, of late years, have brought England and America to the summit of prosperity. Manufacturers, placed under the severe control of men who purchased their offices from government, and who, therefore, exercised them with rapacity, could not hazard any improvement, without infringing the established regulations, and running the risk of having their goods destroyed, burnt, or confiscated. In every trade, official regulations prescribed to workmen the methods of working, and forbade deviation from them, under pain of the most severe punishments. Ridiculous to say, the framer of these statutes fancied he understood better how to sort and prepare wool, silk, or cotton, to spin threads, to twist and throw them, than workmen brought up to the trade, and whose livelihood depended on their talent.

short, by every means in its power, did the government destroy freedom of trade or action, and with it

" To insure a compliance with such absurd regulations, inquisitorial measures were resorted to; the residences of manufacturers were entered by force; their establishments searched and explored, and their modes of working inquired into. Thus their most secret methods were often discovered and pirated by fraudulent competitors.

" The worthy Roland de la Platiere, who was a minister during some part of the French Revolution, and put an end to his life in the reign of terror, gives a deplorable account of the numerous acts of oppression he had witnessed. 'I have seen,' says he, 'eighty, ninety, a hundred pieces of cotton or woollen stuff cut up and completely destroyed. I have witnessed similar scenes every week for a number of years. I have seen manufactured goods confiscated; heavy fines laid on the manufacturers; some pieces of fabric were burnt in public places, and at the hours of market: others were fixed to the pillory, with the name of the manufacturer inscribed upon them, and he himself was threatened with the pillory, in case of a second offence. All this was done, under my eyes, at Rouen, in conformity with existing regulations, or ministerial orders. What crime deserved so cruel a punishment? Some defects in the materials employed, or in the texture of the fabric, or even in some of the threads of the warp!

" 'I have frequently seen,' continues Roland, 'manufacturers visited by a band of satellites, who put all in confusion in their establishments, spread terror in their families, cut the stuffs from the frames, tore off the warp from the looms, and carried them away as proofs of infringement; the manufacturers were summoned, tried, and condemned; their goods confiscated; copies of their judgment of confiscation posted up in every public place; future reputation, credit, all was lost and destroyed. And for what offence? Because they had made of worsted, a kind of cloth called *shag*, such as the English used to manufacture, and even sell in France, while the French regulations stated that that kind of cloth should be made with mohair.

" 'I have seen other manufacturers treated in the same way, because they had made camlets of a particular width, used in Eng-

the power of improvement. The revolution changed
much of this, and trade between the provinces is now

land and Germany, for which there was a great demand from
Spain, Portugal, and other countries, and from several parts of
France, while the French regulations prescribed other widths for
camlets.'

" There was no free town where mechanical invention could find
a refuge from the tyranny of the monopolists—no trade but what
was clearly and explicitly described by the statutes could be exercised—none but what was included in the privileges of some corporation.

" No one could improve on a method, or deviate from the prescribed rules for manufacturing stuffs of cotton, worsted, or silk,
without running the risk of being heavily fined, having his frames
destroyed, and his manufactured goods burnt in the public place
by the hands of the executioner.

" Many inventors were forbidden to reduce their inventions into
practice, when their application for letters patent was not supported
by powerful recommendations, or when they were unable to bid a
high price for the good will of the clerks of office.

" Some merchants of Nantes and Rennes wished to form, on a
new plan, manufactories of wool, silk, and cotton goods. They
possessed new preparations for fixing the colours. As soon as the
establishment was fitted up, the corporation of serge makers con-
tested their right of making woollen stuffs, and the corporation of
dyers claimed the privilege of dying for them. Law proceedings,
carried on for several years, absorbed the capital raised for the purpose of forming a useful establishment, and when at last a favourable decision was obtained, all the resources of the manufacturers
were exhausted; thus the serge makers and dyers succeeded in
ruining dangerous competitors!

" The art of snarling and varnishing sheet-iron was found out in
France in 1761; but to carry it into execution, it was necessary to
employ workmen and use tools belonging to several trades; the in-
ventor, not rich enough to pay the fees of admission into the corporations to which those trades belonged, went abroad and formed
an establishment in a foreign country."—*Pussigna on the French
Law of Patents.*

free, except so far as it is interfered with by the vexatious system of the Octroi: but it left brevets, patents, monopolies by individuals and the state, in numerous departments of internal trade, and a system of restraints by high duties and prohibition, in the foreign.

Every thing is the subject of regulation; even " in some districts of France the period of the gathering of the product of the vine is regulated by authority."* When gathered, and when the wine is ready for sale, it is subjected to heavy duties, altogether amounting to more than 20 per cent. They are excessive, and very unequally levied, and produce about £4,800,000, or near 23 millions of dollars. The octroi, on entering Paris, is 21 francs the hectolitre, being nearly equal to the price of the wine itself.

In the Report upon the commercial relations between France and Great Britain, made by the Commissioners, Messrs. Villiers and Bowring, is given a list of prohibitions upon importation and exportation, with the reasons of the French government for their adoption. Of them the Commissioners say, and with justice,

" It is hardly necessary to remark, that if these reasons for prohibition were pushed to their necessary consequences, all commercial relations would infallibly cease. If the cheapness of a foreign article were a sufficient reason for prohibiting the importation, and the cheapness of a home article for prohibiting its exportation, no exchange at all could take place.

" Many of the arguments which are put forward in justification of prohibitory measures, are mutually destructive of each other. To keep the price of corn low in the interest of the consumer, is

* Redding on Wines, p. 22.

R

assigned as the reason for prohibiting exportation; and to raise the price high in the interest of the producer, as the reason for prohibiting importation: the two objects are incompatible. Again, one set of prohibitions are justified because the articles are dear in France —such as the exportation of wood, timber, charcoal, and others: another set of prohibitions are advocated because the articles are cheap in France—such as the exportation of silk, rags, bark, &c. Reasonings wholly opposed to one another, are, in turn, employed. There is scarcely an argument or calculation, which, if recognised as applying to some articles, is not opposed altogether to the legislation on others.

" It requires merely to state some of the objections to importations, in order to show their narrow and anti-commercial spirit. The introduction of manufactured tin, for example, is opposed because it might benefit England, which is rich in tin mines; as if the importation into France could take place without equally benefiting her. The reasons, too, which are grounded on the superiority of other countries; as, for example, ' dangerous rivalry' in the case of manufactured steel; ' cheapness' of foreign articles in the case of shipping; threatened ' annihilation of the French manufacture' in that of cutlery; ' extra advantages of the English' in plated ware; ' apprehension of the English' in articles of pottery; ' imprudence of admitting English saddlery, as so many persons, regardless of price, prefer it;' ' advantages of machinery' in works of iron;—all are modes of announcing the superiority of foreign articles, and the power which foreigners possess of supplying them on cheaper terms than they can be produced at home.

" There are other grounds of prohibition, by which particular French manufactures are avowedly sacrificed to the interest of other branches of French industry. The importation of extracts of dyewoods is disallowed, for the purpose of encouraging the importation of the dye-woods themselves; the interest of the dyer, the manufacturer, and the consumer, being wholly forgotten. The importation of iron of certain sizes is prohibited, *lest small manufacturers should establish fabrics, and supply the market at less cost than the larger establishments.* Woollen yarn is not allowed to be imported, because it can be produced in France, though the high price must be a great detriment to the woollen manufacturer; and cast iron of a great variety of sorts is prohibited, on the ground that a sufficiency may be obtained at home, though the cost is notoriously more than double that of many articles of foreign cast iron. Molasses are not allowed to be introduced, because the price in France is so low, and the exportation so large, on the ground that importation will lower the prices still more, though the lowness of price would obviously make importation unprofitable; and the fact of considerable exportation is the best evidence that prices are *low* in France. Rock salt was *prohibited in* 1791, and the prohibition is now justified, on the ground that mines *have lately been discovered.* The prohibition of refined sugar is supported on the ground that its admission would not benefit the treasury; but it is clear, if the interest of the treasury were kept in view, that all prohibitions would be suppressed, or superseded by a system of duties. While some articles are prohibited because the production is small in France, and requires protection, others are prohibited (dressed skins for example) because the production is great, and engages a large number of hands."—p. 45.

Having thus, by prohibition, endeavoured to prevent the exportation of various articles of French production that would be required abroad, as well as the importation of various foreign articles that could be introduced with advantage, the next step is to *force* the export of those productions, which, from being higher in France than elsewhere, could not find a market abroad without the aid of government in the form of bounties on export. That system was commenced soon after the close of the war, and in 1817 the whole amount paid was £ 3,500 sterling, but in 1830 it had advanced to £ 600,000, or *one-fifth of the whole revenue from duties.* The table of premiums for 1832 shows that it still increases, having amounted in that year to *nearly a million sterling,* or ONE-FOURTH OF THE WHOLE CUSTOM-HOUSE REVENUE. The increase on the premiums of 1831 is about 50 per cent., and *in that of sugar alone, seven millions of*

francs, the amount paid as bounty on *the export of*
15½ *millions* of kilogrammes of refined sugar, *being*
18½ *millions of francs,* while the import duty *received*
upon 82½ *millions,* was *only* 39½ *millions of francs,* a
little more than double the bounty.

To show how steady is the growth of such a system, the following statements are given:

		Kilogrammes.		Francs.
In 1830—Sugar	imported	69,626,936	duty	33,535,174
	exported	8,410,780	bounty	10,101,678
In 1831—Sugar	imported	81,735,374	duty	39,264,743
	exported	9,679,034	bounty	11,614,840
In 1832—Sugar	imported	82,500,000	duty	39,500,000
	exported	15,500,000	bounty	18,500,000

If the whole quantity entered were exported, the government would pay, after allowing for the loss on
refining it, nearly double what was received.

		Kilogrammes.		Francs.
In 1830—Cotton	imported	29,260,433	duty	6,334,070
	goods exported	1,795,008	bounty	851,294
In 1831—Cotton	imported	28,229,487	duty	6,020,443
	exported	1,979,199	bounty	978,300

By the following, it will be seen that the bounty on
the export of woollens is four times as great as the
duty on the import of wool.

		Kilogrammes.		Francs.
In 1830—Wool	imported, about	8,000,000	duty	4,246,021
	Woollens exported	955,617	bounty	1,970,659
In 1831—Wool	imported	3,836,207	duty	1,733,002
	exported	1,039,257	bounty	2,496,728!

On the import of molasses in 1830, the duty received was 972 francs, and the bounty paid on export was 787,988 francs.

The cost of premiums granted to the whale fishery,

amounted in 1830 to 1142.80 francs per man! but there were several claims unsettled, which the minister said would bring the amount to 1500 or 1600 francs! In addition to this there was a bounty of 180 francs per ton!

In the cod fishery, 12000 seamen are encouraged at an expense of *four millions of francs!*

The same system of interference prevails in regard to the development of the natural resources of France. No mine can be worked without permission from the sovereign, and there are instances of valuable mines remaining unwrought for many years, in consequence of being unable to obtain that permission.

" By the French law, all minerals of every kind belong to the crown, and the only advantage the proprietor of the soil enjoys, is, to have the refusal of the mine at the rent fixed upon it by the crown surveyors. There is great difficulty sometimes in even obtaining the leave of the crown to sink a shaft upon the property of the individual who is anxious to undertake the speculation, and to pay the rent usually demanded, a certain portion of the gross product. The Comte Alexander de B—— has been vainly seeking this permission for a lead mine on his estate in Brittany for upwards of ten years."—*Quarterly Review, Vol. XXXI. p.* 408.

Here we see, on the one hand, an enormous expense incurred for the purpose of inducing the people of France to engage in pursuits that would be unprofitable to the individuals if the nation did not pay a part of the expense; while, on the other hand, an individual is desirous to engage in a pursuit that will enable him to pay a rent to the state, and is refused permission so to do. This is a fair specimen of the whole system. By brevets and monopolies of every kind, the government forbids the people from engaging in pursuits that are profitable, while by the offer of bounties it seduces them to others that are unprofitable.

Under such circumstances, capital accumulates slowly. The people, long accustomed to look to the government to provide them with such improvements in the mode of transport as may be necessary, are not prepared to invest their capital in the making of roads and canals, and even the great city of Paris has neither the one nor the other to connect it with its seaport. The extraordinary deficiency in the means of transportation is well described by M. Cordier, in the passage given at page 92.

The system of centralization pursued by the government, has an additional tendency to cramp the energies of the country. Dupin says, that not a bridge can be repaired without permission from the central board at Paris. A report must first be made from the commune to the arrondissement, thence to the department, and thence to Paris, where it sleeps a year or two, and by the time the order returns through the same channels, the bridge requires to be rebuilt, instead of being repaired. Every thing, indeed, is done in France to prevent improvement, and we see its consequences in the following view of the progress of pauperism.

" ' Dans la plupart des communes,' says M. de Villeneuve, 'les fonds affectés aux Bureaux de Bienfaisance, réunis aux produits des quêtes et des dons charitables, sont toujours insuffisans, surtout pendant la saison rigoureuse. Alors l'administration supérieure est assaillie, de la part des communes et des bureaux de charité, de demandes tendant à autoriser des impositions extraordinaires pour venir aux secours des pauvres. Dans plusieurs villes, en 1828 et 1829, on a même employé secrètement, à cet objet, des allocations destinées à d'autres services. L'impérieuse nécessité était le motif et l'excuse d'actes aussi irreguliers; *ainsi la* TAXE DES PAUVRES (Poor's Rate) *s'est déjà forcement introduite, avec le* PAUPERISME ANGLAIS, *dans cette portion de la France.* * * * L'administration n'a cessé, surtout dans les années 1828 et 1829, d'opposer tous ses efforts au développement officiel de cette taxe. Mais en vain se déguise-t-elle sous le nom de travaux de charité ou de supplément de secours aux Bureaux de Bienfaisance, son existence est consacrée de fait, et la force des choses a fait reconnaitre le droit des pauvres à l'assistance publique. L'opinion générale, dans le département du Nord, est préparé à cette innovation dans la législation française. * * * *Les abus* speciaux à la taxe des pauvres en Angleterre se manifestent graduellement. On remarque que, dans les communes du departement du Nord, le nombre des pauvres est toujours en rapport avec la quotité des fondations charitables.'

" And yet, observes M. de Villeneuve elsewhere,
' la plupart des administrations de bienfaisance *n'osent* entreprendre aucun essai d'améliorations nouvelles, dans la crainte d'exposer, par des innovations sans succès, une multitude en proie à toutes les horreurs du besoin.'—vol. ii. pp. 61, 62."*

Another of the effects is thus described by Dupin. " On a calculé, que sur 25 millions d'adultes, la France n'en compte que *dix* qui sachent lire et ecrire. Il reste donc 15 millions d'individus qui n'ont pas meme acquis les premiers élémens de l'instruction la plus vulgaire."

The population of France doubles in about 105 years, more slowly than that of any other nation in Europe, and the growth of comfort is in about the same ratio as that of population. Even matrimony is subjected to regulation as far as practicable. It is

---

* Economie Politique Chretienne. Par M. de Villeneuve Bargement. Quoted in Foreign Quarterly Review, p. 89. Am. edit.

stated by Mr. Browning,* that " no French soldier can contract marriage without the express permission of the colonel of his regiment, and as this officer has a discretionary power on the subject, assent is by no means general." He states also, that the married men in the French army are to the unmarried as one to twenty-four.

The same inconsistency prevails in this respect that has been pointed out in relation to commerce by Messrs. Villiers and Bowring. While matrimony is forbidden, every facility is given to the disposal of the fruit of illicit connexions.

" In 1809 the number of foundlings in France was 69,000. Since the measure of 1811," (ordering a foundling hospital to be established in each arrondissement,) " it has advanced to 84,500 in 1815; to 102,100 in 1820; to 119,900 in 1825; to 125,000 in 1830; and during the last four years it has advanced with a still more remarkable acceleration. At Paris the proportion of foundlings to births was as one to ten; it is now little less than one to four. * * * * The expense has advanced in a parallel proportion to the numbers. It amounts at present to 11,500,000 francs per annum; the Paris institution alone, costing, last year, 1,731,239 francs."†

The people of France being thus reduced to poverty by regulations and restrictions, the government, by a further regulation, attempts to protect them against some of the consequences of that poverty, and accordingly *monts de piété* are established, whose object is to protect the poor against usury. By heavy penalties it is attempted to secure to those institutions a monopoly of the business of pawn-broking, notwith-

* Political and Domestic Condition of Great Britain, by G. Browning. p. 43.

† Foreign Quarterly Review, No. XXIX. p. 85. Am. edit.

standing which means are found of evading the regulations. As an evidence how little advantage is
derived from interferences, it is stated that a large
portion of the pawning which takes place is for the
purpose of gambling in the petty lotteries. Thus, in
1829, it was remarked at Brussels, where the same
institutions exist, that when the lottery, termed the
Genoese lottery, was suppressed in that city, the
number of pledges during the succeeding five months
was less by 7837, and of redemptions, more by 3609,
than in the corresponding five months of the previous
year.*

Of the very few *rights* possessed of old by the people, some yet remain, but they are of a character to
do injury by lessening the security of property, and
preventing the improvements that would otherwise
take place. Witness the following : " The *droit de
parcours* and *droit de vaine pâture,* or common rights
of feeding stock on the plough and grass lands of
private persons, after the harvest and aftermath until
seed and spring time, are equally general, and, although great hindrances to farming improvements,
afford important conveniences to the peasantry."†

Some idea may be formed of the compensation of
the labourer from the allowance to the pauper.

" The means of subsistence, in France, are cheaper, and the living in most respects of an inferior kind; rye, pulse, and maize, with
potatoes and other vegetable diet, forming 99-100ths of the Frenchman's food. Yet, even with this abatement, the average *quantum*
of relief accorded *seems* out of all proportion with the measure ne-

* Foreign Quarterly Review, No. XXIX. p. 86. Am. edit.
† Ibid. p. 81.

cessary for the lowest scale of existence. The mean value of food distributed to each pauper last year, in the fifth arrondissement,* was 6 fr. 62 c. (the Paris price of sixty-five pounds of the worst bread),—of fuel, 32 c. and of clothing and bedding, 4 fr. 16 c. But even this allowance is high compared with the practice in the department of the North, where the average relief of all kinds, and without discrimination of classes, is only 5 fr. 42 c. and in the arrondissement of Dunkirk only 4 fr. 22 c. We are unwilling to give our own description of the destitute population of Paris, or of the more miserable *canuts* or silk weavers of Lyons; but the following passage, abridged from M. de Villeneuve's work, may suffice—although somewhat obscure—for the manufacturing towns in the North; viz.—

" ' The paupers consist of weavers, unable at times to support their families, and wholly chargeable to public or private charity in case of illness, scarcity, or discharge from work; of workmen, ignorant, improvident, brutified by debauchery, or enervated by manufacturing labour, and habitually unable to support their families; of aged persons, prematurely infirm, and abandoned by their children; of children and orphans, a great number of whom labour under incurable disease or deformity; and of numerous families of hereditary paupers and beggars, heaped together in loathsome cellars and garrets, and for the most part subject to infirmities, and addicted to brutal vice and depravity.'

" More than one-third of the Lille paupers are comprised in the four last classes; and if this arithmetic is correct, it cannot be readily understood how the relief given by the charity-boards can palliate such extensive privation. ' La mendicité s'exerce publiquement *par des bandes nombreuses* qui alarment les propriétaires isolés,' (vol. ii. p. 63;) nevertheless, begging in company is an offence specially punishable with imprisonment from six months to two years, (*Code pénal*, art. 276). The number of beggars is above 16,000, and forms a tenth of the indigent population."†

The following extracts from the Report of Messrs.

* Procès-Verbal de l'Assemblée générale du Bureau de Bienfaisance du 5me Arrondissement. Paris, 1834.

† Foreign Quarterly Review, No. XXIX. pp. 89, 90. Am. edit.

Bowring and Villiers, show what are the usual wages in various parts of France.

" In the iron works at Vandelesse, (Nievre,) the price of labonr is fr. 1.50 per day; (Dupin, p. 293;) at Nevers, for the manufacture of iron cables, fr. 2; at Fourchambault, (where 2, 386 are employed in wood cutting,) fr. 1.60 is the average rate; the workmen in the pot- teries at Nevers gain fr. 1.75 per day; at Nogent, in the manufac- ture of linen goods, the wages are to men, fr. 2, women, fr. 1.25, and children, 60c. to 90c. per day; at Mouy in the woollen manufac- tures, men are paid fr. 1 to 1.50, and boys of 15, fr. 1; in the de- partment de l'Aube, the weavers of fine cloths get fr. 1.75; stocking makers, fr. 1; cotton spinners, fr. 1.50 per day; reelers and winders, fr. 1; tanners, fr. 2 to 2.10; at St. Etienne, the wages paid to the miners are, diggers, fr. 3.50; drawers, fr. 3 per day; at Rive de Gier, fr. 4.25 and 3.50; nailors receive 7c. to 10c. per lb., or from fr. 1 to 1.50 per 1,000. The tenders on silk worms are paid from 150c. to fr. 1 per day. Women employed in reeling silk receive fr. 1 per lb. At the forge of Jarron, (Vienne,) a master founder is paid fr. 8, a founder, fr. 4 to 5, a labourer, fr. 2, and a boy, from fr. 1 to 1.25 per day. At Rive de Gier, the labouring makers of coke re- ceive from fr. 2 to 2.50 per day.

" The ' Ponts and Chaussees' pay their labourers fr. 36 per calen- dar month. (*Dupin*, p. 263.)

" M. Dupin, as the result of his observations and investigations as to the medium price of *manufacturing* labour, calculates fr. 2.26 for the northern, and fr. 1.89 for the southern provinces of France; giving with reference to the whole population, fr. 2.06 as the ave- rage rate."—*Bowring and Villiers*, p. 180.

In answer to queries addressed by the Commis- sioners to the workmen of Paris, it was stated that,

" The terrace-makers and labourers live very economically, not expending more than from 16 to 17 sous per day; in the morning they repair to the low eating houses, called gargottes, where for 7 sous they get soup, and a plate of meat with vegetables; their custom is, to breakfast on the soup and vegetables, and carry the meat away with them for dinner. Thus, these 7 sous—two pounds of bread, 8 sous—and perhaps for wine, 2 sous—make 17 sous."— *Bowring and Villiers' Report*, p. 179.

The average given by M. Dupin includes probably a large body of those descriptions of workmen who receive the highest wages in the finer departments of manufacture. By the above statement of Messrs. Bowring and Villiers it is shown, that in the most extensive manufactures the wages of men vary from one to two francs, and that the majority do not exceed 1½ francs. The proportion which the agricultural population of France bears to the whole, is so much greater than in England, that the average wages must approach much more nearly to those of common labourers than in Great Britain. To estimate them at 10 per cent. below those of men engaged in the cotton manufacture; say fr. 1.35 (25 cents) as the average rate of the wages of men in France; would give probably a higher average than the true one in a nation where, according to M. Dupin, two-thirds of the population, or twenty millions, are deprived of the nourishment of animal food, and live wholly on *chesnuts, maize, and potatoes.*

The freedom with which labour circulates in the United States produces a nearer approach to equality than in any other country whatever. The adoption for France, of the same rule for ascertaining the rate of wages, would most probably make it appear higher than it really is in that country, where labour circulates so slowly as to cause great inequalities.

It has been proposed to colonize Algiers, for the purpose of providing a drain for part of her surplus population. The following extract from M. Pichon, ex-governor of Algiers, will show how far this colony would be likely to form an exception to the rule, that colonies cost more than they produce:—

"Dans un système de colonization comme on l'a fait, en apparence, adopter le gouvernement, ce n'est, comme je l'ai dit, ni vingt, ni trente mille hommes qu'il faut, mais cent mille hommes; et cela avec une dépense qui, indépendamment de la dépense militaire, se compterait par dixaines de millions, seulement pour disposer completement de la Métidja, et la laisser vacante aux *soixante mille* colons dont on a parlé; venant d'où, s'établissant avec quoi, c'est ce qu'on ne dit pas."—*Alger in* 1830, *par M. Pichon, quoted Westminster Review, Vol. XIX. p.* 239.

The colonial system of France is the worst that now exists. The nation is compelled to pay high prices for the products of colonies that cost immense sums to keep, and afterwards enormous bounties to induce other nations to assist in their consumption. It is estimated by Messrs. Villiers and Bowring, that the colonies of France, few as they are, have cost since the peace not less than 40 *millions of pounds sterling*. The addition of a new colony like Algiers would only increase the evil, for as soon as it was ascertained what could be produced there, the importation from other quarters would be prohibited, and a new scale of bounties established.*

* The effect of these regulations and restrictions, bounties and prohibitions, is well described by the vine-growers of the department of the Gironde, in their petition to the French Chambers. "La ruine d'un des plus importantes departements de la France; le detresse des departements circumvoisins; le déperissement général du Midi; une immense population attaquée dans ses moyens d'existence; un

If the "*dixaines de millions*" that must be raised
to maintain such colonies, were left in the pockets of
the producers, or applied to the construction of rail-
roads, France would advance more in twenty years,
than under the system of colonization in a century.
Were they to be so applied, she would require no
" drain for her surplus population," nor would her
engineers, returning from England or this country,
be called upon for the humiliating acknowledgments
of M. Cordier.

———

A reference to Mr. Jacob's Report on the corn
trade will show the situation of Poland, and the
Polish provinces of Prussia.   Every where he found
heavy taxation in money, as well as in military services—a people unaccustomed to freedom of action,
and even where they are now free, incapable of exercising it—a total absence of capital—the want of
implements of husbandry—small stocks of cattle—
communications so bad, that, in many cases, the grain
will not pay the cost of transportation—every thing,

capital enorme compromis; la perspective de ne pouvoir prélever
l'impot sur notre sol appauvri et dépouillé; un préjudice immense
pour tous les départements dont nous sommes tributaires; un dé-
croissement rapide dans celles de nos consommations qui profitent
au Nord; la stagnation générale du commerce, avec tous les desas-
tres qu'elle entraine; toutes les pertes qu'elle produit, et tous les
dommages en materials, en politiques, en moraux, qui en sont l'in-
évitable suite; enfin l'anéantissement de plus en plus irreparable de
tous nos anciens rapports commerciaux; les autres peuples s'en-
richissant de nos pertes, et developpant leur système commerciale
sur les débris du notre.

" Tels sont les fruits amers du système dont nous avons été les
principales victimes."

in short, indicating extreme poverty. A good and cheap government is alone wanting in that country, to make it, in time, as populous and as productive as some of the provinces of Holland, which were formerly as little so as any of those of Poland.

In regard to Prussia, I am not possessed of the statistical information to enable me to speak of it at length. It is sufficient, however, to know, that since property has become more secure; since freedom of action has been granted and slavery abolished; since commerce has become more free by the arrangements in regard to the internal trade of Germany; capital increases, roads and canals are being made, and the situation of the people is steadily improving, notwithstanding a vast increase of population, which doubles in 26 years.

Spain has laboured under all these disturbing causes in full perfection, and its consequence is, that so entire is the absence of capital employed in facilitating the communication between the different parts of the country, that wheat varies in the same year from 18 reals, to 53½ reals per quarter. The average prices of the following articles from September, 1827, to September, 1828, were as follows.

	In Salamanca.	In Catalonia.
Wheat,	18	53½
Barley,	9½	20½
Oats,	6	23
Rye,	12¾	31
Garbanzos,	94	68
Oil,	40	31

" Notwithstanding this enormous difference of price and inducement to exportation, it was calculated that the accumulated surplus
of four or five successive years of good crops in the *silos* and granaries of these plains, (of which Salamanca forms a part,) amounted
at the close of the harvest of last year, (1828,) to 6 millions of fane-
gas, or one and one fifth millions of Winchester quarters." So defec-
tive are the means of transportation, " that in order to deliver
100,000 quarters at the ports, (135 miles distant) 5,000 carts, with
two oxen each, would be required, making the journey in 8½ working days, transporting,   -   -   -   -   90,000
And 5,000 mules, each making four journeys per month,
    with half a quarter,   -   -   -   -   10,000
                                                    ————
                                            * 100,000
                                                    ————

The same quantity of transportation would be
done on the Schuylkill Canal by one hundred and
fifty canal boats, and as many horses, in the same
time.

In describing the situation of the roads in various
parts of Europe, Mr. Jacob says, "they afford a
practical reason for the people of Andalusia, in Spain,
drawing their supplies of wheat and flour from the
United States, when wheat was there 4*s.* 6*d.* per
bushel, while on the plains of Castile it was not more
than 1*s.* 6*d.* per bushel.—*Second Report, p.* 10.

Catalonia had a Constitution, which exempted it
from the oppressive taxation which caused the decay of the rest of Spain, and enabled its people to
prosper and accumulate capital. Its wealth made it
a desirable object of plunder, and after much bloodshed, it was deprived of that Constitution by Olivarez.
It was, however, exempted from that most oppressive
of all taxes, the alcavala, and in consequence, it is

* Foreign Quarterly Review, *Vol. V. p.* 80.

still the richest and most enlightened portion of Spain, as has been shown during the last thirty years. No part of the kingdom showed so great an aversion to submission to the dominion of France, either under Napoleon or Charles X.

———

No nation has experienced fewer revolutions than that of China, and none has enjoyed a peace so durable as that which has prevailed since its conquest by the Mantchoos, nearly two centuries since. Person and property have been secure against those hazards which have affected them in the Netherlands, in Italy, and in Germany, the battle grounds of Europe. Such, however, is the weakness of the government, that it is incapable either of enforcing its laws against foreigners, or of affording protection to its own subjects, and the former are set at defiance by the vessels which visit its eastern coast, while the latter are plundered by pirates which throng the adjacent seas. Unable to put them down by force, the government has been compelled to offer them employment, which has been accepted, until the next favourable opportunity offers for resuming their old trade. Under such circumstances, were even the restrictions withdrawn, the domestic trade of China could not be carried on by sea.

Thus insecure abroad, the people do not find security at home. Office is generally purchased, and as is usual in such cases, it is the duty of the holder to indemnify himself out of those placed under him, for the cost of his purchase. Such is the case with judges, and it is not unusual for both parties to fee them, in the hope of a favourable decision. " Capital is so scarce, and so little feeling of security exists, that money is only lent on pawn, and in that case government restricts the rate of interest to *three per cent. per month*, above which rate it must have a tendency to rise."* In describing the great industry of the people of China, Staunton says, that " they labour as if it were all for their own profit."† Such is doubtless the case with the labourers, but it cannot be the case with the higher classes, or there would not be a total absence of a moneyed interest. " Such a deficiency in a country so wealthy, and a people so industrious, seems to imply in this boasted administration some radical defect, some want of protection for all fortunes that rise above the humblest mediocrity. *There is no system of credit established between the merchants of distant provinces*, no bills of exchange; no circulating medium except a copper coin of one-third of a farthing. In this respect China yields greatly to India, which, amid its political agitation, has formed a great moneyed and banking interest, comprising some individuals of immense fortune."‡

Restrictions of every kind abound. " With a firm hand, they (the Board of Censors,) restrain every thing within the prescribed form, spare the people as well as the emperor the trouble of thinking and acting for themselves, and rigorously resist every im-

---

* Murray's Ency. of Geog. p. 1034.
† Staunton, Vol. II. p. 143.
‡ Ibid.

provement as highly dangerous."* The people are not even permitted to select the mode in which they will make the earth useful to them. " The mountains (of Kwang-se) are rich in ore, and even gold mines are to be found, but the policy of the Chinese government does not allow the working of them on a large scale, *for fear of withdrawing the attention of the people from the cultivation of the soil.*"† No improvement of any description is permitted. " The foreign trade of China is carried on in large unwieldy junks whose structure never can be improved, as the slightest deviation from their present clumsy structure, *would subject the owners to the high duties imposed on foreign merchants.*"‡ Even the extent of trade is the subject of regulation. " The viceroy of the province fixes the number of vessels that shall sail to each particular country, and the species of cargo they shall carry."§

Wherever Europeans can enter into competition with them, they are likely to be left behind, in consequence of this opposition to innovation. Of porcelain, but a few years since, the export was very large, but it has now almost disappeared from the list of exports, in consequence of the superiority of the products of England and France.

It has recently been proposed to introduce into Hindostan the culture of the tea plant. Should it be done, it is not improbable that at no distant period

---

* Gutzlaff, I. 34.
† Ibid. I. 28.
‡ Murray's Ency. of Geog. 1031.
§ Ibid.

that country may supersede China in the supply of it. At present, a very important portion of the cost of inferior teas, consists in the expense of transportation to Canton, a distance of about 750 miles, over thirty of which it is carried on men's backs. All this could be obviated by permitting foreign vessels to load at Amoy, but it is conceived better to have the people employed in *carrying* tea than in *producing* it. Were the exportation from Amoy permitted, the immediate effect would be an increase in the price paid to the cultivator, while the total cost would be reduced. An increased demand would arise out of the reduction of price, and all the people who are now employed in the business of transportation, would then find higher wages in that of production.

Taxation is light compared with that of other countries. The land tax is one-tenth of the product. Duties are levied upon salt, and foreign merchandise, and there are transit duties, but in general the articles consumed by the labouring classes are in a great degree exempted. So desirous, indeed, is the government to secure a full supply of food, that vessels bringing cargoes of rice are exempted from the customary charges. In this respect the despotism of China shames the liberal governments of Europe and America, which have always selected for taxation the articles consumed chiefly by the working classes. Timkowski[*] states the whole taxation of the empire at 39,667,272 liang, equal to nearly sixty millions of dollars, or about twelve millions of pounds

---

[*] Timkowski. Russian Embassy to China. Vol. II. p. 458.

sterling; but it is uncertain whether or not this includes the local expenditure. Staunton states the revenue at .200 millions of ounces of silver, equal to 225 millions of dollars, which, with a population of 333 millions, would give 68 cents per head. The Rev. Mr. Jones, on the authority of the Bulletin des Sciences, May 1829, states it at eighty-four millions of ounces of silver, of which thirty-three millions are paid in silver, and fifty-one millions in grain, rice, &c. Eighty-four millions of ounces are equal to ninety-five millions of dollars, which, with the present population of 367 millions, would be but 27 cents per head.

There is no tax for the support of religion, and but little for that of the army. The chief part of the troops labour for their own support, and the calling is held in little esteem. "They are reckoned far below the civilians, who are thrice as well paid, and who treat the military officer like a police agent, which has brought the whole body into disrepute."* In almost every part of Europe and America, the most important posts are occupied by marshals and generals; but in China, "unlike to the rest of the world, where labour and military talents, occasionally united to natural eloquence, were originally the foundation of all wealth and greatness, while literature was little more than an amusement, the study of the written morals, history and politics of China was the *only road* not merely to power and honour, but to every individual employment in the state."†

* Gutzlaff. I. 40.　　　　† Staunton. II. 107.

In regard to industry, they are models for all other people. " At this season of harvest an active cheerfulness seemed to pervade both sexes. They appeared to be sensible of labouring for their own profit. Many of the peasants are owners of the lands they cultivate."* Extraordinary good humour and cheerfulness are their characteristics, and there is perhaps no nation in which decency and regularity are so universal ;† where crime is less.‡ Their economy is equal to their industry.

The population is stated by Mr. Gutzlaff at 367 millions, on a surface of 1,298,000 square miles, being equal to 290 to each square mile. In the province of Ke-ang-se there are 1,126, while in that of Shen-se there are only fifty to a mile. In the three presidencies of Bengal, Madras, and Bombay, there is a population of 89,470,152 upon 421,673 square miles, giving an average of 212. Bengal has 316, Madras 95, and Bombay 105 to the mile.

Mr. Gutzlaff states his belief that the population is not over-rated, and if his views be correct, it follows that the quantity of land for each individual in China, is one-fourth less than in Hindostan. Her lands are generally fertile, and cultivated in the most extraordinary manner. They are watered by immense rivers, two of which are 2,000 miles in length, and numerous canals have been constructed at vast expense.

We here find a nation increasing rapidly in numbers, and forbidden to extend their field of action.

* Staunton, II. 143.   † *Ibid.* I. 269.   ‡ *Ibid.* II. 39.

They are not permitted to leave the empire, by which they might transport themselves to new lands; nor are they permitted to vary their modes of operation, by which old lands might be rendered more productive, or by which labour employed in manufactures might be made to increase the quantity or improve the quality of the commodities brought to market. " Notwithstanding the paramount importance attached to works of utility, the Chinese have made no progress in the application of the mechanical powers; they cannot even construct a common pump; and all their great works are the mere result of indefatigable labour performed by a multitude of human hands."*

Population increases rapidly, but production is not permitted to keep pace with it, and the nation is in precisely the opposite situation of that described at page 29, where the ratio of production increases more rapidly than that of population. Forbidden to avail themselves of machinery, the amount of production is small, and the most untiring industry is required to obtain the means of support; the necessary consequence is, that very little remains to become capital. Even were it, under these disadvantageous circumstances, to increase more rapidly than it does, the insecurity that appears to exist would prevent its investment in machinery, were it not, as it is, forbidden to be so used.

Peace and security from invasion, light taxation, great industry and strict economy, enable the Chinese to obtain a better support than falls to the lot of

* Murray's Geography, p. 1039.

the Hindoos, but restrictions and insecurity prevent them from availing themselves of their advantages, and thus impede the growth of capital. Barrow says he never saw a beggar. Beggars, however, there certainly are, but they are always well clothed, and it is believed that the Chinese are better clad than any other nation in the world. Infanticide is often adduced as an evidence of great distress, but Mr. Morrison, who had as good opportunity as any European of knowing the facts, declared that he had never been able to find it.

China possesses every requisite but an enlightened government for becoming one of the most prosperous nations of the earth, but the doctrines of her rulers are in accordance with those of some of our writers, who would tax machinery for the purpose of limiting production, and while she thus refuses the aid of science, her people must continue in a state of poverty.

CHAPTER XVI.

HAVING thus completed the survey of some of the most important nations, I propose now to ascertain as nearly as practicable, with the imperfect means at my command, what is the actual difference in the reward of labour, between the United States, England, the Netherlands, France, China, and Hindostan.

Mr. Jacob, (First Report, p. 230,) gives a statement of the average prices of wheat of the best quality in the markets of Europe, during the year 1825, from which the following prices are taken.

	Per Quarter.		
	s. d.		s. d.
Amsterdam,	28 10 ⎫		
Rotterdam,	28 7 ⎬ average,		29 2
Antwerp,	30 00 ⎭		
New York,	- - - - -		28 9
France,	- - - - -		35 4
Mr. M'Culloch's Dict. of Commerce gives for England,			68 7

The price above given for New York, is exceedingly low; much lower than the usual price; and can hardly be correct. At page 27 is given a statement of the average price of flour in Philadelphia in that year, by which it will be seen to have been $4 84, but the average of ten years was $5 32, which would give about 35s. per quarter for wheat.

The ordinary average of France was stated by Count Chaptal, in 1819, at 42s. 10d. per quarter, but it has probably fallen to the rate mentioned by Mr. Jacob. The price in Havre in December,

Francs.		Francs.	
1829, was 52.10 per 100 kilos.		1832, was 43 per 100 kilos.	
1830, 56.10 " "		1833, 40 " "	
1831, 60 " "		1834, 42 " "	

T

being an average of 49 francs, or 42s. 9d. sterling per quarter, or nearly the same price stated by Chaptal. Owing, however, to the difficulty of transportation, the price varies greatly in the different parts of the kingdom. Desirous not to over-rate it, the price assumed shall be that of Mr. Jacob, 35s. 4d., which is a little less than the average price in Havre for 1832, 33, and 34.

Wheat was at an unusually high price in England in 1825, and it would not be correct to take that year for the purpose of making a comparison. I will therefore take the average for eleven years, from 1820 to 1830, which was 61s. 2d.* The price in

---

* In 1833, the price of the finest wheaten flour in London, was 50s. per sack; the highest price of the finest wheaten flour in Paris, was 46 francs per 150 kilogrammes, equal to only 28s. 6d. the English sack of 280 pounds.—(Hist. Mid. and Working Classes, p. 543.) These prices are in almost exact accordance with the averages that are above assumed for England and France. By the following article it will be seen that the reduction in price that has taken place in England, has altered materially the proportions above given.

" The highest quotation of white wheat of the first quality at Hamburgh, is 80 rix dollars current the last, which answers to 25s. 10d. the quarter, and the highest quotation of red wheat of the first quality, is 76.2 dollars current the last, which answers to 24s. 7d. the quarter, and therefore the mean price at Hamburgh of white and red wheat is 25s. 3d. per quarter. The highest quotation of white wheat of the first quality in Mark Lane, is 50s. the quarter, and the highest quotation of red wheat of the first quality, is 44s. the quarter, and therefore the mean price in Mark Lane of white and red wheat, is 47s. the quarter. It appears, therefore, that wheat is 86 1-8 per cent. dearer in London than in Hamburgh, and that with the sum of £2 7s., a man may buy 14 1-8 bushels of wheat at Hamburgh, whereas with the same sum he can buy only eight bushels at London.

" The highest price of Zealand white wheat of the first quality at Amsterdam, is 175 florins the last, which equals 28s. 3d. the quarter, and the mean price in London being 47s. the quarter, it follows that wheat is 66 3-8 per cent. dearer in London than in Amsterdam.

the United States being 35s. and 78 to 80 cents per
day being the usual wages of a labouring man, the
labour requisite to procure a quarter of wheat would
be nearly - - - - days, 11

	Wheat.		Labour.		
In England,	61s. 2d.	72 cents or 3s.			20⅓
The Netherlands,	29 2	30 "	1	3d.	23⅓
France,	35 4	25 "	1	½	33½

To make a fair comparison it would be, however,
necessary to ascertain the comparative cost of many
other commodities besides that of corn, by which a
considerable change would be produced in the relative position of the inhabitants of those countries.

The people of the United States have corn, and
provisions generally, very cheap. Tea and coffee are
imported free of duty, and are sold at a very small
advance upon their cost at the places of production.
Sugar is at a much smaller duty than in France and
England. Fuel is cheap. Most descriptions of manufactured goods are higher than in England, particularly those of wool and iron; and the rate of interest
being higher, house rent is also higher. Making allowance for these differences, it is probable that the English labourer would be required to work sixteen days

" The highest price of red wheat of the first quality at Antwerp,
is 8 3-4 florins current the hectolitre, which is equal to 36s. 5d. the
quarter, and the highest price of red wheat in London being 44s.
the quarter, it follows that red wheat is 20 3-8 per cent. dearer in
London than at Antwerp.

" The mean average of the prices of wheat of the first quality at
Hamburgh, Amsterdam, Antwerp, and Stettin, is 28s. 1d. the quarter, and the mean price of wheat of the first quality in London being
47s. the quarter, it follows that the mean price in London is 67 3-8
per cent. higher than in the above mentioned places."—*Times, March*
30, 1835.

to obtain the same amount of commodities that would be obtained by the American labourer in eleven days.

In the case of the Netherlands the same remarks are to be made as in that of the United States. Provisions are cheap, as trade in them is free; and their great system of canals facilitates the transmission of domestic and foreign products at small cost, so that the variations in price cannot be very great. Manufactured goods are lower than in the United States, while provisions are not higher, if so high. Notwithstanding the difference in money wages, almost as large an amount of commodities can be obtained by the labourer as in England. A strong evidence of the comfortable situation of the people is to be found in the fact, that the magazines and journals count one subscriber for every 100 persons, while in England there is only one for 184, and in France only one in 437.*

In France, prohibitions, heavy duties, monopolies, and restrictions, meet us at every step. Roads are bad, and limited in extent, and canals and rail roads are few in number. Transportation is consequently expensive, and the differences of price are very great. The domestic trade is interfered with by the octroi, which prevents the free transmission of merchandise from one part of the kingdom to another. According to the price of wheat, the difference in the reward of the American and French labourer would be as 11 to 33½, but taking into consideration the difference in other articles of consumption, it would be probably about as 11 to 28.

* Foreign Quarterly Review, March, 1835.

The following extracts will tend to show what is
the rate of wages in India.

" In a late statistical account of Dinagepore, a province of Bengal,
there are statements of the annual expenses of different classes of
society; and among them one of the expenses of a labouring man
with a wife and two children. The amount is only, rupees 22.10.11
—or near £3 per annum; being at the rate of 15 shillings a head.
The article of clothing for this family of four persons is only 6 shillings per annum."*

"Colonel Munro states the average price of agricultural labour
in the 'Ceded Districts,' to be about 5s. per month, or 2d. per day.
He framed tables, dividing the population (about two millions) into
three classes, and ascertained the annual expense of each individual,
for clothing, food, and every other article, to be as follows:—
First class, containing about one-fourth of the popu-

lation, average per head,	-	-	-	£2 0 0
Second class, containing about one-half of the popu-lation, average per head,	-	-	-	1 7 0
Third class, containing about one-fourth of the popu-lation, average per head,†	-	-	-	0 18 0

In estimating them at two rupees per month, it is
believed much more likely to exceed than to fall short
of the average. Mr. Senior (see page 63) estimated
them at from one to two pounds of silver per annum,
or 2½ to 5 rupees per month. By reference to page
114 it will be seen, that wages are spoken of by Mr.
Colebrooke as being two anas a day (about three rupees per month), but that he considers that more than
can be realized by the cultivator. The usual price paid
to the men engaged in the cultivation and preparation
of indigo, is two rupees per month. Assuming that as
the average of money wages, and the price of rice in
the interior, as given by Mr. Colebrooke, at 12 anas

* Committee's Report, p. 9.—Quoted by Rickards, I. p. 48.
† Rickards, I. p. 68.

per maund of 74 pounds, it would require, *in the rice
country*, the labour of two months and a half to earn
480 pounds, being the equivalent of a quarter of wheat.

In Calcutta the labourer receives three rupees per
month, while servants and mechanics have from four
to six rupees: the average may be three and a half
rupees. By reference to M'Culloch's Commercial
Dictionary, article Calcutta, under the head of Exports, it will be seen that the average price of the
rice exported was 1 rupee 7 anas per *Bazar maund*
of 82 pounds, and of wheat 1 rupee 8 anas. By a recent price current the average price of rice was 1.7,
and of wheat 1.6. At these prices, and allowing the
average of wages to be 3½ rupees per month, it would
require the labour of 2½ months to obtain 480 pounds
of rice, or as much as would be obtained in the United States by the labour of eleven days.

In Southern India rice is much higher, and it is probable that a much larger amount of labour may be required to obtain the same quantity of food. It is proper
to observe that a large portion of the rice of India is
exceedingly inferior in quality, and of course low in
price. Even that which is exported sells at very low
prices in England compared with that of the United
States.*

---

* The price of rice in the London market (duty paid), 23d June
1831, was as follows:

			£.	s.	d.	£.	s.	d.
American—Carolina		per cwt.	1	11	0	to 1	13	0
East India { Bengal, yellow		"		12	6		13	6
white		"		14	0		15	6
cargo,		"		11	0		11	6
Patna,		"		17	0		19	0
Java and Madagascar,		"		10	0		11	0

M'Culloch's Com. Dictionary, p. 908.

The means of ascertaining the condition of the labouring population of China are not such as could be desired, but Timkowski* has furnished a list of prices at Pekin, that will enable us to make some comparison between their situation and that of similar persons in Europe.

He says servants in the first houses have, per month, 3300 tsian,† or *cash*, equal to $ 4 50.

Servants in houses of the second class have, in addition to their board, from 1000 to 1500 tsian, equal to an average of $1 75 per month, or $21 per annum.

At page 91 are given the wages of house servants in Dumfries, at $ 56 to $ 60 per annum. In many parts of Prussia, under similar circumstances, wages do not exceed $ 10 per annum.

The prices of provisions are as follows:

Rice, per 20 pounds,	- - - -	400 tsian.
Eggs, per hundred,	- - - - -	400 to 600 tsian.
Cabbages, per hundred,	- - - -	300 to 550 tsian.
Millet flour, per 20 pounds,	- - -	275 tsian.

Wages are as follows:—

	Tsian.
A joiner, per day,	300 equal to 15 lbs. rice.
A carpenter, do.	200 equal to 10 lbs. rice.
A paper hanger, do.	200 equal to 10 lbs. rice.
A working man, do.	130 equal to 6½ lbs. rice.

The average price of bread in Paris for several years, as given by the police to Messrs. Bowring & Villiers, was 60 centimes for 2 kilogrammes. The

* Russian Mission to China, vol. II. p. 199.
† Of these 137½ are equal to a franc, or 18⅔ cents.

wages are also given in the same report, by which
it is seen that

		Francs.	Bread.
The cabinet maker has per day,		3 to 3.50	equal to 23 pounds.
The carpenter,	do.	3 to 3.50	equal to 23 pounds.
Hatter, shoemaker, &c.	do.	3	equal to 22 pounds.
Terrace makers & blacksmiths, do.		2	equal to 14 pounds.

In Canton, rice sells at $1 40 to $1 80 per picul
of 133⅓ pounds English. Mr. M'Culloch says from
a halfpenny to three farthings per pound, equal to
$1 33 to $2 per picul. A day labourer has from nine
candareens to one mace (say 13 cents) per day, finding himself. His wages will purchase from 9½ to 13
pounds of rice, according to quality, being perhaps
25 per cent. less than is obtained by the labourer in
Paris. A mechanic receives one mace (13⅘ cents)
per day, and his board. Allowing 313 days to the
year, he would earn 3200 pounds of the *best* rice by
his year's work. A brewer or cooper, in Paris, receives 500 francs per annum and his board.* With
500 francs he could purchase 3610 pounds of bread.
A butcher has 1000 francs.* A pastry cook from
600 to 900 francs.* The average, being 750 francs,
would purchase 5415 pounds of bread.

I see no reason to believe that the rate of wages
in France exceeds that of China more than 50 per
cent., or that the Chinese labourer could not obtain
as much in 40 or 42 days, as is obtained in France
by the labour of 28 days. The materials for forming
a judgment are, however, very small, and this view
of the case may not prove correct.

* Bowring and Villiers' Report.

CHAPTER XVII.

I PROPOSE now to submit to the reader a scale of the advantages (or productive powers) possessed by the several nations to which I have referred, that he may see at a glance how far it accords with the state of the labouring classes as described in the last chapter. It is necessary to bear in mind what has been the situation of the various countries during the last fifty years, as, although property was secure, and trade free, in the Netherlands, at the time of preparing the statements that have been used, it had been far otherwise at very recent periods, and a long course of peace and tranquillity is necessary to enable a nation to recover from the effects of such wars as have been waged in her territory. It is also necessary to recollect, that although capital abounded in Holland, a large portion of it was invested abroad, and the owner of what was thus lent to aid foreign manufacturers or ship-owners, was useful at home to the same extent only as the Irish absentee landlord was of service to the people of Paris or Rome.

This table is not offered as being accurate, but simply as an approximation sufficiently near to illustrate my argument.

	U S.	G.B.	Neth.	France.	China.	Hind.
Security of person and property,	100	100	45	50	20	10
Freedom of action, - -	100	70	65	40	00	00
Freedom of commerce, -	80	50	60	30	00	00
Habits of industry, - -	90	80	100	55	100	50
Capital, *land included*, -	90	100	45	50	15	15
	460	400	315	225	135	75
Deduct taxation,	20	100	50	50	6	10
	440	300	265	175	129	65

It has been estimated that eleven days' labour in the United States would be sufficient to obtain a quarter of wheat. Taking the above sum of 440, and multiplying it by that number of days, the product would be 4840, which I propose should represent a quarter, or eight bushels, of wheat. Say, 11 days.

The powers of the English labourer being 300, he would require, to obtain the same value of commodities, - - 16 days.

The labourer in the Netherlands, - 18 days.

The advantages of the French labourer being only 175, he would require nearly 28 days.

The Chinese would require - - 38 days.

The Hindoo, whose powers of production are estimated at only 65, would require 74 days.

These results correspond very nearly with the estimates of the previous chapter, but it is possible that many persons may be disposed to question the correctness of the quantities assumed, and which have produced those results. It has been a matter of controversy whether the amount of taxation in France was greater than in the United States, while it is above stated to be more than twice as great. I entertain no doubt of its being as given above, but statistical information is needed on that and many other points for the correct formation of such a table. Again, notwithstanding the tendency of insecurity and restrictions to produce a want of industry, the people of China and the Netherlands are set down in the preceding table as more industrious than those of the United States and England. Taxation is light in China, and the common people, feeling themselves secure, labour with extraordinary assiduity, while the industry of the class which is possessed of capital, is restrained by the causes to which I have referred. It is difficult here to assign proper quantities to security and industry, but it is probable, that, taking into view the situation of the two classes, the former might be increased to 30 or 40, while the latter might be reduced to 70, 80, or 90. In the case of the Netherlands, for the same reason, it would perhaps be proper to reduce industry to 80, and the sum of the powers of production to 245, which would make it necessary to give the labour of 20 days instead of 18 as above stated. The increased attention that is given to statistics will, I doubt not, in a few years, enable future writers to give much more accurate views than can now be done, and every improvement in that science will tend more and more to prove that the condition of the working classes improves as security is obtained without interference with their freedom, and without taking from them too large a portion of the fruits of their labour.

CHAPTER XVIII.

Having thus passed in review several of the principal nations, the reader will probably be disposed to admit that there are abundant reasons for the state of things that exists, and will now be prepared for a brief examination of the views of some of the writers who insist that all the poverty and wretchedness that exist, arise out of the erroneous arrangements of the Deity.

Mr. Mill (Elements of Political Economy,) takes the same view of the influence of capital as that which will be found at p. 30. He says, " If the ratio which capital bears to population increases, wages will rise; if the ratio which population bears to capital increases, wages will fall." Being, however, a full believer in the Malthusian theory, that population is always disposed to increase so rapidly as to be threatened with starvation, and only kept down by the apprehension thereof, he asserts that population has increased much faster than capital, as " is proved incontestably by the condition of the population of most parts of the globe. In almost all countries, the condition of the great body of the people is poor and miserable." I do not doubt their poverty, but do doubt their being as poor as they were, one, two, or three centuries since, and if they are not so, capital must, according to Mr. Mill's own theory, have increased more rapidly than population. That they are not so, is evidenced by the case of Great Britain; by that of Prussia, where population is increasing more rapidly than in any other part of Europe, and where improvement in the condition of the people keeps pace with the increase of population; and by that of the late kingdom of the Netherlands, whose population at its present rate of increase would double itself in 63 years. Even were such not the case, and were they as poor, or even poorer than they had been, it would be necessary, before admitting such to be the natural course of things, to examine how far the measures of the various governments had tended to promote or to repress the growth of capital. If upon such examination it were found, that in some of them, all the disturbing causes, treated of in the previous chapters, had been in full operation, and in others a portion of them, it might well be doubted if its slow increase had not arisen from those interferences alone, which are abundantly sufficient to keep any people " poor and miserable." In accordance with the above doctrine, Mr. Mill asserts, that " whether, after land of superior quality has been exhausted, capital is applied to new lands of inferior quality, or in successive doses, with diminished returns upon the same lands, the produce of it is continually diminishing in proportion to its increase. If the return to capital is, however, continually decreasing, the annual fund from which savings are made, is continually diminishing. The difficulty in making savings is continually augmented, and at last they must entirely cease." The means of accumulating

U

capital being thus cut off, it follows that "how slow soever the increase of population, provided that of capital be still slower, wages will be reduced so low, that a portion of the population must regularly die of want." He says that population does increase more rapidly than capital, and we must therefore be gradually approaching that state of things which he describes.

The first dose of capital applied to land, was probably in shape of a spade, and the next that of a plough, and it is unlikely that the return in the second case, was less than in the first. Among the most recent are the cradle and horse-rake, and it is highly improbable that any farmer will admit that capital thus applied, pays him less interest than that previously applied in the shape of a reaping-hook and hand-rake.

The "inferior soils" of Mill, Ricardo, and others, mean those which by reason of their inferiority of quality, or distance from market, are last brought into cultivation. It is evident that both situation and quality must enter into the consideration of the character of land, as that of second, third, or fourth quality near New York or Philadelphia would be sooner brought into cultivation, and command a higher rent, than that of first quality in Ohio or Indiana. The latter are emphatically the "inferior soils" referred to, and yet fresh doses of capital are daily administered to them, and to lands in Illinois, Missouri, Tennessee, Mississippi, and Alabama, and so far are they from being attended with a "diminished return," that circulating capital is there worth 12,

15, or 18 per cent. per annum, and is used to greater profit by the borrower than in the older states, when obtained at 5 or 6.   Those distant lands are brought into cultivation in consequence of the " doses of ca-pital" being administered in the form of canals, turn-pike and rail-roads, by which the transport of their products is facilitated; but the result would be the same if the lands were less distant and of inferior quality, and the capital were applied in the form of manure, or improved methods of culture.   Yet Mr. M'Culloch refers to the culture of lands in Indiana and Illinois in support of this theory!

Such theories are so totally opposed to the evi-dence afforded by all Europe, and particularly Great Britain, as well as this country, that it is difficult to account for their production.   They would be amusing, were it not that they are adopted by men in elevated stations, whose modes of thinking influ-ence the happiness and prosperity of the people over whom they are placed.   There is no doubt that popu-lation *may* increase with great rapidity, and it is probable that it will increase at a much more rapid rate than it has done, but if governments can be induced so to modify their systems as to permit the labourer to enjoy the product of his labour, his situ-ation will become more comfortable with every such increase.   Even now it does so in Prussia, the Nether-lands, and Great Britain, and still more so in the United States, where the demand for labour and its reward, are, with a population of fifteen millions, vastly greater than when there were but five millions.

Such being the case, it is difficult to believe in the

awful consequences to be apprehended from this
enormous increase; or to dread starvation, when mis-
government is not carried too far. The disciple of
Mr. Malthus would ask if there can be a doubt as to
the geometrical increase of population, and arithmetical increase of food, or that if population should
double in fifteen or thirty years, it would be attended
with the horrible effects that have been predicted.
So the advocate of restrictions upon trade objects to
taking off the duties upon coffee, on the ground that
the increased demand must increase the price at the
place of production, and that the duty will be paid to
the grower, in place of the government. The advocates of the corn laws, when the approach of famine
has made it necessary to import a large quantity,
and they see that it is paid for in bullion, deem it
conclusive evidence of the incorrectness of the assertion of their opponents, that a free trade in corn
would promote the demand for British goods. All
are restrictionists, and all equally in error. By prohibiting the trade in corn in ordinary seasons, the one
does all in his power to depress the people of Prussia
and Poland, and keep them in a state of poverty, preventing the accumulation of capital, and the growth
of a taste for British wares, and then uses the fact of
their poverty as a reason why the system should be
continued. By heavy duties upon coffee, the consumption is discouraged, and the owners of plantations are compelled to root up their trees, which
cannot be replaced for several years, and when the
production is thus reduced to the demand, we are
told that the system must be persevered in, lest the

coffee planter should obtain an increased price for a short period of time, until the production could again overtake the demand. By enormous taxes and ruinous wars; by every expedient that could be devised; the people of the eastern continent have been ground to the earth; unable, in many places, to command more than the mere necessaries of life, there could be no accumulation of capital; their trade restrained so that in many places corn has not been worth the cost of sending to market, while the want of capital prevented improvement of communications; compelled, as in Hindostan, to pay in rent and taxes more than half the gross product of their lands, and rendered unable to improve the miserable tools with which they were cultivated; and after having thus done all in our power to prevent the growth of capital, and consequent increase of food, we are asked if we believe the demand, being doubled in twenty or thirty years, could be supplied. To this, the reply would, of course, be in the negative; but if rulers had been content to leave to the labourer the product of his labour, allowing his capital to increase, the population of the earth might now be infinitely greater than it is, without a deficiency of food, and it might go on to an extent that would now be deemed incredible, the condition of the people steadily improving with the increase in number. Even in Ireland,* the condition of the people is decidedly better

---

* " From various criteria of prosperity we have a remarkable testimony to that of Ireland; for whilst the proportion of uninhabited houses is just the same as in Scotland, that of the houses building is one in 81 of those inhabited, or exceeding above eleven per cent.,

than it was, and yet in that unfortunate country all the disturbing causes have been in full action. Every thing has tended to repress the growth of capital, and keep them in a state of poverty, preventing them from either improving their own waste lands, or transferring themselves to the richer lands of Canada or the United States. *Here,* transfers of population are daily going on to an immense extent, but *there,*

the like proportion in England. We have often heard a cry, too, that in consequence of the Union, Dublin had been deserted, and multitudes of houses become uninhabited. Now, the fact is, that the proportion of uninhabited houses is less in Dublin than in the metropolis or either of the sister kingdoms:—the uninhabited houses in London, Edinburgh, and Dublin, being respectively one in 11, 17, and 18. So much for clamour, and so much for facts of statistical investigation to put clamour down; or, if it cannot be silenced, the light, at least, may exhibit the screech-owl."

The following statement is from a pamphlet by Mr. Pratt, the barrister appointed to certify the rules of Savings' Banks and Friendly Societies, and shows a marked improvement in the condition of the people of Ireland.

"The increase in the deposits of the Irish savings' banks, has been proportionably much greater than in the English.

"In England and Wales, the augmentations since 1831 do not exceed 8 per cent. of the gross sum invested, while in Ireland the increase has been above 25 per cent. Of course it will be said that the condition of the Irish people being inferior to the English, there exists greater room for improvement in the one case than in the other, and that this circumstance explains the more rapid expansion of savings' banks in Ireland. The observation is undoubtedly true, but it leaves the fact of the increasing prosperity of the sister kingdom unshaken. It is clear that Ireland is not only in a state of progressive improvement, but that she is improving at a quicker rate than this country."

"The exports from Ireland to the single port of Liverpool in 1833, were £ 7,456,692."—*Speech of Mr. S. Rice, April,* 1834.

such is their poverty, that unless sent by the government, they are utterly unable to leave the country; to be useful to it either at home or abroad.

Having done all in our power to make man " poor and miserable"—to prevent the growth of capital or any improvement in his situation—and finding that there is a great deal of poverty in the world, we inquire the cause, and find it arises out of a mistake in the Deity, who fitted man to increase in a geometrical ratio, while he permitted the fruits of the earth to increase in an arithmetical ratio only, thus making poverty and misery inseparable accompaniments of the human race. This result is highly satisfactory to us, as it transfers to the Deity what should rest upon our own shoulders, and we then invent the starvation check; discourage matrimony that we may promote profligacy, and thus check population; while the earth is as yet, in a great measure, untouched, and is capable of supporting thousands of millions in those parts where cultivation is almost unknown.

All these attempts at interference should be regarded like those with trade, and it is not to be doubted that the time will come when they will be considered equally absurd. The trade of population is the only one that has heretofore been free, and it is to be regretted that those who are in favour of loosing the shackles which have bound all others, advocate restrictions upon that which has heretofore escaped. As yet we know nothing of the productive powers of the earth. In the United States food has increased in the same ratio with population, while they supply a large portion of the world with other productions of the soil, cotton and tobacco. In England, within the last century, the improvement has been immense, arising from improved methods of cultivation, yet she is far behind Flanders, which, " two centuries since, was a barren waste." There, " the produce of wheat is often not less than thirty-two bushels to two of seed; of oats, sixty bushels to three; and of other grain in proportion, whilst in scarcely any part of Great Britain does wheat yield more than eight or ten times."*

The following remarks, upon the present state of English agriculture, are from a review of a work on that subject, by Mr. Lowe, in a British journal for November last.

" The most fertile soils, miserably tilled, according to the prescriptive rule of 'follow my leader,' are every where found contiguous to examples of skill and industry which raise abundant crops; and the contented boor sits down to his starved returns, quite satisfied with what rude implements, wasteful defects, and ignorant blindness, have permitted him to gather like his predecessors!

" How different would it be, were the opposite course pursued; were all the British Empire, for instance, as ably and intelligently cultivated as the Lothians and Lowlands of Scotland! Were Mr. Lowe's practical lessons universally acted upon, we should then hear no more of a surplus population beyond the supply of food; of the necessity of exporting our hearty peasantry to Australian or other colonies; of the dreadful sufferings of the labouring poor. The honest toils of the field would largely supersede the depraving employment of the workhouse; and the reward of those toils would be plenty of wholesome food to sustain the humblest classes of our fellow-creatures."

Throughout a large part of the Russian, Polish, and Prussian provinces on the Baltic, Mr. Jacob de-

* For. Quar. Rev., Vol. V. p. 375.

scribes the people as in a state of extreme poverty—
totally destitute of capital—unable to stock their land,
or to supply themselves with any but the poorest implements, and yet subject to enormous taxation, in
money and military services. Were that taxation
dispensed with, or reduced to a moderate amount,
there can be no doubt that capital would increase,
agriculture would be improved, communications
would be opened, and the lands might become as productive as those of Great Britain or the Netherlands.

At page 108 is given a view of the state of agriculture in those countries, where it is shown that the
return to the cultivator does not usually exceed four
times the seed. An examination of those statements
would show that similar causes produce similar effects
in Europe and Asia. There is no country of Europe
that so much resembles Hindostan in its fate as Poland, and there we find, in the situation of the labouring classes, an almost exact parallel. As many days'
labour are necessary to obtain a quarter of wheat,
with the further disadvantage that the Hindoo scarcely requires any clothing, while the climate of Poland
makes it indispensable.

In an able article on America in the Encyclopedia
Britannica, it is stated, that notwithstanding the difference in size between the eastern and western continent, the proportion of the former that is unfit for
cultivation, in consequence of sterility, or absence of
water communications, is so much greater, that the
latter is capable of subsisting an equal population.
The writer then proceeds to estimate the extent of
its ability, and taking Germany as the basis, where

population varies from 100 to 200 to a square mile, he assumes 150 to be the limit in latitude 50°, according to which, and making due allowance for the superior productiveness of the lower latitudes, he finds that this continent is capable of subsisting 3,600 millions. The same quantity for the eastern continent would made 7,200 millions, or eight, if not nine times, the present population. We know, however, that agriculture in Germany and in France, where there are 160 to a square mile, is in a very backward state, and it cannot be doubted that the application of capital would very speedily double the product, and that in many parts of Europe it might be trebled, quadrupled, or quintupled. Long before the population shall have attained the extent above mentioned, Germany will support 300 persons to a square mile better than she now does 150. If to that be added the economy of the products of the earth that is to arise out of the substitution of steam for horse power; estimated in Great Britain to be now equal to the support of eight millions, or *one-half of its present population;* and the vast extent of land in Australasia, it will be seen that the ability of the earth to afford food is immense, perhaps equal to thirty thousand millions. It is perfectly true, that if population were to proceed every where at the rate at which it does in this country, it would soon attain this extraordinary amount. We know, however, that it does not, and we also know that in every country where the government will permit it, there is a steady improvement of condition with the increase of population: we know that the difficulty is not to supply food, but to find

a market for it: that in a very large part of Europe
the cultivators are "poor and miserable," solely because they are not at liberty to exchange their products freely for what they want: that in consequence
thereof, prices have been so much reduced in many
places as to render them totally unable to pay rent:
and with this knowledge we may be content to let
population take its own course, and instead of fetter-
ing it by restrictions, endeavour to improve the condition of the people by increasing their liberty of action and lightening their burdens. Let this be done,
and capital will increase more rapidly than population, and the surplus of Europe being enabled to
transfer itself to this continent, the whole world may
become a garden. Doing this, we may safely trust
that population will limit itself, and that the wisdom
of the arrangements of the Deity, in regard to man,
will be as evident as it is in every other part of the
creation. We shall find that, as in every thing else,
"laissez nous faire" is the true doctrine: that when
allowed to come into action, there is already established a system of checks and balances, action and
re-action, as far superior to that which has haunted
the imagination of *some* of the writers on population,
as is that which regulates the motions of the planets
to that of a windmill: and that if to man was granted
the power of increase in a geometrical ratio, there
was at the same time implanted a principle which
secures him against its effects, the desire of bettering
his condition; which, *if allowed to begin to act,* will
be abundantly sufficient, with the increased fruitful-
ness of the land, arising out of the application of

capital, to prevent the necessity of the starvation
check.

Mr. Malthus tells us, that wherever food is abundant, population increases rapidly; but it might be as
correctly said, that where population increases rapidly, food is abundant, and we have full evidence
that with increased population, the dangers of famine
are greatly decreased, where man is not too much
trammeled. " *A'cote' d'un pain, il nait un homme,*"
is a saying in some parts of the continent, but experience would show that it would be equally correct
if read thus, " *a coté d'un homme, il croit un pain,*"
—or would grow, if permitted. At the time Mr.
Malthus formed his theory, he had but few facts in
regard to *civilized* man upon which it could be based.
The experience of this country had been too short to
enable him to use it with any advantage, and he was
obliged to argue from the state of man as he exists
in the eastern hemisphere, " checked like a bond-
man," fettered by laws and regulations, and oppressed
by claims for the support of government and of individuals. To argue from facts thus obtained, is like
constructing a theory of the tides from a collection
of observations on mill dams. I am not aware of a
fact in his book in regard to man in a state of civilization, that goes to support his theory, or that is not
much better evidence that man has been misgoverned,
and his increase repressed thereby, than that it has
been repressed by inability of the earth to afford him
support.

The only disease under which mankind labours is
oppression. Let that be removed, and he will speedily

recover, and show by the increase of population and consequent division of labour, increased productiveness of labour, and growth of capital, that such was the case. All other medicines must fail, even that of Dr. Chalmers, who contends that relief from taxation would do little good, and that the only want is the extension of education. Relieve the people from oppression, and they will educate themselves. If not disturbed in its growth, capital will increase more rapidly than population, and with its increase will be increase of education, and of all comforts, moral and physical.

CHAPTER XIX.

I WILL now submit for the consideration of the reader, the conclusions at which I have arrived. They are—

I. That government was instituted for the protection of person and property.

II. That the best government is that which secures the attainment of the object, with the smallest sacrifice of freedom of action and of the produce of labour.

III. That where it is attained at the smallest cost, there is the most rapid accumulation of capital.

IV. That there is a tendency to the more rapid increase of capital than of population, when not prevented by human interferences.

V. That the more rapid the increase, the greater will be the demand for labour, and the more rapid the increase of production.

VI. That the greater the amount of production, the larger will be the quantity for each individual member of the community, if equally divided; but the extent of the portion actually assigned to the labouring class must depend, *first*, upon the ratio which capital bears to population, and *second*, upon the extent of the demands for the support of government, and the manner in which they are assessed.

VII. That the rate of wages depends on the extent of the fund assigned for the support of the labouring population compared with the number to be supported.

VIII. That *high wages*, or a large " fund for the support of the labouring class, in proportion to the extent of that class," are an infallible evidence of prosperity, and of the rapid increase of capital, and that the doctrine of Mr. M'Culloch in regard to *high rate of profit* is not borne out by the facts.

IX. That nothing is required to secure to the mass of the people in Europe, a rate of wages equal to that of the United States, but peace and tranquillity; security of person and property at small cost; permission to citizens or subjects to exercise their talents in such modes as they may deem most advantageous to themselves; *cheap government*, which, allowing them to enjoy nearly all the proceeds of their labour, and having in return their affections, is thereby rendered *strong government.*

Whether or not we shall ever see such governments in Europe, it is very difficult now even to guess, but it is to be hoped that by slow degrees, rulers will see that their interests and those of the people are the same. Whenever they shall do so, the reign of peace and freedom of trade will commence; population will increase at a more rapid rate than it has ever done, and every increase of population bringing with it new divisions of labour, will insure a higher degree of perfection, and a more rapid increase of the supply of the means of support; leaving the theory of starvation, and the commercial theory of " ships, colonies, and commerce," to be forgotten together. " National prosperity," says Mr. M'Culloch, " does not depend nearly so much on advantageous situations, salubrity of climate, or fertility of soil, as in the adopting of measures fitted to excite the inventive powers of genius, and to give perseverance and activity to industry. The establishment of a wise system of public economy can compensate for every other deficiency. It can render regions naturally inhospitable, barren, and unproductive, the comfortable abodes of an elegant and refined, or crowded and wealthy population. But where it is wanting, the best gifts of nature are of no value; and countries possessed of the greatest capacities of improvement, and abounding in all the materials necessary for the production of wealth, with difficulty furnish a miserable subsistence to hordes distinguished only by their ignorance, barbarism, and wretchedness."

CHAPTER XX.

I will add here a few words in regard to the disclaimer, by Professors Senior and Whately, of any consideration of that which I deem the great object of political economy, and its chief claim to attention, viz. *the promotion of the happiness of nations.* The former says, "it is not with happiness, but with wealth that I am concerned as a political economist;" and the latter speaks of the science as one "whose strict object is to inquire into the nature, production, and distribution of wealth, not in connexion with human happiness."

The political economist sees that a large portion of mankind are "poor and miserable." He sees that the disease with which they are afflicted, is poverty, and that the remedy for the evils under which they labour is to enable them to accumulate property, or articles having exchangeable value. He sees that the possession of a sufficient quantity of such articles will redeem them from the "miserable" state in which they are, and the object of his studies is to ascertain the causes which have prevented such accumulations in times past, and to point out the course by which they may be promoted in future. As well might a physician called to a patient labouring under a disorder which rendered him "poor and miserable," assert that his object was only to remove the disease, not restore his patient to health, as the political economist that his science had regard to the wealth, and not to the happiness of nations. Mr. Senior says truly, that "in fact wealth and happiness are very seldom opposed," and as evidence thereof, adduces the great increase of the duration of life in the course of the last fifty years, as a strong proof of great increase of comfort.

The object of the political economist is to ascertain what is the mode in which the labour of a nation can be applied, so as to enable the labourer to command the greatest amount of comforts with the smallest sacrifice.* It is obvious that if he can devise a mode by which twelve hours of labour per day shall enable the workman to command twelve yards of cloth, instead of half that number, which he had hitherto had for an equal quantity of time, he renders him service. By doing so, he does not compel him to make any greater sacrifice of his ease than he had before done, but, on the contrary, enables him, if so disposed, to live as he had done, with half the labour; or to live better than he had done by the devotion of the same quantity of time. He has his option. Fortunately, the desire to improve his condition prevails to a sufficient extent to induce the great mass of mankind to continue their exertions, and with the surplus produce, add to the

---

* "The great practical problem involved in that part of the science which treats of the *production* of wealth, must resolve itself into a discussion of the means by which labour may be rendered most efficient, or by which the *greatest amount of necessary, useful, and desirable products may be obtained with the least possible outlay of labour.*"—*Principles of Polit. Econ.* p. 75.

list of their enjoyments. Every improvement in the condition of a people, tends to new improvements. Adam Smith says, that the best labourers are always to be found where wages are highest, the truth of which is fully proved by a comparison of those of Great Britain or the United States, with those of Ireland and Hindostan.

It is difficult to imagine a case in which the wealth of a community can be increased by measures tending to lessen the happiness of its members. Wealth may accumulate, even in Hindostan or Ireland, but the increase is not a consequence of the injudicious measures of the government. If it do so, it is because maladministration is not carried quite far enough to prevent it. The adoption of the measures recommended by the political economist could not fail to promote the increase of wealth, as well as an increase of happiness. If the absentee go abroad for economy; if instead of expending £ 5000 in Ireland, he live in Italy for £ 1000, and the balance be added to his capital, and judiciously expended by an agent in the improvement of his lands, or in the promotion of manufactures, (the only mode in which wealth can be increased by absenteeism,) then absenteeism is decidedly advantageous, and tends to promote the happiness of the community by increasing the demand for labour, and its reward. It may, indeed, be asserted without fear of contradiction, that it is not possible to increase the wealth of a nation, without increase of happiness in the community, even if it consist of slaves. If the cotton planters, by economy and industry be enabled to accumulate capital, they must find means of investing it, by which the demand for slaves will be increased, and the price will be raised. Their increased value then, operates as an additional reason for care and attention, and we find accordingly, that the situation of the slave does, as a general rule, improve with his increased value.

The ingenious author of numerous articles on various branches of this science, in the Quarterly Review, avails himself of this admission of Messrs. Senior and Whately, and asserts, "that the amount of wealth in a country is no measure of its prosperity, understanding by that term the aggregate of comfort, ease, and happiness enjoyed by its inhabitants," and in proof thereof, adduces the following case:—

"Let us suppose a country, A., to raise large quantities of corn by the labour of a body of agriculturists, who, from the condition on which alone they are allowed to cultivate the soil, have but a bare subsistence left to them, and live in a state of extreme misery. The corn remaining beyond their consumption, is the property of the land owner, who exports it in exchange for luxuries and rich stuffs for his own consumption. Now, there can be no question that the total wealth of A. is increased by this trade, because for the wealth exported in the shape of corn, wealth of *greater value*, in the shape of luxuries, is imported. But is the trade which thus produces an increase of wealth in A. of a beneficial character? Does it tend to increase the prosperity of the inhabitants of A.? Suppose the trade did not exist, and that the same quantity of corn we first supposed to be exported, was consumed in maintaining the population of A. in abundance, instead of penury; whatever circumstances occasioned this different state of things, of a political or other nature, it is evident that the condition of the inhabitants of A. would be vastly superior to what we supposed, than before, though *the total amount of wealth possessed by them would be less.*"—*Quarterly Review, Vol. LXVI. p.* 48.

One error in this reasoning is the assumption, that

if the produce was not exported, it would remain for the support of the agriculturists. Another consists in separating the landlord from the producers. The whole constitute but one community, and the mass of enjoyment is undoubtedly increased by the foreign trade. Suppose, however, that the trade did not exist, and that the same quantity of corn first supposed to be exported, were consumed by the landlord in its original shape, would the situation of the inhabitants of A. be improved thereby? Suppose, instead of corn, its inhabitants were employed in producing peaches and pine apples, which were consumed by the landlord, instead of wines and rich stuffs, how would their situation be improved? Suppose, instead of exporting it, it were sent to the capital, and there invested in pictures by Lawrence, Wilkie, or Leslie, would the inhabitants of A. benefit thereby? Would any of these changes cause them to live in abundance, instead of penury? They would not. The whole income of the land owner might be spent on domestic productions, without the smallest increase of comfort to the labourer. What is to be complained of, is the manner in which the produce is divided.

The reviewer will, perhaps, allow us another supposition. Suppose the exchangeable value of the labour of the inhabitants of A. were doubled, in consequence of a great reduction of the rents, but that instead of applying the excess to the improvement of the condition of their families, the labourers were one and all to apply it to the purchase of gin, and spend all their leisure time in the consumption of it, would their situation be improved? The result would be the same, a state of "extreme misery," and as good an argument might be made in the one case against the reduction of rents, because the additional sum left to the labourer, might, perhaps, be spent in gin, as against the foreign trade, because the proceeds of the corn might come home in wines and rich stuffs, to be spent by the land owner. If the whole proceeds over what is required to support the people in the state described, be consumed, it matters little whether its consumption be the work of the labourer or the landlord. The result in either case is the same, as in both cases the growth of capital is prevented, and without it, there can be no improvement of condition.

Suppose the landlord, anxious to improve his income, were to look into "The Wealth of Nations," what would he find there? He would find advice to economize his expenditure; to let his capital increase; to improve his estate; and to make good roads leading to his market, by which his revenue would be increased. Suppose he were influenced only by the desire to improve the condition of the inhabitants, he would find the same advice as tending to his own benefit, and to that of all connected with him. He would not find advice to erect hospitals or alms-houses; or to distribute the surplus among the people, to enable them to idle away half of their time; but *he would be advised to invest it in such manner as would be profitable to himself;* to conform to the dictates of *an enlightened self interest;* by which he must increase the demand for labour, and its exchangeable value, thereby offering an incentive to industry, and an opportunity of rising from the wretched situation to which they had been reduced.

There is no doctrine of political economy, the object of which is not to promote happiness, and Adam Smith would have been perfectly justified in entitling his book, "AN INQUIRY INTO THE NATURE AND CAUSES OF THE HAPPINESS OF NATIONS."

THE END.

ERRATA.

Page 141, line 18, *for* estate, *read* state.
" 143, line 6, *for* estate, *read* state.
" 161, line 22, *for* lands they possess are,
read land they possess is.
" 171, last line, *for* labourer, *read* labour.
" 185, line 28, *for* annum, *read* mensem.
" 244, line 9, for *A'cote*, read *A coté*.